About Island Press

Island Press is the only nonprofit organization in the United States whose principal purpose is the publication of books on environmental issues and natural resource management. We provide solutions-oriented information to professionals, public officials, business and community leaders, and concerned citizens who are shaping responses to environmental problems.

In 2000, Island Press celebrates its sixteenth anniversary as the leading provider of timely and practical books that take a multidisciplinary approach to critical environmental concerns. Our growing list of titles reflects our commitment to bringing the best of an expanding body of literature to the environmental community throughout North America and the world.

Support for Island Press is provided by The Jenifer Altman Foundation, The Bullitt Foundation, The Mary Flagler Cary Charitable Trust, The Nathan Cummings Foundation, The Geraldine R. Dodge Foundation, The Charles Engelhard Foundation, The Ford Foundation, The Vira I. Heinz Endowment, The W. Alton Jones Foundation, The John D. and Catherine T. MacArthur Foundation, The Andrew W. Mellon Foundation, The Charles Stewart Mott Foundation, The Curtis and Edith Munson Foundation, The National Fish and Wildlife Foundation, The National Science Foundation, The New-Land Foundation, The David and Lucile Packard Foundation, The Pew Charitable Trusts, The Surdna Foundation, The Winslow Foundation, and individual donors.

About The Nature Conservancy

The mission of The Nature Conservancy is to preserve plants, animals, and natural communities that represent the diversity of life on Earth by protecting the lands and waters they need to survive.

Since 1951, the Conservancy, a nonprofit membership organization headquartered in Arlington, Virginia, has worked with local conservationists both in the United States and internationally to identify and protect critical habitat. To date, the Conservancy and its members, who now number over 820,000, have been responsible for the protection of more than 8 million acres in the United States and Canada, and have helped like-minded organizations in Latin America, the Caribbean, Asia, and the Pacific safeguard more than 53 million acres. The Conservancy is well known for its expertise in land acquisition for conservation purposes; in the United States, the organization owns more than 1,300 preserves-the largest private system of nature sanctuaries in the world.

The Conservancy recognizes that local organizations have the best insight into local conservation issues. It therefore works to support partners, ensuring that they have the resources and skills to make decisions that will guarantee a rich natural legacy.

For more information about The Nature Conservancy and its work in Latin America and the Caribbean, visit its website at www.tnc.org.

Nature
in Focus

Conservation efforts will not succeed without a knowledge of the character and location of the biodiversity we seek to protect. This book is dedicated to those who strive for biodiversity protection through conservation science.

Nature
in Focus
Rapid Ecological Assessment

Roger Sayre

Ellen Roca

Gina Sedaghatkish

Bruce Young

Shirley Keel

Roberto L. Roca

Stuart Sheppard

Illustrations by Tamara R. Sayre

The Nature Conservancy

ISLAND PRESS
Washington, D.C. • Covelo, California

ISLAND PRESS is a trademark of The Center for Resource Economics.

Library of Congress Cataloging-in-Publication Data
Nature in focus : rapid ecological assessment / Roger Sayre . . . [et al.].
     p.   cm.
    Includes bibliographical references.
    ISBN 1–55963–754–4 (paper)
    1. Ecological surveys—Methodology.   2. Biological diversity
conservation.   I. Sayre, Roger.
QH541.15.S95.N38   2000
577'.028—dc21

                                                    99–37188
                                                    CIP

Printed on recycled, acid-free paper

Manufactured in the United States of America
10 9 8 7 6 5 4 3 2 1

Contents

Chapter 6. Fauna Surveys   93

Chapter 7. Assessing Threats   119

List of Tables, Figures, Boxes, and Color Maps

Tables

Figures

Boxes

Color Maps

Color maps can be found in the insert following page 76.

Foreword

Conservationists and conservation biologists sometimes feel trapped. They are caught between the uncertainty of relatively superficial knowledge of biological diversity and the imperative to advance conservation rapidly in the face of a powerful array of destructive forces. This situation presents a challenge of how to conserve what one does not know about.

While this is a problem in any area of the world—even where the biota is relatively well known if not all its dynamics understood—it is of towering importance in the developing world. There, where scientific understanding and capacity is dramatically uneven and where in some instances scientific institutions are weak and most relevant scientific knowledge is squirreled away in minds and institutions in the industrialized nations, the conservation challenge is vast. Often such countries are a patchwork of the environmental problems of both the developed and the developing world.

It was out of this crucible of ignorance and conservation urgency that Rapid Ecological Assessment (REA) was born. REA is a comforting term, implying that there is actually something constructive to be done to enhance scientific understanding of conservation priorities and to enable effective conservation initiatives. For most in the conservation and related science professions, however, REA has remained somewhat mysterious, more a name than anything else. Roger Sayre and his coauthors have done the profession and society at large a favor by rendering accessible what today is a quite sophisticated activity.

About a decade of experience with REA exists today, starting with the first effort in the Mbaracayú rain forests of Paraguay in 1988. One of the most recent efforts involving a major portion of the Brazilian state of Amapá dealt with *cerrado* and a variety of other habitats. As it happens, I was closely associated with the latter exercise as a member of an overall advisory committee for Champion Paper, which requested the study. The assessment was done quickly, with reassuring detail and a solid scientific footing. The result was a state-of-the-art product that all concerned could use to make decisions or recommendations with full confidence.

The excellence of that particular product and, indeed, of all REAs is due in large part to partnering with relevant scientific institutions and scientists. In the Amapá REA, the major partner was the Museu Paraense Emilio Goeldi at Belém, the oldest scientific institution in the Amazon (1865) and a repository for most of the scientific specimens collected during the REA. The Museu's senior scientist, Fernando Novaes, used to tell me about his expeditions to Amapá during quiet moments of our fieldwork on the outskirts of Belém in the late 1960s. Building on Novaes's intellectual legacy, Goeldi scientist David Oren led the necessary fieldwork to update and fill in some of the blanks. The reward for such institutions and scientists is conservation action, which guarantees secure study sites in perpetuity.

This particular approach is of course not the only way to confront the challenge. The authors have been conscientious in citing other obvious approaches. The value of this volume is that the entire process is laid out in full detail, enabling anyone to undertake an assessment and enabling the process to evolve and improve. We should all be grateful to Roger Sayre and his coauthors for taking such an open and workmanship approach. Everybody's reward will be more and better conservation.

—Dr. Thomas Lovejoy

Acknowledgments

Many individuals contributed to the development and review of this document. Although the work was authored by scientists from The Nature Conservancy's Latin America and Caribbean Region, the information contained herein represents the accumulated experiences of a much larger body of colleagues both within and external to the Conservancy. The individuals who have worked on Rapid Ecological Assessments (REAs) over the past ten years number in the hundreds, and acknowledging each of these individuals by name would prove overwhelmingly difficult. Their contributions to the development of the REA methodology and the streamlining of the REA process are gratefully acknowledged.

Robert Livernash provided valuable editorial assistance in the compilation of this work. Nicole Panagopoulos managed the document revision, finalization, and delivery process; Karin Wall worked on an earlier version. Thea Jaster and Lisa Vonder Haar helped with the field forms and other materials. Eva Vilarrubi provided invaluable encouragement and assistance with the publication aspects of this project.

For pioneering the REA methodology in the first place, we acknowledge the contributions of Claudia Sobrevila, Robert Jenkins, Paquita Bath, Bruce Stein, Dennis Grossman, Kathleen Sullivan, Douglas Muchoney, Susan Iremonger, Andrea Cristofani, and other REA "veterans." Their REA experiences are as rich and varied as the biodiversity they sought to characterize. Andrea Cristofani, in particular, exemplified and inspired positive energy, hard work, and infectious enthusiasm on many REAs. Two of the authors of this book, Shirley Keel and Roberto Roca, also participated in REAs from the beginning, contributing significantly to the development of the flora and fauna components, respectively. Certain past and current staff of the Conservancy, by their direct assistance and helpful attitudes, deserve special mention: Claire Teixeira, Douglass Baker, Xiaojun Li, Connie Campbell, Michelle Libby, Timothy Boucher, Xavier Silva, Luis Corrales, Jane Mansour, and Marcelo Guevara.

For review of parts or all of this manual, we thank Timothy Fahey, Eric Fajer, Tom Lovejoy, Kent Redford, Deborah Jensen, Brad Northrup, Robb Wright, Howard Daniel, John Tschirky, Kelvin Guerrero, Alberto Yanosky, and Timothy Tear. Their perspectives were diverse, and their comments were useful. For in-country leadership, fruitful collaborations, and enduring friendships which materialized on many REAs, we thank Celeste Acevedo, Wilfrido Sosa, Raúl Gauto, Marcia Aparecida de Brito, Jorge Chávez, Pedro Vásquez, Nélida Rivarola, Dilia Santamariá, Iván Valdespino, Jonathan Littau, Nella Stewart, Peter Reeson, Enrique Coronado, Claudio Méndez, Olga Valdez, César Castanheda, María José Durán, Fernando Salazar, Miguel Scarcello, Osmany Salas, Fernando Fernández, Felipe Campos, Ronald León, Tirso Maldonado, Kelvin Guerrero, José Miguel Martínez, Francisco Núñez, Angela Guerrero,

David Oren, and Ricardo Soto. We ask these REA Team leaders to extend our gratitude to all the members of their teams.

For contributing ideas and written and graphical materials that helped in the elaboration of this work, we acknowledge Douglass Baker, Pedro Vásquez, Susan Iremonger, Luis Corrales, Douglas Muchoney, Connie Campbell, Timothy Boucher, and Michelle Libby.

Robb Wright, Marcelo Guevara, Luis Barbosa, and Kevin Skerl provided high-quality maps from different REAs with which they were associated and have always been supportive of REA mapping efforts. For dedication to advancing the mapping dimension of REAs, we are also indebted to Santiago Hernández, Luis Tolentino, Tomás Montilla, Hannelore and Helmut Bendsen, Pedro Vásquez, Emilia Moreno, César Munoz, Luis Paniagua, Luis Barbosa, David Grigg, Delia Tillet, and other REA mappers. We thank ESRI and ERDAS for creating, supporting, and often donating the best spatial information technologies for conservation mapping, and for evolving those technologies over the years in response to user requirements. All of the maps in this book were produced using Arc® technologies.

We thank the many guides, camp-hands, and local communities who have welcomed REA teams into their landscapes. Their expertise in locating biodiversity, using machetes, and cooking is unparalleled. We thank as well the many helicopter and fixed-wing aircraft pilots who have flown REA overflight missions, allowing and helping us to equip their aircraft with global positioning system (GPS) technologies.

We especially acknowledge the funding assistance for implementing terrestrial REAs that has been received from the U.S. Agency for International Development (USAID), the Biodiversity Support Program (BSP), the U.S. Department of Defense (DoD), the U.S. Department of the Navy, Champion Forest Products International, EOSAT, the InterAmerican Development Bank (IDB), the John D. and Catherine T. MacArthur Foundation, the Moriah Foundation, the Munson Foundation, Fundación Moisés Bertoni, Fundación Peruana para la Conservación de la Naturaleza (FPCN), the Jamaica Agricultural Development Foundation, the World Wildlife Fund (WWF), and many national governments and Conservation Data Centers. Partial support for the preparation of the manuscript for this book was provided by the Office LAC/RSD/EHR, Bureau for Latin America and the Caribbean, U.S. Agency for International Development, under terms of Grant No. LAG-0782-A-00-5026-00. The opinions expressed herein are those of the authors and do not necessarily reflect the views of the U.S. Agency for International Development.

Overview

Rapid Ecological Assessment After Ten Years

Roger Sayre

The Earth supports an extraordinary variety of living things—plants, animals, insects, and more, totaling perhaps 10 million species. This biological diversity ranges from magnificent to microscopic—from redwood forests, whales, and elephants, to bacteria and viruses. Most species have never been scientifically described.

Many of these species are imperiled, largely because of the growth of human populations and the rapid expansion of human activities. The root causes include conversion of forests and grasslands to agricultural and other uses, habitat fragmentation, urban expansion, introduction of nonnative species, overharvesting of commercial species, and inadequate enforcement of environmental statutes.

Current extinction rates are on the order of ten thousand times higher than at any previous time in the Earth's history. Each loss is irretrievable; an extinct species cannot be restored. Certainly, in the aggregate, these losses are undermining the Earth's natural infrastructure and posing new threats to those species that remain.

The economic value of the Earth's natural heritage is being recognized more and more. For example, recent studies suggest that the vast array of services provided by living species and the natural world—plant pollination, cleaning of water and air, flood and pest control, nutrient cycling—are worth billions of dollars annually. If lost, the services provided by these species may be impossible (or at least prohibitively expensive) to replicate by other means.

For the past several decades, concerns about biodiversity loss have prompted many positive responses. The international community has put about 8 percent of the world's land area under protected status, adopted national and international laws to protect threatened and endangered species, and agreed to a new

Convention on Biological Diversity. Yet, while some of the planet's biodiversity is "captured" in protected areas, most of it is not and is subject to substantial threat by humans. The lack of an active conservation management program in many protected areas frequently causes threats to biodiversity in parks, especially in developing countries. Clearly, much more needs to be done in the area of biodiversity protection.

As awareness increased, many nations expressed interest in protecting their natural heritage. Yet comprehensive, reliable information about biodiversity resources was rarely available, especially in developing countries. Before any government, community, or environmental organization could act to save living resources in any given area, they first had to find out what resources were there.

In an ideal world, such assessments should be exhaustive and minute. Given the urgency of the situation and the limited financial resources available, however, something that was less than ideal—but still scientifically viable—was desperately needed.

To date, the principal response to this problem has been Rapid Ecological Assessment (REA), a biodiversity survey methodology developed over the past ten years by The Nature Conservancy. REAs combat the lack of available biodiversity information by producing preliminary, integrated, and spatially explicit information about species distributions and vegetation types. REA is defined in box 1.

What are the key features of an REA? Briefly, the REA process emphasizes:

- *Speed.* From initial planning to final publication of a report, an REA usually takes about one year. Getting an REA done quickly helps both to reduce costs and to produce useful information before the

---

A Rapid Ecological Assessment (REA) of a terrestrial area or region is a flexible, accelerated, and targeted survey of vegetation types and species. REAs utilize a combination of remotely sensed imagery, reconnaissance overflights, field data collection, and spatial information visualization to generate useful information for conservation planning at multiple scales.

REAs are implemented by teams of conservation scientists and resource managers organized into groups by disciplinary and functional specializations. REAs result in a mapped and documented characterization of classified landscape units, and a description of the species-level biodiversity within these units. They produce baseline biophysical data, maps, documents, recommendations, and increased institutional capabilities for effective conservation work. REA data can be produced and analyzed at different spatial scales depending on conservation goals.

REA is a useful planning tool for conservation, and as such, REAs are increasingly implemented for the rapid characterization of the biodiversity of an area. REAs are particularly well suited to the efficient characterization of the landscape and species-level biodiversity of large areas for which relatively little is known.

REA is a multifaceted concept and has been referred to as an approach, a methodology, a tool, a strategy, a process, a program, a conservation assessment, and by a variety of other descriptions. REA is, in fact, all of these, and we refer to REAs in these different contexts throughout the book. In general, however, we will refer to REA as a methodology.

Finally, it is important to keep in mind that there are many types of analyses that should not be confused with REA. For example, an REA is not an exhaustive inventory of the biological resources of an area; a biodiversity monitoring program; a rigorous statistical assessment of ecological relationships; an environmental impact assessment; a management plan; basic research to understand ecological processes; a rapid rural appraisal (RRA) or some other socioeconomic survey instrument (although human context analyses are often conducted in conjunction with REAs); a change-detection analysis of landscape characteristics; a predictive or descriptive model for explaining the distribution of biodiversity; or a representativeness assessment for designing networks of sites, which will collectively conserve the representative biodiversity of a region.

Box 1. What Is Rapid Ecological Assessment?

study area is altered.

- *Careful planning and training.* Careful planning in the beginning saves both money and time, while upfront training ensures consistency in approach.
- *Landscape and species-level assessments.* REAs characterize biodiversity at two levels of organization, landscape level (coarse filter) and species level (fine filter).
- *New mapping technologies.* New spatial technologies—such as geographic information systems (GIS), remote sensing (RS), and global positioning systems (GPS)—combine with increasingly powerful personal computers and innovative software to create extraordinary conservation mapping tools.
- *Careful scientific documentation.* Classification, sampling, and survey methods have been developed and refined to help carry out biodiversity assessments in a short period of time.
- *Capacity building and partnerships.* Fostering cooperative relationships among conservation partners builds local capacity and improves the odds that ensuing decision making will have local support.

Since their development in the 1980s, REAs have gone through a considerable evolutionary process in a relatively short time. In the next section, we review the history of REAs.

REAs: Early Development and Evolution

The REA methodology, both as originally conceived and currently, is a rapid characterization of vegetation types and associated flora and fauna. This information is used to direct conservation planning efforts at sites and to contribute to national biodiversity inventories. REAs were intended to be suitable and efficient for large, relatively unknown areas.

The first site-level REA, which was conducted in 1988 in the rain forests of Mbaracayú, Paraguay (Conservation Data Center–Paraguay, 1991) (box 2), identified the area's highest-priority habitats for conservation consideration. Nine of the nineteen natural plant communities described in this REA did not occur in any other Paraguayan protected area. Twenty-one nationally endangered plant species were recorded, and 191 bird species were observed, of which 44 were endangered. A plan to implement conservation management zoning in the reserve was adopted to protect this biodiversity. Two more REAs were subsequently implemented in 1989 and 1990 in Brazil, one at the state level (Mato Grosso; Aparecida de Brito et al., 1991a) and one at a site (Rio Sepotuba; Aparecida de Brito et al., 1991b) that was identified as a high-priority conservation area in the state-level assessment. An island-wide REA of Jamaica (Grossman et al., 1991) followed, which revealed priority areas for biodiversity conservation at the national level.

For the Conservancy's Latin America and Caribbean programs, the methodology quickly became an important conservation tool. These early REAs allowed experimentation with the flexibility and usefulness of the methodology and provided experiences and lessons learned for the development of an REA manual.

The Original REA Manual

In 1991, the Conservancy published the original REA manual (Sobrevila and Bath, 1992) (figure 1) in Spanish, with the intent of making it available to the Conservancy's like-minded conservation partners and other conservation organizations. Many of the Conservancy's Latin American and Caribbean conservation partners contributed to the development of the manual. Many other organizations have since employed the methodology in their conservation efforts. The original Spanish-language REA manual had a limited printing and distribution and was never translated, but it has become recognized as an important source of information on rapid biodiversity assessments (UNEP, 1995; Jermy et al., 1995).

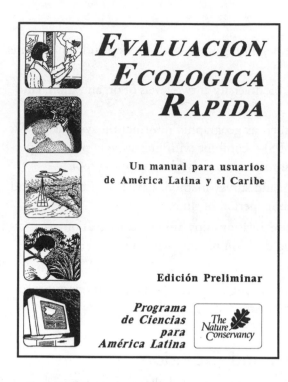

Figure 1. The original Spanish-language REA manual, published in 1992.

The Need for a New Manual

While the concepts presented in the original REA manual are still valid, the tools available to carry out an REA have changed so much that a new manual is needed. The original manual described REA as a sequential set of prescribed steps and activities and focused essentially on the methodological aspects of REA. This revised and expanded manual describes refinements in the methodology and adds new emphasis on planning and managing REAs. It also provides greater detail about the spatial information processing aspects of REA.

We expect that REA will continue to evolve in the future, and we developed the new manual to provide an overview of the current state of REA. We hope that the value of REA in generating critical information for conservation action continues to be recognized, and that the conservation benefits from REA are increasingly realized.

Purpose and Audience

We hope that this manual will enable conservationists to understand how and why REAs are conducted and will assist any interested organization in the planning and implementation of an REA. While books on biodiversity are commonplace, few address how biodiversity can be rapidly characterized and quantified for conservation decision making. A great and urgent need to characterize landscape- and species-level biodiversity exists, but relatively few references on how to accomplish this characterization are available (Margules and Austin, 1991; Sobrevila and Bath, 1992; Margules and Redhead, 1995; Jermy et al., 1995; Institute of Environmental Assessment, 1995; and Spellerberg, 1992).

This manual provides the reader with a detailed approach for assessing biodiversity in a more rapid and integrative manner than traditional inventory permits. It is a definitive reference, which presents both a conceptual model for REA and practical guidelines on how REAs are planned and implemented. The work is intended primarily for conservation practitioners and biodiversity scientists who desire either to understand the REA methodology or to participate in REA initiatives. The book also is useful for conservation managers, policymakers, and donors because it explains concepts and methodologies in non-

Mbaracayú Forest Nature Reserve protects one of the largest remaining tracts of privately owned, dense, humid, subtropical forest in South America. Eighty-seven percent of the 65,000-hectare reserve located in eastern Paraguay is covered by subtropical forest, warm temperate forest, natural grasslands, rivers, and wetlands. The overall goal of the REA was to assess the site's suitability as a privately owned nature reserve. Specific REA objectives in support of this goal were as follows:

- To identify natural communities and their conservation status.
- To identify representative plant species for each natural community.
- To survey bird species occurring in the study area.
- To compare bird diversity among sampling points.

The REA focused on the diversity of plant communities and plant and bird species as indicators of conservation value and significance. The sampling effort for birds was intense to allow calculations and comparisons of bird diversity among sampling points. The ornithologists augmented transect data with information from local people and published data sources.

Important Findings

The REA resulted in the characterization and classification of nineteen natural communities, nine of which did not occur in any other Paraguayan protected area.

Field biologists determined that all except one plant community were intact and of ecological importance. Botanists located twenty-one endangered plant species, including cedro *(Cedrela fissilis)* and tree fern *(Alsophyla atrovirens)*. Ornithologists recorded the presence of 191 bird species, 44 of which are threatened, including rare cracids, the rufous-faced crake *(Laterallus xenopterus)*, and the endangered helmeted woodpecker *(Dryocopus galeatus)*.

This REA contributed significantly to the subsequent zonation of the reserve by providing the type of critical baseline data that are needed to develop science-based management plans. The REA also helped direct further research, such as the identification of medicinal plants.

Major Recommendations

- Zone the proposed reserve to adequately protect areas of high bird diversity, waterways, and plant communities of high ecological significance and conservation concern.
- Work with property owners to control sediments flowing into the major waterways.
- Conduct more studies on birds and other animal groups in certain sampling sites.

Box 2. The first REA; Mbaracayú, Paraguay. Conducted in 1988 by Fundación Moisés Bertoni and other collaborators, this REA established a biodiversity baseline, prioritized habitats, and led to a conservation zonation of the protected area.

technical language. Although the examples used are drawn primarily from the Conservancy's experience in Latin America and the Caribbean, the approach is universally applicable.

Evolving Technologies for an Enduring Methodology

The REA methodology has evolved continuously since its inception. Improvements and simplifications in mapping technologies have contributed to an emphasis on digital mapping in REAs, and lessons learned from implementing a number of REAs have refined the approach.

REAs are difficult to describe in generic terms, and every REA to date has been a study in individuality. For example, an REA of *cerrado* savanna habitats in the Brazilian state of Amapá (Oren et al., 1998) was completed in 1998, ten years after the first REA in Mbaracayú. In contrast to the pioneering Paraguayan REA, in which all mapping was prepared by hand cartography after the project was completed, the Amapá REA was a sophisticated, digital mapping effort, with complex radar imagery interpretation, GPS-located field sampling, GPS-controlled overflight navigation, and acquisition of digital still photography of communities and species. These technologies allowed for the use of an alternate data source (radar), increased quality (spatial accuracy) of derived information, and an increased ability to integrate, analyze, and present REA information, all of which would have been either impossible or significantly more difficult and expensive ten years earlier.

Since the publication of the first manual, the rapid development of spatial information technologies (GIS, GPS, RS) has revolutionized the REA methodology by (1) enhancing ability to collect and analyze imagery and field-derived information, (2) facilitating the integration of information from different sources and differing scales, and (3) generating useful and visually appealing products.

The basic REA methodology has remained essentially unchanged. REAs continue to focus on landscape-level conservation, maintaining a coarse-filter/fine-filter emphasis that conserving landscapes (coarse filters) will result in the conservation of the species (fine filters) that are contained within them. The coarse-filter/fine-filter paradigm applies to information collection as well (figures 2 and 3). Coarse-resolution information generated from remote sensing and overflights is both refined and focused in a fine filter of more detailed complementary information from the field.

I. Coarse Filter: Landscape-Level Assessment

Objective

Describe, Classify, and Map Vegetation Communities

Tools

Image Interpretation, Overflights, GIS, GPS

Products

Vegetation Community Classification and Preliminary Map

II. Fine Filter: Species-Level Assessment

Objectives

Verify Vegetation Community Classification and Map

Survey Species in Identified Communities

Tools

GPS, Field Survey Methods

Products

Refined Vegetation Classification and Map, General Species

Lists, Species of Concern Lists, and Information for Site

Prioritizations

Figure 2. The coarse-filter/fine-filter paradigm of REA. REAs characterize biodiversity at both landscape (coarse filter) and species (fine filter) levels, employing coarse-grained (satellite image interpretation, overflights) and finer-grined (field sampling) assessment methodologies. Information from each assessment is ultimately integrated to develop conservation strategies and management recommendations.

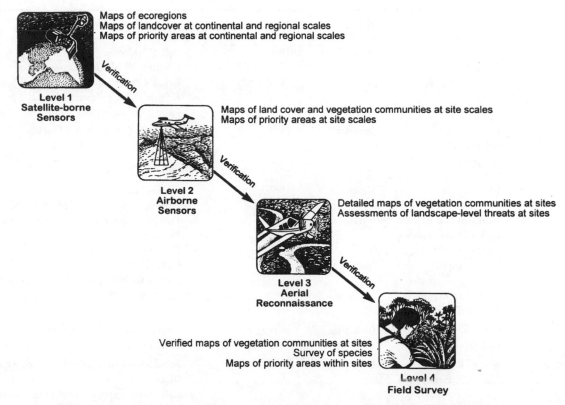

Figure 3. Scale dimensions, data sources, sampling methodologies, and products from the REA process. The focus and scale of the process always increases from general to specific. (Modified from Sobrevila and Bath, 1992.)

REAs are targeted at conservation of biodiversity (e.g., plants, animals, and natural communities). Because this biodiversity occurs in ecosystems, and because species and ecosystems are functionally related, REAs represent ecosystem-level conservation efforts as well. REAs are therefore designed to help conserve both biodiversity and ecosystems.

Experience to Date

The REA concept has now endured for ten years. We are aware of some fifty REAs that have been conducted in a variety of tropical landscapes, all using the REA model developed by the Conservancy. Of these fifty REAs, the Conservancy has participated directly in thirty-three (table 1, figure 4). REAs have contributed to improved conservation at sites and to improved conservation capacities in many organizations mandated to conserve biodiversity (table 2). Specifically, REAs have resulted in the establishment of protected areas, development of management plans and zonation, design of biological corridors, selection of priority conservation areas, identification of future research needs, and development of threats abatement programs.

REAs have also improved scientific knowledge about biodiversity. Several REA reports have described new species to science or have made first reports of particular species in certain areas or regions. Plant and animal specimens collected in REAs are always provided to museums, along with accurate locality information.

Internationally, the Conservancy's biggest program is in Latin America and the Caribbean, so the bulk of the Conservancy's experience with REA to date has been in these areas. This is not to suggest that the REA methodology—or this manual—is useful for only Latin America and the Caribbean. The REA methodology is applicable anywhere. The Conservancy has been involved in an REA in the Solomon Islands (Leary, 1993), and an REA in the Yunnan province of China was initiated while this manual was being developed.

Table 1. REA locations and primary collaborating organizations. Although most REAs have had a terrestrial focus, a number of marine REAs have also been implemented. A diversity in the types of implementing organizations is evident (e.g., government agencies, conservation NGOs and data centers, consultants, museums, and universities).

Country	Site	Type	Year	Implementing Organizations
Belize	Bladen Nature Reserve	Terrestrial	1994	Belize Audubon Society Ministry of Natural Resources
	Port Honduras	Marine	1996	Belize Center for Environmental Studies Florida and Caribbean Marine Conservation Science Center
Brazil	Champion International Corporation's land holdings	Terrestrial	1998	Museu Paraense Emílio Goeldi
	Mato Grosso	Terrestrial	1989	CDC-Brazil Fundação Estadual do Meio Ambiente
	Pantanal National Park and surrounding region	Terrestrial	1992	Fundação Brasileira para a Conservação da Natureza IBAMA
	Rio Sepotuba	Terrestrial	1990	CDC-Brazil Fundação Estadual do Meio Ambiente
	Serra do Divisor National Park	Terrestrial	1998	Fundação SOS Amazonia IBAMA
China	Great Rivers National Park System	Terrestrial	in progress	Yunnan Provincial Government Yunnan Province
Colombia	Sierra Nevada de Santa Marta National Park	Terrestrial	1998	Fundación Pro-Sierra Nevada de Santa Marta La Unidad Especial de Parques Nacionales del Ministerio del Medio Ambiente
Costa Rica	Osa Peninsula	Terrestrial	1997	Fundación Neotrópica
	Talamanca Biological Corridor	Marine/Terrestrial	1998	ProAmbiente
	Tempisque Region	Terrestrial	1995	Fundación Neotrópica
Cuba	U.S. Naval Station Guantanamo Bay	Marine/Terrestrial	1997	ProAmbiente Florida and Caribbean Marine Conservation Science Center
Dominican Republic	Parque Nacional del Este (National Park of the East)	Marine/Terrestrial	1997	PRONATURA Dirección Nacional de Parques Secretaría de Estado de Agricultura Espeleogrupo Acuario Nacional, Fundación Mamma
	Madre de las Aguas Conservation Area	Terrestrial	in progress	Fundación Progressio Museo de Historia Natural Jardín Botanico Nacional Dirección Nacional de Parques
Ecuador	Podocarpus National Park	Terrestrial	1995	Fundación Natura CDC-Ecuador Fundación Arcoiris
	Mache Mountains	Terrestrial	1996	CDC-Ecuador, Fundación Natura Fundación Jatun Sacha World Parks Endowment
Guatemala	Maya Biosphere Reserve	Terrestrial	1993	APESA
	Sierra de Lacandon National Park	Terrestrial	in progress	Defensores de la Naturaleza
	Sierra de las Minas Biosphere Reserve	Terrestrial	1993	Centro de Datos para la Conservación de Guatemala

Country	Site	Type	Year	Implementing Organizations
Honduras	El Cusuco National Park	Terrestrial	1996	Centro de Estudios Conservacionistas (CECON) Fundación Defensores de la Naturaleza Fundación Ecologista "Héctor Rodrigo Pastor Fasquelle" BioConsult S. de R.L.
Jamaica	Blue and John Crow Mountains National Park	Terrestrial	1994	CDC-Jamaica Forest Department of Agriculture
	Island-Wide	Terrestrial	1991	Rural and Physical Planning Unit of the Ministry of Agriculture CDC-Jamaica
	Montego Bay Marine Park	Marine	1994	CDC-Jamaica Montego Bay Marine Park Natural Resource Conservation Authority of Jamaica
Panama	Bocas del Toro Province	Marine/ Terrestrial	1998	ANCON
	Panama Canal Watershed Protection Area	Terrestrial	1995	ANCON
	U.S. Department of Defense Land Holdings	Terrestrial	1997	ANCON
Paraguay	Defensores del Chaco National Park	Terrestrial	in progress	CDC-Paraguay Museo de Historia Natural Dirección de Ordenamiento Ambiental Fundación para el Desarrollo Sustentable del Chaco
	Eastern Region	Terrestrial	1990	CDC-Paraguay
	Mbaracayú Forest Nature Reserve	Terrestrial	1988	CDC-Paraguay
Peru	Pacaya-Samiria National Reserve	Terrestrial	1993	CDC-Peru (Universidad Nacional Agraria La Molina)
Solomon Islands	Arnavon Islands	Marine/ Terrestrial	1993	Isabel Provincial Fisheries Isabel Ministry of Natural Resources
U.S. Virgin Islands	Island-wide: St. Croix, St. John, St. Thomas	Marine/ Terrestrial	in progress	CDC-Virgin Islands U.S. Park Service U.S. Fish and Wildlife Service University of Virgin Islands The Department of Planning and Natural Resources

REAs are most useful in information-poor areas of the world. For well-studied landscapes (e.g., temperate North America or Europe), an abundance of information about biodiversity permits the use of sophisticated conservation science tools [gap analysis (Scott et al., 1996) and range-wide conservation assessments of single species (Buttrick, 1992)].

Other Approaches

Somewhat surprisingly, relatively few parallels to REA—as well as few alternative methodologies—appear to exist in other regions of the world.

The Rapid Assessment Program (RAP) methodology (Roberts, 1991; Foster et al., 1994), developed

Figure 4. Locations of several Latin American and Caribbean REAs. Note the variety in size of sites for which REAs have been conducted, ranging from areas as small as tens of hectares (e.g., Guantanamo, Cuba) to millions of hectares (e.g., Pacaya-Samiria, Peru).

by Conservation International, is an elegantly simple and very rapid assessment approach. It is based on assembling a multidisciplinary team of renowned experts who conduct field surveys at predetermined locations and immediately write up their list-oriented results with conservation recommendations. To date, about a dozen RAP field expeditions have been conducted, mainly in Latin America (see http://www.conservation.org for more information on RAP).

The BioRap approach (Margules and Redhead, 1995), on the other hand, is a computer-intensive methodology that employs complex spatial modeling software and derives several environmental and biodiversity data sets, which are then integrated and analyzed to select priority sites for conservation. Environmental variables are mapped, spatially modeled, and used to predict distribution patterns of biological entities. The BioRap approach utilizes available information on the distribution of biodiversity and does not include a specific field survey component to generate this information. BioRap has been used extensively in Australia.

Taxonomic minimalism (Beattie and Oliver, 1994) is a survey approach that emphasizes the use of taxonomic ranks instead of species identification at the level of Latin binomials. Assessment of biodiversity at the level of genus, family, order, or even phylum, while less taxonomically "resolved," can be more rapid and less expensive. The use of morphospecies is another example of taxonomic minimalism. Morphospecies are groups of organisms identified by similar morphological characteristics, with no reference to established classifications. For example, litter invertebrates can be separated as spiders, beetles, ants, and so on and then further classified by size, color, and other characteristics.

The All Taxa Biodiversity Inventory (ATBI) (Janzen and Hallwachs, 1994) is a species-level total inventory (from viruses to big trees) of a large site. Based on parataxonomy, in which technicians are trained to collect and prepare specimens for formal taxonomic treatment, ATBI documents which species are present, how to tell them apart, where they can be found on the site, how to obtain them, and what their natural history is. ATBI has been used in Costa Rica.

REA differs from each of these other assessment techniques in two main areas: (1) its reliance on imagery (satellite or aerial photography) interpretation to delineate landscape-level biodiversity features, which are then characterized and sampled for species-level elements of biodiversity, and (2) its emphasis on partnerships with local scientists and on conservation capacity building. Partner involvement is always built into the REA project design from the beginning. Partners are engaged with an eye toward conservation management of the area subsequent to the REA. The maps produced from the landscape characterizations are similarly oriented toward management of the site.

Defining Parameters

Three common questions about REAs include "What will be done?", "What kind of environment is being assessed?" and "Who is doing the work?" The defining parameters of an REA include its objectives, the type of environment characterized (e.g., terrestrial versus marine), and the number and kind of collaborating institutions involved. (For more information, see chapter 3.)

Objectives

Clearly, REAs incorporate multiple objectives. The most common REA objectives generally resemble the following examples:

- Characterize the distribution of vegetation and certain taxa in the study area.
- Produce baseline biophysical information necessary for the development of subsequent management plans, environmental impact assessments, and legislative policy.
- Conduct a threats analysis for the biodiversity of the area.
- Train local scientists in REA methodology.
- Produce informational and data products (data, reports, maps, lists, classifications, descriptions, and threats identification) for management, educational, and fundraising purposes.

A review of these objectives reveals a great variety in the following:

- the landscapes being studied (site, park, watershed, corridor, islands);

- the management orientation (develop management plan, monitor, implement threats analysis, create zoning scheme, revise park boundaries);
- the science orientation (develop vegetation classification, identify endangered species, quantify plant and animal diversity); and
- the capacity-building orientation (train personnel, enhance organizational capacity, contribute to national inventory).

Note that none of these objectives includes environmental impact assessment because REAs do not describe the effects of proposed projects on the environment. REAs can, however, contribute appropriate baseline ecological information for impact assessments, with the caveat that REAs do not definitively characterize either (1) the distribution of all taxa, or (2) the ecological processes occurring in the study area.

Terrestrial versus Marine

The scope of an REA includes a consideration of terrestrial versus marine habitats, or both. Although the process for each habitat is similar, the sampling methodologies differ considerably, and this book emphasizes terrestrial REAs. REAs with both marine and terrestrial dimensions are logistically difficult to implement if sampling for both is to be conducted at the same time. There is no need to simultaneously execute the marine and terrestrial assessments, and in fact the ideal sampling times for each may not coincide.

If an REA of a terrestrial and adjacent marine system is implemented and mangroves are present, considerable planning is necessary to determine how the mangroves should be sampled and which team (marine or terrestrial) should conduct the survey. Although most REAs historically have focused on either the marine or the terrestrial dimension, they can focus on freshwater aquatic habitats as well (wetlands, lakes, rivers, subterranean waters). Methodologies for freshwater aquatic REAs are not well established due to a general lack of experience in these environments (but see Chernoff, 1998). Aquatic community classification methodologies, however, are becoming increasingly available (Lammert and Higgins, 1997), and adaptation of the REA methodology to aquatic environments should be relatively straightforward.

Institutional Partners

The number of collaborating institutions—which can include government organizations, non-governmental organizations (NGOs), and university researchers—also defines an REA. An REA always has a primary implementor, which is typically a strong conservation NGO in the area that is often charged with a mandate to manage the site. While for management purposes it is best to limit the number of collaborating institutions to a few, this limitation is not always possible because the necessary disciplinary expertise is spread among many individuals from multiple institutions. The primary implementor organizes the logistical arrangements, coordinates the activities of the collaborators, financially administers the project, and serves as the main point of contact with other collaborating institutions.

Donors for the project—which can include the U.S. Agency for International Development (USAID), other U.S. government agencies (e.g., the Department of Defense), The World Bank, multilateral development banks, international aid programs, local governments, foundations, corporations, and individuals—often play a participatory role. This participation can be achieved through the invitation of donors to REA workshops (as either observers or participants, depending on their level of interest and expertise) and by providing opportunities to review documents.

How REAs Can Be Used

REAs serve a variety of conservation purposes and are implemented at a variety of scales. The following sections describe different REA applications.

Regional Conservation Planning

Effective conservation planning at regional scales requires two types of assessments: ecological assessments (including REA) and representativeness assessments.

Ecological assessments are analyses that generate information about the biota and ecological processes of an area or region. REA is a type of ecological assessment that is more directed at characterizing distributions of biota and placing less emphasis on the understanding of ecological processes. Ecological assessments identify landscape- or species-level conservation targets within a single site or study area.

Representativeness assessments are a different type of analysis with a regional conservation focus and scale. Representativeness assessments use information about biodiversity distribution to design regional conservation strategies (Austin and Margules, 1986). These conservation strategies usually involve designing portfolios of sites within a given region that will conserve representative examples of the biodiversity within that region. A representativeness assessment analyzes multiple areas for potential inclusion in a site-based network design.

Representativeness assessments require information produced from ecological assessments as input. REAs therefore are important not only at the level of site-based conservation, but also at regional conservation scales. Some REAs, in fact, have focused primarily on regional level assessments to identify priority conservation sites (Acevedo et al., 1991; Aparecida de Brito et al., 1991a; Grossman et al., 1991). REA at regional scales holds promise for informing ecoregional planning initiatives as well. Ecoregional planning based on representation of distinct natural communities in conservation strategies and protected-area networks has become a fundamental conservation goal for many conservation organizations (Dinerstein et al., 1995; The Nature Conservancy, 1997a). REAs generate useful information on vegetation units and representativeness at ecoregional scales.

Site Conservation Planning

At site-based conservation scales (e.g., a national park), REAs provide baseline biodiversity information for an area and identify the conservation targets (vegetation types and species) for which conservation management goals and strategies are formulated. REAs also provide basic ecological information, information about threats and, increasingly, information about the human context at sites. Thus, information produced from REAs or other ecological assessments should be considered basic and essential input for the site conservation planning process (figure 5). The site conservation planning process described in figure 5 is a standardized model for site-based conservation employed by the Conservancy and its network of partner conservation organizations in the United States and internationally (Fawver and Sutter, 1996). Site management plans should not be developed without an understanding of the conservation targets; this understanding is derived from ecological assessments. In general, site conservation planning involves several steps. REA is clearly central to the site conservation process because site conservation planning cannot proceed without conservation target information as input.

Community-Based Conservation

When REAs are implemented at sites, local communities should be studied and the human context of conservation should be analyzed. Integrating information about species and vegetation types with infor-

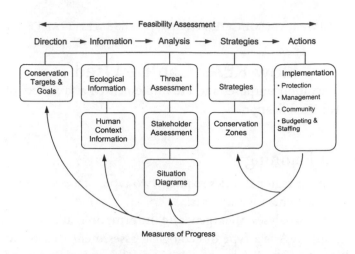

1	What are the conservation targets and long-term goals for those targets?	*TARGETS & GOALS*
2	What ecological and biological attributes sustain the targets over the long-term?	*ECOLOGICAL INFORMATION*
3	What are the characteristics of the human communities at the site?	*HUMAN CONTEXT INFORMATION*
4	What current and potential activities interfere with the maintenance of ecological processes that sustain the targets?	*THREAT ASSESSMENT*
5	Who are the organized groups and influential individuals at the site, what are their interests, what impacts might we have on them, and how might they help or hinder us in achieving site goals?	*STAKEHOLDER ASSESSMENT*
6	What can we do to prevent or mitigate threatening activities, and how can we influence important stakeholders?	*CONSERVATION STRATEGIES*
7	What are the areas on the ground where we need to act?	*CONSERVATION ZONES*
8	What actions are necessary to accomplish our goals, who will do them, how long will they take, how much will they cost?	*IMPLEMENTATION*
9	Can we succeed in our goals, based on assessment of both ecological possibilities and programmatic strengths?	*FEASIBILITY*
10	How will we determine whether we are making progress toward our goals?	*MEASURES OF PROGRESS*

Figure 5. The site conservation planning (SCP) approach. SCP can be thought of as a series of steps and questions; answers constitute the major components of the site conservation plan. REAs generate information about conservation targets (natural communities and species) and threats, the primary inputs to the SCP process.

mation about the local human context is another component of site conservation planning (figure 5). This analysis of the human context is a participatory and iterative process of social inquiry that integrates existing tools and methodologies to assess and describe the relationships between the local communities and a conservation site (Borrini-Feyerabend, 1997; Byers, 1996; FAO, 1990; Feuerstein, 1986; National Environment Secretariat, 1990; Poole, 1995; Slocum et al., 1995). Local people are often the primary users of the resources from the study site, and a better understanding of resource-use conflicts, power structures, and gender relationships in the nearby communities facilitates conservation planning (see, for example, Redford and Mansour, 1996; Western and Wright, 1994). Because humans are an essential part of the biodiversity equation and conservation solution, an analysis of local peoples and their communities should always be conducted in parallel with REAs.

Applied Science

REA is an application of science for the satisfaction of conservation objectives, and the REA methodology and process are always contextualized within a clear understanding of the specific REA objectives and expected outcomes. REA should not be construed as basic research because every REA represents science conducted for some stated management purpose. If the specific objective of an REA is, for example, to identify the biodiversity in an area to inform the development of a management plan, then the REA is an applied science approach to rapidly generate useful biodiversity information for management plan formulation. If the specific REA objective is to identify critical habitats for designation as a strict protection management category, then the REA represents applied science to inform zonation or protected area establishment. If the specific REA objective is to identify abundance of a population to evaluate harvest regulations, then the REA offers applied science in support of specific resource management decisions.

Measuring Success

The success of an REA is measured in terms of the conservation benefits produced, the quality of information generated, the training provided, and an improved stewardship for the resources of the area. The conservation impacts are sometimes obvious, such as the establishment of the area as a national park, or the incorporation of a zoning scheme into a management plan. REAs also are successful when they result in the generation of information that contributes to an enhanced scientific understanding of biodiversity, such as in the discovery of new, rare, and endangered species. One obvious aspect of REA success is the discovery of species new to science. In general, only if an REA produces information that contributes to an improved, conservation-oriented management of an area can the REA be considered successful. Table 2 highlights several such REA "successes."

REAs also provide training opportunities to scientists and managers. REA is a very useful conservation planning tool, and individuals trained in the use of this tool are valuable conservation assets. This capacity-building dimension of REA is important because it provides the potential for accomplishing similar work in the future.

In addition to direct conservation impacts and training benefits, REAs should be considered successful if they produce an enhanced potential for interinstitutional conservation collaborations. REAs can contribute to improved policy environments and also can serve as focal points for galvanizing interest in local environmental issues.

Organization of the Manual

This manual can be approached in two ways: first, as a description of the REA process; and second, as a description of the essential tools and techniques that are used to conduct an REA.

Table 2. Types and frequency of conservation benefits realized from REAs. REAs have improved conservation at sites in a variety of ways, but principally through the development of a stronger management approach. These data are from a survey of conservation impacts from REAs (Sedaghatkish, 1999).

Conservation Benefits from REAs	No. of Sites
New Protected Area	2
Management Plans	10
Increased Management Presence	9
Land Acquisitions	6
Zoning/Boundary Changes	11
Ecological Monitoring	9
Restoration Activities	6
Creation/Design of Biological Corridors	4
Increased Habitat Protection	10
Environmental Education Programs	7
Threats Abatement Activities	8
Research Programs	11
Sustainable Development Activities	6
Community-Based Conservation Activities	9

The ten-step REA process, which is described at the beginning of chapter 1, falls roughly into four phases. The first phase is conceptualization and initial planning. The second phase includes planning and training workshops and initial landscape characterization. The third phase is field implementation, and the fourth phase is information and reporting. The ordering of chapters in this book generally follows the sequence of these phases.

The essential tools and techniques are described throughout this manual and include the following: vegetation classification and survey, sampling, GIS, satellite image processing, aerial photography, GPS, mapping, map production, plant survey methods, fauna survey methods, threats assessments, data management, and information integration. The presentation of materials describing the REA process and the REA tools is mixed throughout the manual.

The manual is divided into five parts. Part I deals with process and planning issues and includes the second and third chapters. Chapter 1 presents an overview of the REA process and sampling framework. All readers should review the process description because it presents the sequence of steps that are followed in virtually all REAs. The sampling framework description also is important because it describes the emphasis on characterizing and mapping vegetation as the framework for all field sampling efforts. Chapter 2 reviews the planning and management dimensions of REA. Because REAs are usually multi-institutional projects, they require special attention to project management.

Part II focuses on the mapping and spatial dimensions of REAs. Chapters 3 and 4 are intended for readers with an interest in either understanding or undertaking the mapping of biodiversity in an REA context. Chapter 3 describes the spatial information technologies (GIS, GPS, and RS) and their conservation applications, and Chapter 4 describes the mapping of an REA. Chapter 4 also contains a set of seventeen color maps. Twelve of these maps describe the sequence of mapping activities in one case-study REA in Parque Nacional del Este (National Park of the East) in the Dominican Republic (The Nature Conservancy, 1997b); the remaining five maps are examples from other REAs. All readers are encouraged to review the color maps section for a quick and visually striking impression of the REA process. A detailed textual description of the Parque Nacional del Este REA case study is presented in appendix 1.

Part III deals with fieldwork issues, including vegetation and fauna surveys and threat assessments. Chapters 5 and 6 describe the surveys of vegetation and fauna, respectively, and are designed for readers who wish to understand the species-level sampling and analysis components of REA. Chapter 7—a general description of threats assessments—is oriented toward readers desiring to understand how threats to biodiversity in an area should be characterized.

Part IV concerns information management, integration, and reporting issues. Chapter 8 describes the information management aspects of REAs and how large amounts of data produced by different REA teams are integrated and synthesized into a cohesive set of management recommendations for the study site. Chapter 9 describes how the REA effort is documented, published, and disseminated.

Part V (chapter 10) comments on the future of REA.

The appendices contain (1) a detailed case study of the same REA for which the color maps in chapter 4 were developed (Parque Nacional del Este, Dominican Republic; The Nature Conservancy, 1997b), (2) a full set of REA field forms for sampling, and (3) a sample generic scope of work between the soliciting and implementing entities of an REA, which can be used as a model agreement for collaboration.

Literature Cited

Acevedo, C., J. Fox, R. Gauto, T. Granizo, S. Keel, J. Pinazzo, L. Spinzi, W. Sosa, and V. Vera. 1990. *Areas prioritarias para la consevación en la región oriental del Paraguay.* Asuncíon, Paraguay: Conservation Data Center.

Aparecida de Brito, M., C. Sobrevila, J. C. Dalponte, G. A. Borges, and T. Grant. 1991a. *Setting Conservation Priorities in the State of Mato Grosso, Brazil.* Unpublished report. Washington, D.C.: The World Bank.

Aparecida de Brito, M., C. Sobrevila, T. Grant, and J. Walsh. 1991b. *Rapid Ecological Assessment of Rio Sepotuba, Mato Grosso, Brazil.* Unpublished report. Washington, D.C.: The World Bank.

Austin, M. P., and C. R. Margules. 1986. Assessing representativeness. In *Wildlife Conservation Evaluation,* edited by M. B. Usher. London: Chapman and Hall.

Beattie, A. J., and I. Oliver. 1994. Taxonomic minimalism. *Trends in Ecology and Evolution* 9:488–490.

Borrini-Feyerabend, G., ed. 1997. *Beyond Fences: Seeking Social Sustainability in Conservation.* 2 vols. Gland, Switzerland: International Union for the Conservation of Nature.

Buttrick, S. C. 1992. Habitat management: A decision making process. *Rhodora* 94:258–286.

Byers, B. A. 1996. *Understanding and Influencing Behaviors in Conservation and Natural Resources Management.* African Biodiversity Series, no. 4. Washington, D.C.: Biodiversity Support Program.

Chernoff, B. 1998. *Biodiversity and Conservation of Aquatic Systems: Rapid Assessment Programs, Establishing Priorities, and Ethical Considerations.* In Symposium on Biodiversity and Conservation, 58.2, edited by N. Castagnoli. In Proceedings of the Pan American Veterinary Congress XV.

Conservation Data Center-Paraguay. 1991. *Estudios biológicos en el area del proyecto Mbaracayú, Canindeyu, República de Paraguay: Caracterización de las comunidades naturales, la flora y la avifauna.* Asuncion, Paraguay: Conservation Data Center.

Dinerstein, E., D. M. Olson, D. J. Graham, A. L. Webster, S. A. Primm, M. P. Bookbinder, and G. Ledec. 1995. *A Conservation Assessment of the Terrestrial Ecoregions of Latin America and the Caribbean.* Washington, D.C.: The World Bank.

Food and Agriculture Organization (FAO). 1990. *The Community's Toolbox: The Idea, Methods and Tools for Participatory Assessment, Monitoring and Evaluation in Community Forestry.* Community Forestry Field Manual 2. Prepared by D'Arcy Davis Case. Bangkok, Thailand: FAO Regional Wood Energy Department.

Fawver, R., and R. Sutter. 1996. Threat Assessment. Chap. 9 in *Site Conservation Planning Manual.* Unpublished technical document. Arlington, Va.: The Nature Conservancy.

Feuerstein, M-T. 1986. *Partners in Evaluation: Evaluating Development and Community Programmes with Participants.* London: MacMillan.

Foster, R. B., T. A. Parker III, A. H. Gentry, L. H. Emmons, A. Chicchón, T. Schulenberg, L. Rodríguez, G. Lamas, H. Ortega, J. Icochea, W. Wust, M. Romo, J. A. Castillo, O. Phillips, C. Reynel, A. Kratter, P. K. Donahue, and L. J. Barkley. 1994. *The Tambopata-Candamo Reserved Zone of Southeastern Perú: A Biological Assessment.* Washington, D.C.: Conservation International.

Grossman, D. H., S. Iremonger, and D. M. Muchoney. 1991. *Jamaica: A Rapid Ecological Assessment. Phase I: An Island-Wide Characterization and Mapping of Natural Communities & Modified Vegetation Types.* Arlington, Va.: The Nature Conservancy.

Institute of Environmental Assessment. 1995. *Guidelines for Baseline Ecological Assessment.* London: Chapman and Hall.

Janzen, D. H., and W. Hallwachs. 1994. *All Taxa Biodiversity Inventory (ATBI) of Terrestrial Systems. A Generic Protocol for Preparing Wildland Biodiversity for Non-Damaging Use.* Draft report of a National Science Foundation Workshop, 16–18 April in Philadelphia, Pa.

Jermy, C., D. Long, M. Sands, N. Stork, and S. Winser, eds. 1995. *Biodiversity Assessment: A Guide to Good Practice.* London: Department of the Environment/HMSO.

Lammert, M., and J. Higgins. 1997. *A Classification Framework for Freshwater Communities: Proceedings of The Nature Conservancy's Aquatic Community Classification Workshop.* Arlington, Va.: The Nature Conservancy.

Leary, T., ed. 1993. *Rapid Ecological Survey of the Arnavon Islands: A Report to the Landowners of the Arnavon Island Group.* Solomon Islands: The Nature Conservancy and Environment and Conservation.

Margules, C. R., and M. P. Austin, eds. 1991. *Nature Conservation: Cost Effective Biological Surveys and Data Analysis.* Canberra, Australia: CSIRO.

Margules, C. R., and T.C. Redhead. 1995. *BioRap: Guidelines for Using the BioRap Methodology and Tools.* Canberra, Australia: CSIRO.

Nature Conservancy, The. 1997a. *Designing a Geography of Hope: Ecoregion-based Conservation in The Nature Conservancy.* Arlington, Va.: The Nature Conservancy.

Nature Conservancy, The. 1997b. *Evaluación Ecológica Integral: Parque Nacional del Este, República Dominicana. Tomo 1: Recursos terrestres.* Arlington, Va.: The Nature Conservancy.

NES (National Environment Secretariat). 1990. *Participatory Rural Appraisal.* National Environment Secretariat in Kenya, Clark University, Egerton University, and the Center for International Development and Environment of the World Resources Institute.

Oren, D., J. Cardoso da Silva, G. Colli, A. Nunes, H. Higuchi, M. Fernandes da Silva, S. Soares de Almeida, and L. Barbosa. 1998. *Rapid Ecological Assessment of the Chamflora Lands, Amapá.* Belém, Brazil: Museu Paraense Emilio Goeldi.

Poole, P. 1995. *Indigenous Peoples, Mapping and Biodiversity Conservation.* Washington, D.C.: Biodiversity Support Program and World Wildlife Fund.

Redford, K., and J. Mansour, eds. 1996. *Traditional Peoples and Biodiversity Conservation in Large Tropical Landscapes.* Arlington, Va.: The Nature Conservancy.

Roberts, L. 1991. Ranking the rainforests. *Science* 251:1559–1560.

Sedaghatkish, G. 1999. *Rapid Ecological Assessment Source Book.* Arlington, Va.: The Nature Conservancy.

Scott, J. M., T. H. Tear, and F. W. Davis. 1996. *Gap Analysis: A Landscape Approach to Biodiversity Planning.* Bethesda, Md.: American Society of Photogrammetry and Remote Sensing.

Slocum, R., L. Wichhart, D. Rocheleau, and B. Thomas-Slayter, eds. 1995. *Power, Process and Participation: Tools for Change.* London: Intermediate Technologies Publications.

Sobrevila, C., and P. Bath. 1992. *Evaluación ecológica rápida: Un manual para usuarios de América Latina y el Caribe.* Arlington, Va.: The Nature Conservancy.

Spellerberg, I. 1992. *Evaluation and Assessment for Conservation.* London: Chapman and Hall.

UNEP (United Nations Environment Program). 1995. *Global Biodiversity Assessment.* Edited by V. H. Heywood, and R. T. Watson. Cambridge, England: Cambridge University Press.

Western, D., and R. M. Wright. 1994. *Natural Connections: Perspectives in Community-Based Conservation.* Washington, D.C.: Island Press.

PART I

THE REA PROCESS AND PLANNING

Chapter 1

The REA Process and Sampling Framework

Roger Sayre

There are two aspects of REA that are fundamental to the understanding of the overall concept: the ten-step implementation sequence, and the sampling approach and framework. This chapter begins by characterizing the ten steps in the REA process. It then describes the sampling framework, beginning with a discussion of classification and mapping of vegetation types. This is followed by a discussion of the difference between vegetation classifications and imagery-based classifications, and how these two are reconciled. The chapter concludes by addressing species-level sampling, sampling intensity, and sampling plans.

The Process

The typical REA process is a ten-step sequence of events, with each step consisting of a set of related activities. The sequence is as follows:

1. Conceptual Development
2. Initial Planning
3. Initial Landscape Characterization
4. Planning Workshop
5. Training Workshop
6. Field Implementation
7. Report Generation by Discipline
8. Information Integration and Synthesis
9. Preparation of Final Report and Maps
10. Publication and Dissemination of Products

Although not all REAs incorporate each of the ten steps in the exact order depicted above, REAs generally follow this sequence.

Conceptual Development

In the Conceptual Development phase, the idea to conduct an REA emerges, and initial discussions about the merits and shortcomings of the approach are held. The need to generate biological information for an area can be identified by governments, local people, international scientists, in-country conservation non-governmental organizations (NGOs), and other parties. If the need to generate this information can be coupled with a financial mechanism for accomplishing the work, an REA is conceptualized. The primary implementor usually conceptualizes the REA and is ultimately responsible for all planning and implementation.

Initial Planning

The Initial Planning stage follows closely upon the conceptualization of the REA. During this phase, the primary implementor officially proposes to do an REA and usually attempts to identify the geographic extent, determine the objectives, secure financing, identify collaborators, develop time frames, and solicit input from the scientific community, the government, and the local people. Financial security for the project should be established before the REA is highly publicized in case funding does not materialize and the REA cannot be executed. Identifying collaborating institutions and individuals is critically important and requires a thoughtful consideration of the role, reputation, availability, cost, biases, and political constraints of the potential collaborators.

Initial Landscape Characterization

The Initial Landscape Characterization phase entails the interpretation of imagery (satellite images or aerial photographs) to classify the landscape under study into a system of vegetation units, typically vegetation types or land use–land cover classes. Delineating these discernible landscape features from imagery (entitation) reveals the number and distribution of all unique vegetation types. Classification of the study area into vegetation types is fundamental to the REA concept, and it distinguishes REA from other rapid biodiversity assessments. The classification is preliminary, and the vegetation types need not be identified during the initial entitation because they will necessarily be verified in subsequent fieldwork. It is, however, extremely important to assign all of the land area that constitutes the study site into some system of vegetation units. This delineation of classes is necessary for two major reasons: (1) to characterize and map biodiversity at the landscape level, and (2) to establish a sampling framework within which to conduct field sampling. Once the area has been preliminarily delineated into vegetation types, the number and logistical details of the field visits can be organized. The Initial Landscape Characterization step often involves helicopter or aircraft overflight reconnaissance missions to begin the process of identifying unknown vegetation units and to provide a greater familiarity with the area.

Planning and Training Workshops

The Planning Workshop is the most critical step in the process. During this workshop, all identified collaborators come together to develop a shared vision. The workshop produces a consensus on the objectives, which often change from previously formulated objectives. The workshop also results in a workplan, derived by consensus, that assigns specific tasks, identifies responsible individuals, and establishes benchmarks and deadlines.

The Training Workshop can be coupled with the planning workshop or held at a later date. This workshop provides training related to technically oriented activities, such as mapping, field plot establishment, and data collection. The training workshop allows disciplinary specialists to obtain instruction in the use of standardized sampling techniques and field forms. Experienced REA scientists provide this instruction.

Field Implementation

During the Field Implementation phase, field data collection activities are undertaken. The field team consists of highly specialized scientists with expertise in several disciplinary areas. These scientists are often organized into groups representing taxonomic disciplines (e.g., botany, herpetofauna, and avifauna). The groups sample the area by visiting a number of pre-established sampling locations within representative vegetation types identified during the Initial Landscape Characterization. Field sampling operations require a great deal of logistical coordination. For maximum efficiency and concentration of effort, fewer, well-coordinated, longer-duration, team-based field sampling initiatives are preferred to several short sampling efforts by individual scientists. All field data are precisely georeferenced using global positioning system (GPS) technologies for subsequent mapping and data analysis.

Report Generation by Discipline

The Report Generation by Discipline phase includes the data analysis and presentation of results by individual groups following the completion of data collection activities. Each group produces a stand-alone document detailing objectives, methodologies, major findings, and conclusions. These reports constitute the major input into the integration and synthesis of all of the REA-derived information for the preparation of the final REA report. Many of the individual collaborators withdraw from the REA initiative after generating their own taxa- or discipline-based reports for three reasons: (1) their individual reports constitute major contributions to science and biodiversity management in and of themselves, (2) someone else is identified to integrate the final information and prepare the report, or (3) the lack of continued funding precludes subsequent dedication of effort.

Information Integration and Synthesis

After all of the individual discipline reports are submitted to the primary implementor, the Information Integration and Synthesis phase begins. This work is best done by a small team of individuals with both extensive knowledge of the area and broad ecological perspectives. The integration step involves reviewing all of the single discipline reports and maps, analyzing the results with a multidisciplinary focus, extracting the most important information from each report, repackaging this information in a new multidisciplinary context, and developing conclusions and recommendations for site management that will be presented in the REA report.

The integration step is the most difficult part of the REA process. It is not a trivial exercise to review several documents, extract the most useful information from each, and combine all of this information into a cohesive synthesis. The original vision of the REA is frequently lost at this juncture because it can be challenging to relate large amounts of raw information to the satisfaction of the objectives. The difficulty of accomplishing this work can also be exacerbated by a growing impatience to finish the project. The integration step is normally accomplished in a workshop format.

Final Report, Publication, and Dissemination

The last two phases—Preparation of Final Report and Maps, and Publication and Dissemination of Products—require a great effort to turn the draft document from the Information Integration and Synthesis into a concise, useful, visually appealing document and associated maps. Many draft versions are commonly produced, and they should be widely reviewed for content and style. Donors may wish to review documents prior to publication. If the document is to be translated into another language, substantial staff and/or financial resources are necessary. The decision to translate should be made early in the REA process so that the translation work may begin as soon as possible after an acceptable final report is produced.

These ten steps describe the process of an REA and can be used to measure progress. We now turn our attention to the REA sampling framework.

The Sampling Framework

Vegetation types constitute the sampling framework of an REA. Species are surveyed within vegetation types. Vegetation types are organized and described in vegetation classification systems.

Vegetation Classification

A vegetation classification is a grouping of similar types of vegetation according to logical criteria. The classification is usually organized hierarchically, and it contains descriptions of the types of classified units (FGDC, 1996; Grossman et al., 1998). A vegetation classification is presented as an ordered, hierarchical, and logical list of characterized vegetation types in some area or region. A partial example of a vegetation classification from an REA in Guantanamo, Cuba (Sedaghatkish and Roca, 1999) appears in box 1-1. Different classification systems are used in different regions of the world and are based on vegetation structure (physiognomic criteria), vegetation composition (floristics), or a mixed classification combining both structure (at upper hierarchy levels) and composition (at lower hierarchy levels) (FGDC, 1996; Grossman et al., 1998). For each REA, an appropriate vegetation classification is selected to describe the vegetation types that will be sampled and characterized.

Vegetation Types

Vegetation types commonly mapped in REAs include vegetation communities and vegetation cover classes. Vegetation communities are natural assemblages of coexisting and interacting plant species that depend on and modify their environments (Mueller-Dombois and Ellenberg, 1974). They are often named with both physiognomic and floristic descriptors (FGDC, 1996; Grossman et al., 1998). Vegetation cover classes, on the other hand, are broader groupings of similar kinds of vegetation, such as forests, wetlands, and scrublands (Anderson et al., 1976). Imagery with relatively high spatial resolution (aerial photographs or high-resolution satellite imagery) often permits the delineation of actual vegetation communities, whereas lower resolution imagery may permit only the delineation of vegetation cover. We use the term *vegetation types* throughout this book to represent either vegetation communities or vegetation cover classes.

Vegetation types frequently represent logical management units because they have a discernible spatial extent for which conservation management strategies can be formulated. Because REA results provide the information necessary for making conservation management decisions, the most useful representation of REA information is in the context of ecologically based landscape units with their associated elements of species biodiversity. Mapped vegetation types are often ideal for this purpose.

TROPICAL ARID FOREST
Phyllostylon forest
Phyllostylon brasiliensis Forest Alliance
Association: *P. brasiliensis—Senna* sp.—*Stenocereus histrix*
Phyllostylon cactus forest
Phyllostylon brasiliensis Forest Alliance
Association: *P. Phyllostylon brasiliensis* Forest

MANGROVE FORESTS/SCRUB
Red mangrove tidal forest
Rhizophora mangle Tidally Flooded Forest
R. mangle Medium Island Forest
Black mangrove scrub
Avicennia germinans Tidally Flooded Shrubland
Association: *A. germinans/Batis maritima* Shrubland

PALM WOODLAND
Bucida woodland
Bucida spinosa Seasonally Flooded Woodland Alliance
Association: *B. spinosa—Harrisia taylori/Cordia globosa* Woodland
Cordia woodland
Bucida spinosa Seasonally Flooded Woodland Alliance
Association: *Cordia densata—Ciskerwylum frutioocumo—Capparis ferruginea/Cordia globosa—Lycium tweedianum* Woodland

PALM SCRUB
Coccothrinax scrub
Coccothrinax fragrans Shrubland Alliance
Association: *C. fragrans* Shrubland
Croton—Coccothrinax scrub
Coccothrinax fragrans—Croton (rosmarinoides, stenophyllus) Shrubland Alliance
Association: *C. fragrans—Croton (rosmarinoides, stenophyllus)* Shrubland

TROPICAL ARID SCRUB
Cactus scrub/Thorn scrub
Stenocereus peruvianus Woodland Alliance
Association: *S. peruvianus—Plumeria tuberculata* Woodland
Randia aculeata Shrubland Alliance
Association: *R. aculeata—Tabebuia myrtifolia* Shrubland
Colubrina scrub
Colubrina elliptica Shrubland Alliance
Association: *C. elliptica* Shrubland

SPARSELY VEGETATED ROCK
Coastal rock pavement
Rachicallis americana Sparsely Vegetated Alliance
Association: *R. americana/Caribea littoralis* Sparse Vegetation
Open shrub outcrop
Melocactus harlowii Sparsely Vegetated Alliance
Association: *M. harlowii—Agave albescens* Sparse Vegetation

Box 1-1. Vegetation classification (partial) from an REA of U.S. Naval Station at Guantanamo Bay, Cuba (Sedaghatkish and Roca, 1999).

Mapping vegetation types necessarily involves interpreting remotely sensed imagery to characterize landscape units (Lillesand and Kiefer, 1994). This interpretation is accomplished by a preclassification of imagery, a field verification effort, and a classification and map refinement process, all described in subsequent sections.

Imagery-Based Classification

A remotely sensed image (aerial photograph or satellite image) contains polygon features that represent areas of differing land cover or vegetation. For example, when looking at a satellite image or color aerial photograph, areas with a variety of different spectral characteristics can usually be discerned. Delineating these features onto a map base results in a set of polygons, which can then be classified. This activity is completed in the Initial Landscape Characterization step and results in a map of preliminarily classified polygons, often referred to as the "unknown polygon map" (figure 1-1). These mapped polygons constitute the remote sensing classification, which is differentiated from a nonmapped vegetation community classification. The vegetation classification can be spatially distributed (mapped) by assigning the different vegetation units described in the classification system to the polygons resulting in the image and then

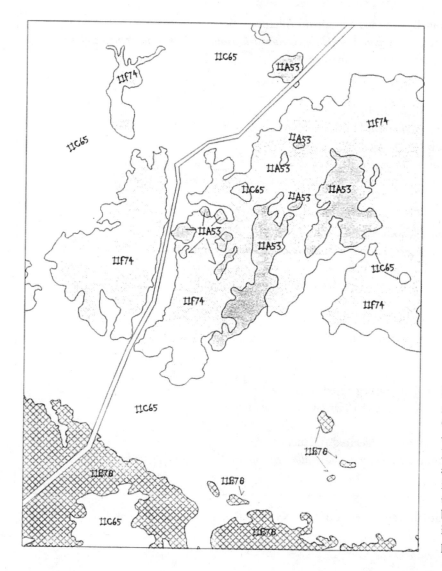

Figure 1-1. An unknown polygon map from an Initial Landscape Characterization analysis. Unique vegetation types are coded with a label that may contain information about the vegetation unit (e.g., which individual, from which spectral signature class, in which sampling region), but the true identity of the polygons is not determined until the field sampling and verification work.

verifying that the actual vegetation units at a particular location on the ground correspond with the mapped unit at that same location (Lillesand and Kiefer, 1994).

Reconciling Classification Systems

The mapping of a vegetation classification by assigning described vegetation types into features delineated from image interpretation can be a difficult endeavor, and it occasionally creates conflict between vegetation classification ecologists and remote sensing specialists. This conflict occurs because (1) some described vegetation types cannot be distinguished in the imagery, and (2) distinguishable features in aerial photographs and satellite imagery may not always correspond with described vegetation types. For example, although a vegetation ecologist may identify a pine forest, a spruce/fir forest, and a hemlock forest as three distinct vegetation types, these types may not be separable in a remote sensing classification in which all types might be singularly grouped as needle-leaf evergreen forests. The map produced ultimately, which shows the spatial distribution of vegetation types, will likely represent a compromise between the vegetation that can be identified in an image and the vegetation types that are described in a classification and verified in the field.

Because REAs are rapid, preliminary, and nonexhaustive, predicting where vegetation communities should exist based on a knowledge of the abiotic factors that control their distribution is beyond the scope of an REA. From a practical and simplistic management standpoint, interpreting unique landscape units from imagery and then sampling them on the ground to determine their actual identity is much wiser. Due to limitations of time and budget, not all polygons in the unknown polygon map (e.g., figure 1-1) will be visited on the ground for verification. Again, the final product will represent the best compromise between remotely sensed data and what is verifiable on the ground. The REA mapping approach is, in essence, a remote sensing classification supported by fieldwork.

The Field Sampling Approach

Field sampling occurs at point locations inside preselected examples of each vegetation type. Sampling locations are not determined using grid-based sampling strategies or environmental gradient transects (gradsects). The selection of the actual vegetation units to be sampled is derived from a study of the unknown polygon map (e.g., figure 1-1) produced during the Initial Landscape Characterization. This map contains the set of all vegetation units (polygons) in the study area, a subset of which is chosen for sampling. Two types of vegetation sampling occur during fieldwork: (1) sampling at point locations to verify vegetation type and identify dominant floristic groups, and (2) sampling in plots at a subset of these locations to obtain quantitative information for plant diversity estimates.

REAs always include mapping of the distribution of vegetation types in the study site, which requires that many examples of these vegetation types be visited for field verification. Thus the vegetation team determines the selection of the vegetation units to be sampled, which will include representative examples of all vegetation types in the site. Fauna sampling is conducted in all vegetation types, but typically at fewer replicate sampling locations within each vegetation type due to the sometimes complex methodologies for surveying animals (e.g., pitfall traps and mistnests). Moreover, the fauna team often identifies additional sampling locations that do not necessarily correspond with locations determined by the vegetation team for vegetation type verification. In these cases, the vegetation team agrees to sample these "extra" locations as well.

In plant surveys, sampling locations are point locations whose coordinates are precisely geolocated with a GPS receiver. Species are identified out to 20 meters in a 360-degree "sweep" around the point. Plots established at the sampling location for quantifying diversity are generally 20 meters × 20 meters (forests) or 10 meters × 10 meters (shrublands/grasslands).

Selecting Sampling Locations

Sampling locations within vegetation units are selected by visual inspection of the image and corresponding unknown polygon map; they are based on representativeness, known or suspected biological value, accessibility, proximity to other different landscapes, level of threats, and availability of information. Whereas traditional ecological inventory emphasizes highly objective field sampling based on random coordinate-pair sample locations, transects, or sampling grids laid out over the entire study area (Magurran, 1988; Heyer et al., 1994; Wilson et al., 1996; Kent and Coker, 1992), REA emphasizes sampling in mapped vegetation types. This sampling is frequently determined by access and efficiency. Although replicate units are sampled, the sampling process is not designed to be as statistically rigorous as traditional ecological inventory. Knowledge of the large-scale disturbance history of the area is also very important because disturbance history influences the biota.

The Distribution of Vegetation Types and Fauna

REAs use vegetation types as a practical framework for surveying faunal taxa, but the extent to which animal distributions are influenced by the spatial organization of vegetation is highly variable and difficult to precisely characterize. For example, some fauna respond more to the structural variables in a forest than to the species composition (MacArthur, 1964; Chadwick et al., 1986). REAs are not intended to rigorously determine habitat affinities of faunal groups. Rather, the occurrence of fauna in the vegetation type (or types) in which they are encountered is emphasized. In REA, vegetation types are considered to be the most biologically useful framework for the preliminary description of animal distributions.

Plants are generally distributed according to temperature, precipitation, and geomorphology (Holdridge, 1967; Austin, 1987; Austin and Smith, 1989). Moreover, historical factors, such as barriers to dispersal and past and present interspecific interactions, also influence plant distributions (Mueller-Dombois and Ellenberg, 1974; Connell, 1980). Microclimatic and local physical environmental conditions can control the distribution of vegetation even at submeter scales. In some instances, the distribution of animal communities will be tightly coupled with the distribution of vegetation types. This may be because these animal communities are intimately associated and perhaps even dependent upon the vegetation, or it may simply be because the animal communities are distributed according to ecologically controlling variables and could be similarly present at the location with an entirely different vegetation type.

Animal mobility and seasonal and diurnal behaviors require an animal sampling effort different from the normal one-point-in-time vegetation sampling effort. For this and other reasons, we recommend (1) preliminary sampling of animal populations within the vegetation communities that are to be characterized in an REA, and (2) additional sampling as necessary (resources permitting) to characterize the spatial and temporal distribution of certain fauna. The habitat preferences of some species are relatively well understood; this information should be used where available to refine sampling approaches for fauna. Additional information on species-level sampling is provided in chapters 5 (vegetation) and 6 (fauna).

Sampling Intensity

The intensity of sampling depends upon the amount of information desired and the resources to support fieldwork. Discussions about sampling intensity should be held during the Initial Planning phase. Time constraints may limit the ability to accomplish replicate sampling in multiple examples within the same vegetation community. In general, there are two types of biodiversity sampling approaches. The most popular and least expensive REA sampling methodology involves characterizing vegetation and the distributions of certain taxa at one moment in time by mapping vegetation types and recording occurrences of species encountered during fieldwork. The second type of sampling aims to at characterize species abundances, and fieldwork frequently includes a seasonality component. Characterizing species abundances, or relative abundances, is more often associated with standard species inventory work, and it requires exhaustive sampling, which is normally outside the scope of a typical REA.

The sampling principle is based on representativeness, with replicates, in all distinct vegetation types. This means that all vegetation types identified from the image interpretation must be visited, and each type should be sampled in multiple locations to capture variation within the same vegetation type. Repeated samples within vegetation types are necessary for confidence in the final map of vegetation types.

Subdividing the study area into different sampling "regions" based on ecological units is often appropriate. For example, watersheds serve well as spatial planning units because (1) they are easy to delineate and map, (2) they are sensible management units for nonconservation purposes (e.g., agricultural production and water development) as well, and (3) they are easily recognized on the ground by humans. Watersheds have been successfully employed as spatial planning and sampling units in REA (FPSNSM, in press). However, establishing sampling regions within the site is more commonly based on considerations of practicality, such as access, study area size, human presence, management urgency, and logistical planning. Sampling emphasis is often restricted to natural areas or to those areas with minimal human-caused alteration. A number of specific polygons are targeted in the sampling plan for visitation. The number and locations of polygons to be sampled are determined from analysis of the unknown polygon map. Decisions about which polygons to sample are usually not based on a statistical analysis, but rather on a combination of practical and rule-of-thumb considerations.

For practicality, sampling should be planned in areas where a maximum number of distinct classes exist in relative proximity, which will enhance sampling efficiency. The decision about which polygons will actually be sampled is made by group consensus and is usually based primarily on objectives, resource constraints, and accessibility. Typically, large polygons with easy access will be chosen for ground-truthing. Other representative polygons with difficult access may have to be verified by aerial survey.

Regardless of the sampling intensity, all vegetation types must be sampled. In typical biological inventory fieldwork, sampling locations are statistically determined and often randomly located. REA sampling is rarely statistically rigorous, but it is as thorough as access and resources permit. A sampling plan should detail the decisions about which polygons were chosen for sampling. The actual techniques used to sample plants and animals vary according to the objectives and budget of an REA. Suggestions on choosing appropriate sampling methods are provided in chapters 5 and 6.

The Sampling Plan

The sampling plan is a document that identifies areas to be sampled during fieldwork, designates field teams responsible for conducting the fieldwork, and establishes a chronogram with schedules for the sampling activities. The sampling plan details the strategy for sampling the entire study area, which is often subdivided. Table 1-1 shows a sampling plan from an REA in the Chaco region of Paraguay.

Table 1-1. A modified sampling plan from an REA in the Defensores del Chaco National Park, Paraguay. Three sampling regions were identified, and sampling locations (Obs. Pt.) were determined in replicate examples of each tentatively identified vegetation type. This plan is modified from the actual plan, which identified many more than forty-four sampling locations.

				Sampling Method at Each Observation Point					
Survey Site Name	Tentative Vegetation Types	Obs. Pt.	Date	Veg/flora	Date	Mammals	Birds	Amphibians	Reptiles
Agua Dulce	Gallery forest	1	12/8	Obs.	14/8	Transect	Obs.	Transect	Transect
Agua Dulce	Gallery forest	2	12/8	Obs.	14/8	Transect	Nets	Plot	Transect
Agua Dulce	Gallery forest	4	12/8	Obs.	14/8	Transect	Nets.	Transec	Transect
Agua Dulce	Aspidosperma quebracho-blanco dense forest	6	11/8	Obs.	14/8	Transect	Obs.		
Agua Dulce	A. quebracho-blanco open forest	7	11/8	Obs.	14/8	Transect			
Agua Dulce	A. quebracho-blanco dense forest	8	11/8	Obs.	14/8	Transect			
Agua Dulce	A. quebracho-blanco tall forest	10	11/8	Obs.					
Agua Dulce	A. quebracho-blanco tall forest	11	11/8	Plot					
Agua Dulce	Palm savanna	12	13/8	Plot			Obs.		
Agua Dulce	Tall quebrachal	13	13/8	Obs.					
Agua Dulce	A. quebracho-blanco open forest	14	13/8	Obs.					
Cerro Léon	A. quebracho-blanco dense forest	15	14/9	Obs.	15/9	Transect	Obs.	Transect	Transect
Cerro Léon	Aspidosperma quebracho-blanco dense forest	16	14/9	Plot	15/9	Transect		Plot	Transect
Cerro Léon	A. quebracho-blanco open forest	17	14/9	Plot	15/9	Transect			
Cerro Léon	Calycophyllum multiflorum riverine forest	18	14/9	Obs.	15/9	Transect	Obs.		
Cerro Léon	A. quebracho-blanco/C. multiflorum transitional forest	19	14/9	Obs.	17/9	Transect			
Cerro Léon	A. quebracho-blanco open forest	20	14/9	Plot	17/9	Transect			
Cerro Léon	A. quebracho-blanco/C. multiflorum transitional forest	21	14/9	Obs.	17/9	Transect			
Cerro Léon	A. quebracho-blanco open forest	22	13/9	Obs.	17/9	Transect			
Cerro Léon	Elionurus muticus savanna	23	13/9	Obs.	17/9	Transect	Obs.		
Cerro Léon	E. muticus savanna	24	13/9	Plot	17/9	Transect			
Cerro Léon	A. quebracho-blanco open forest	25	13/9	Obs.		Transect			
Cerro Léon	C. multiflorum riverine forest	26	13/9	Obs.		Transect			
Cerro Léon	A. quebracho-blanco open forest	27	13/9	Obs.		Transect			
Cerro Léon	A. quebracho-blanco forest/eastern tall forest transition	28	16/9	Obs.					
Cerro Léon	Plateau vegetation	29	16/9	Obs.					
Cerro Léon	Plateau vegetation	30	16/9	Plot					
Cerro Léon	Hillside forest	31	16/9	Obs.					
Cerro Léon	Hillside forest	32	16/9	Plot	16/8	Transect	Obs.	Transect	Transect
Cerro Léon	Forest on foothills	33	16/9	Obs.					
Cerro Léon	Forest on foothills	34	16/9	Plot					
La Jerenza	Aspidosperma pyrifolium open forest	35	1/9	Obs.			Obs.		
La Jerenza	A. pyrifolium open forest	36	1/9	Obs.	1-6/9	Transect			
La Jerenza	E. muticus savanna	37	1/9	Obs.	1-6/9	Transect			
La Jerenza	A. pyrifolium dense forest	38	1/9	Obs.	1-6/9	Transect			
La Jerenza	A. pyrifolium dense forest	39	1/9	Obs.					
La Jerenza	A. pyrifolium open forest	41	3/9	Obs.					
La Jerenza	A. pyrifolium dense forest	43	3/9	Obs.	1-6/9	Transect			
La Jerenza	E. muticus savanna	44	3/9	Obs.	7-9/9	Transect			

Literature Cited

Anderson, J. R., E. E. Hardy, J. T. Roach, and R. E. Witmer. 1976. *A Land Use and Land Cover Classification System for Use with Remote Sensor Data.* U.S. Geological Survey Professional Paper 964. Washington, D.C.: U.S. Government Printing Office.

Austin, M. P. 1987. Models for the analysis of species response to environmental gradients. *Vegetatio* 69:35–45

Austin, M. P., and T. M. Smith. 1989. A new model for the continuum concept. *Vegetatio* 83:35–47

Chadwick, N. L., D. R. Progulske, and J. T. Finn. 1986. Effect of fuelwood cutting on birds in Massachusetts hardwood forests. *Journal of Wildlife Management* 50:398–405.

Connell, J. H. 1980. Diversity and the co-evolution of competitors, or the ghost of competition past. *Oikos* 35:131–138

FGDC (Federal Geographic Data Committee). 1996. *Vegetation Classification and Information Standards.* Reston, Va.: FGDC Secretariat.

FPSNSM (Fundación Pro Sierra Nevada de Santa Marta). In press. *Evaluación ecológica rápida: Definición de áreas críticas para conservación en la Sierra Nevada de Santa Marta, Colombia.* Santa Marta, Colombia: FPSNSM.

Grossman, D. H., D. Faber-Langendoen, A. S. Weakley, M. Anderson, P. Bourgeron, R. Craword, K. Goodin, S. Landaal, K. Metzler, K. Patterson, M. Pyne, M. Reid, and L. Sneddon. 1998. *International Classification of Ecological Communities: Terrestrial Vegetation of the United States.* Vol. 1. The National Vegetation Classification System: Development, Status, and Applications. Arlington, Va.: The Nature Conservancy.

Heyer, W. R., M. A. Donnelly, R. W. McDiarmid, L. C. Hayek, and M. S. Foster, eds. 1994. *Measuring and Monitoring Biological Diversity: Standard Methods for Amphibians.* Washington, D.C.: Smithsonian Institution Press.

Holdridge, L. R. 1967. *Life Zone Ecology.* San José, Costa Rica: Tropical Science Center.

Kent, M., and P. Coker. 1992. *Vegetation Description and Analysis.* Ann Arbor, Mich.: CRC Press.

Lillesand, T. M., and R. W. Kiefer. 1994. *Remote Sensing and Image Interpretation.* New York: John Wiley and Sons.

MacArthur, R. H. 1964. Environmental factors affecting bird species diversity. *American Naturalist* 98:387–397.

Magurran, A. E. 1988. *Ecological Diversity and its Measurement.* Princeton, N.J.: Princeton University Press.

Mueller-Dombois, D., and H. Ellenberg. 1974. *Aims and Methods of Vegetation Ecology.* New York: John Wiley and Sons.

Sedaghatkish, G., and E. Roca. 1999. *Rapid Ecological Assessment: U.S. Naval Station Guantanamo Bay, Cuba.* Arlington, Va.: The Nature Conservancy.

Wilson, D. E., F. R. Cole, J. D. Nichols, R. Rudran, and M. S. Foster. 1996. *Measuring and Monitoring Biological Diversity: Standard Methods for Mammals.* Washington, D.C.: Smithsonian Institution Press.

Chapter 2

Careful Planning: A Key to Success

Roger Sayre and Ellen Roca

Thoughtful planning is the most important part of the REA process. A well-planned REA will be easier to implement and coordinate, and will prove more cost effective. The conservation benefits of an REA will be proportional to the amount of careful planning invested at the outset. This chapter describes the planning dimensions of REAs. We begin by discussing the needs for conducting REAs, the formulation of objectives, and the determination of the disciplinary scope of an REA. We then describe the REA team and how it participates in the planning and training workshops and fieldwork. We conclude with a brief discussion of safety considerations.

Assessing the Need for an REA

The need for an REA depends on the amount of information already available for the area under consideration and the urgency of obtaining new information about its habitats and species distributions. An REA always generates information for a specific application, and the need for an REA is established when there is a clear consensus about the need for the information. Areas for which considerable biodiversity information already exists are usually not good candidates. REAs develop detailed but basic information about the distribution of biodiversity on a particular landscape; if a current general understanding of that biodiversity is evident (e.g., cover type classes have been described and mapped and species lists have been developed), an REA is probably not appropriate. If the existing biodiversity information is considered to be high quality, noncontroversial, and generally current, an REA is inadvisable. REAs are not appropriate for marginal improvement or updating of existing biodiversity information because the rare species and habitats missing from existing lists still may remain undetected in an REA.

Marginally surveyed or unsurveyed areas are more appropriate for REA consideration, especially when a general lack of biodiversity information precludes sound conservation planning. Good candidate sites are frequently large, poorly understood, and highly threatened.

Formulating Objectives

The formulation of objectives that are sound, measurable, realistic, attainable, and timely is the most critical step in the planning process and must occur before any training or sampling efforts. The objectives become the yardstick for all future activities and resource allocations. Any activity that does not contribute to the satisfaction of the objectives should not be implemented. Draft objectives are usually formulated by the organization that establishes the initial need for the REA. This organization is usually the primary advocate of the REA and is often the primary implementor as well. Occasionally, however, governments establish the need for REAs, develop the objectives accordingly, and act as the primary implementor. Ideally, objectives are formulated by group consensus between government officials, the implementing agency, and local interests.

To illustrate the variety and general flavor of objectives that have been associated with REAs to date, a partial list of REA objectives, as they appear in REA planning documents and reports, follows:

- Provide information for the identification of important ecological sites.
- Characterize the vegetation types of the Park.
- Generate information about terrestrial and marine resources, threats, and potential uses of the Park for management.
- Train personnel in the use of satellite images and aerial photographs for the mapping of terrestrial and marine habitats.
- Identify and evaluate the threats to the natural systems and design a monitoring program.
- Conduct a speleological study of the caves of the Park and produce recommendations for their management.
- Develop a natural community classification and inventory for the study site.
- Generate baseline data for monitoring activities in the Park.
- Enhance the data management capability of the Conservation Data Center.
- Generate biological and ecological data to develop an initial management plan and threats analysis matrix.
- Produce a map showing vegetation communities, hydrography, roads, development activities, and special conservation areas.
- Collect and provide data in an archivable form compatible with national database formats.
- Document and assess the status and distribution of the island's marine and terrestrial resources and provide conservation management recommendations.
- Recommend priority actions for the management, development, and conservation of the watershed.
- Map the flora and fauna of the Park at the vegetation community level.
- Identify species that are threatened and/or in danger of extinction.
- Define new ecologically based boundaries for the Park.
- Conduct a comprehensive biophysical characterization of the Corridor.
- Foster cooperative relationships among conservation partners in the inventory, management, analysis, and application of ecological and conservation data.
- Develop preliminary data sets for future use in inventories that are more detailed and in ecological characterizations.
- Characterize natural communities, provide descriptions listing key species, and assess their importance for conservation.

- Study spatial patterns of benthic communities, including fringing mangrove forests, and describe natural and anthropogenic disturbances to these communities.

As shown by this list, REAs can have a wide variety of objectives.

The strength of these objectives should be assessed by considering the following questions:

- Is the objective focused on biodiversity and relevant to the situation at hand?
- Is the objective realistic, and can it be achieved?
- Is the objective measurable?
- Is the objective timely?

Good objectives have all the qualities listed above. Time spent in drafting, reviewing, and refining objectives is always fruitful; clarity in objectives can help prevent unwarranted delays in subsequent planning, implementation, and analysis.

Once formulated, the objectives should be widely disseminated to a public that includes all stakeholders in the area. REAs should never be conducted "secretly." Every attempt should be made to inform local interests and government officials about the survey, even if individuals representing these groups contributed to the formulation of the objectives. The format for disseminating these goals and objectives can include community workshops and presentation in the media. Local understanding about the nature of the REA, and local consensus on its utility, can help facilitate the process.

Establishing the Scope

The disciplinary scope of a terrestrial REA refers generally to the level of landscape classification and the number of taxonomic groups that will be assessed. A typical disciplinary scope for an REA might include vegetation communities, vascular plants, mammals, birds, reptiles, and amphibians. Additional taxa are sometimes included.

Objectives should ultimately determine the taxonomic groups to be included. REAs are usually resource constrained, and therefore the most visible, easily surveyed, and well-known taxa are surveyed. The suggestion to limit taxonomic representation to these well-known taxa (plants, mammals, birds, reptiles, and amphibians) is based on practical and financial considerations and does not imply a greater ecological importance. Indeed, a characterization of insect diversity would contribute to a substantially improved understanding of the local ecological dynamics. If the scientific expertise and financial resources are available, and the sampling for these organisms can be integrated into the general workplan, broader taxonomic representation is encouraged.

Most REAs to date have been limited to the well-known taxa. The disciplinary scope of the REA should be established early in the planning process. The disciplinary scope is sometimes limited by the lack of available scientific expertise. The choice of taxa to investigate should be reflected in both the REA objectives and in all official descriptions of the scope of work.

Organizational Issues

Three important organizational aspects of the planning process are funding, team-building, and role clarification in REA agreements. The following three sections discuss these aspects.

Soliciting Funding

Financial support options for REAs include development banks, international governments, international development agencies, international conservation organizations, foundations, corporations, military landowners, and individuals. Every attempt should be made to secure funding in the initial planning phase, and as many of these donor types as possible should be contacted. A succinct (two- or three-page) fundraising proposal with clearly stated goals and uses of the solicited funding should be developed. It should include a list of products wherever possible and should clearly state that credit for the financial support will be acknowledged in project documentation. It should be tailored to the donor's interests, and the technical content of the proposal should reflect the technical inclination of the donor. Face-to-face follow-up after the donor receives the proposal is encouraged.

The proposal should contain a realistic budget section, which is determined according to requirements for salary, operating expenses, equipment costs, imagery acquisition and processing, overflights, international travel, institutional overhead, and so on. If the full amount required for funding the REA cannot be obtained, the scope of the REA should be re-evaluated and scaled back.

Team Composition

The REA team is the group of individuals officially responsible for executing the REA. This team will include scientists responsible for generating results and administrators responsible for managing the process. The REA team, collectively, is the primary implementor of the REA. This team may vary in number from few to many and may represent one or more collaborating institutions. Multidisciplinary, multi-institutional teams are common because single organizations usually cannot provide all of the coordination, technical support, and financing necessary to conduct an REA.

The number of disciplinary specialists depends on objectives and available resources, but as a rule of thumb, each taxonomic group under study should have a specialist and an assistant. The REA team should be limited to a manageable group, not exceeding twenty to thirty individuals. For the study of vegetation types, plants, mammals, birds, and reptiles and amphibians, the core team would be ten scientists (five study groups, two individuals per group). The number of team members increases with the inclusion of the mappers, data managers, logistical specialists, guides, rangers, visiting scientists, and others.

REA Agreements

The participation and roles of organizations and individuals in an REA should be spelled out in a written, signed, legally binding agreement between those who finance or oversee the REA and those who implement the work. Many types of documents serve this purpose, including Memoranda of Understanding or Agreement (MOUs or MOAs), Scopes of Work (SOWs), Terms of Reference (TORs), and contracts and are prepared by the REA managers and are as detailed as possible, with specific work expectations, deadlines, expected products, and financial disbursement descriptions. A generic SOW agreement is presented as appendix 3.

Leadership and Communication

Strong leadership and effective communication are critical for the success of any REA. Leaders should be identified early on in the planning process. Explicit communication strategies will greatly enhance the REA effort.

Leadership Roles

The primary implementing agency usually designates an overall Project Leader, as well as a Logistical Coordinator and a Technical Director or Chief Scientist. REAs are very difficult to orchestrate, and require the separation of the management function from the science function. Combining these functions in the same individual is often perceived as a way to sidestep resource constraints, but this combination is not recommended. An individual charged with managing the logistical and administrative details of an REA will find it challenging to make a significant scientific contribution as well.

The Project Leader provides primary oversight. The Chief Scientist is responsible for the scientific integrity of the effort and is appointed by the Project Leader, although this appointment may be by consensus among all participating scientists. The Logistical Coordinator is responsible for operational considerations, a role that requires strong leadership and logistical coordination skills. This individual commonly leads field expeditions as well.

The field team usually also includes guides and camp staff. These individuals are chosen for their knowledge of the area; local inhabitants are recommended.

Channels of Communication

Successful planning and implementation of an REA necessarily involve a great deal of complex communication among all participants. Each organization that is substantially involved in the REA should designate a point person. To facilitate communication and to avoid problems resulting from failed or misdirected communications, all interinstitutional communication should be channeled through these point persons. All REA participants should be made aware of this preferred communication channel and should do their utmost to respect it. Channeling communication in this way tends to eliminate duplicate, erroneous, incomplete, and misdirected communication, all of which tend to reduce the efficiency and quality of work.

Costs and Timing

Considering the costs of an REA and the time necessary to complete the effort is important. The decision to go forward with an REA is often strongly influenced by the perceived financial and time investments.

Costs

The costs of an REA include salary expenditures, equipment and imagery purchases, travel expenses (both in-country and international), workshop expenses, contracts, and publication and dissemination costs. The ultimate cost of an REA varies with the scope of the effort, the level of necessary detail, and the size of the area under study, but as a rule of thumb a terrestrial REA costs between $75,000 and $250,000. Any considerations of seasonality tend to extend the life, and therefore the costs, of an REA. REAs with minimal field sampling requirements are obviously more economical than heavy sampling initiatives. Coarse-level, image-based analyses directed at landscape characterization with little field verification will be substantially less expensive than fine-level, field-based, species-oriented REAs.

Any REA that incorporates the process outlined above and is budgeted at less than $30,000 may be underfunded. For example, an aerial photo acquisition mission alone can cost between $20,000 and $120,000. The primary implementing collaborator should have sufficient funding in hand or officially approved before beginning any cost-accruing activities.

The costs of an REA in terms of time are substantial and thus very important to consider. REAs tend to dominate the workplans of both individuals and institutions, especially the primary implementing organization, for periods of one year or longer. Sometimes the salary costs are contributed by participating organizations, if the REA fits an institutional goal or mission, but frequently they are not. A commitment to do an REA should always be based on an evaluation of institutional conservation priorities, not on a perceived opportunity for financial gain. REAs are often underfunded and typically involve a substantial amount of volunteerism. On the other hand, well-scoped, well-funded, and carefully managed

REAs can also represent a significant source of income for an institution, primarily as a source of salary support and the purchase of computer mapping technologies.

To the extent possible, REA team members should be compensated for their work. Compensation levels should be commensurate with local professional salary levels, and they should not represent the disproportionately high wages commanded by international consulting firms. It is recognized that compensation is not always possible, or that it is sometimes possible but not for all participants. Decisions about which individuals should be compensated are made by the Project Leader. Individuals who take time out of their regular employment at other institutions should seek authorized approval for the period of time they intend to work on the REA to the exclusion of their regular duties.

The Life of an REA

Compared to a more exhaustive, traditional biological inventory, an REA is rapid. Few REAs, however, have ever been initiated and completed in less than one year. The ten steps of the REA process, implemented over the course of a year, generally correspond to the following quarterly schedule:

Months 1–3
Conceptualization
Initial Planning

Months 4–6
Initial Landscape Characterization
Planning Workshop
Training Workshop

Months 7–9
Field Implementation

Months 10–12
Individual Report Generation
Integration and Synthesis
Final Report/Map Generation
Publication/Dissemination

This approximate chronology is ideal and does not consider either seasonality considerations or delays at any step, which will increase the duration of the REA. Fieldwork is usually initiated immediately after the planning and training workshops, but season and weather may delay getting into the field. Delays during the field implementation period sometimes occur because of difficulty mobilizing multidisciplinary teams. Delays may also arise during the Integration and Synthesis step, where the difficulty finding the right person for the job, organizing in one place all of the individual reports, and reviewing and synthesizing the relevant findings from each report into a single flowing report can be substantial. If the REA includes a seasonality component, the time required to complete the REA will exceed one year.

Workshops

Two workshops—a planning workshop and a training workshop—are an important aspect of REA methodology. These workshops are often combined into one multi-organizational, collaborative REA strategy development session.

The Planning Workshop

The REA planning workshop is a four- to five-day meeting of all collaborators to identify working groups and group leaders, formulate and reformulate objectives, develop a workplan, and assign tasks to responsible individuals. An REA should always incorporate a planning workshop prior to engaging in fieldwork or substantial analysis of information. This workshop should be conducted at the actual REA site, if possible, in a facility capable of handling large groups. The planning workshop is often combined with a technical training session, but four days of planning are usually necessary to engineer the vision of an REA.

Invitees to the workshop should consist of all the individuals from the principal implementing institutions as well as a limited number of stakeholders from the region. These latter participants can be invited as "observer status" (expenses not covered), depending on their interest and need in participating in the REA.

A workable agenda should be structured as follows:

Day 1:
• Introduction of the REA Concept
• Presentation of REA Case Studies as Models
• Presentation of State of Knowledge for Area
• Statement and Discussion of REA Objectives

Day 2:
• Introduction to Concept of Workgroups (e.g., Vegetation Ecology/Botany, Zoology, Mapping, and Executive/Administration)
• Break-Out into Workgroups
• Development of Workgroup Strategy to Include:
    —Designation of Group Leader
    —Designation of Rapporteur
    —Objectives
    —Activities
    —Data Management/Voucher Specimen Processing
    —Responsible Individuals
    —Deadlines
    —Products

Day 3:
• Presentation of Strategies by Workgroups
• Discussion/Reconciliation of Timelines
• Development of Draft Workplan Incorporating Individual Strategies

Day 4:
• Presentation of Workplan Document
• Discussion of Workplan
• Development of Master Timeline
• Revision of Draft Workplan
• Affirmation by Signature

The main product of the planning workshop is a workplan, which contains a definite assignment of tasks and responsibilities, and deadlines for task completion. Box 2-1 presents a hypothetical workplan for

1. Introduction

This workplan describes a collaborative effort among several governmental and nongovernmental conservation organizations to develop, map, and verify a terrestrial vegetation community classification for [site]. The workplan was developed primarily from discussions held during a project planning meeting. Funding for the project will be provided from [funding institution] to [implementing institution].

2. Objectives

The objectives of this collaboration are: develop, map, and field verify a terrestrial vegetation community classification for improved conservation planning and management.

3. Project Description and Protocol

The need for an appropriately scaled vegetation community classification and map has been identified as a priority by a suite of organizations concerned with the conservation of the biodiversity of [site]. This project will emphasize habitat characterization and mapping and will involve species-level sampling for the following taxa: mammals, birds, reptiles, amphibians, and fish.

A land-use planning survey has been completed, and a decision was made at the planning workshop to use it as a starting point data layer. The vegetation scientists expressed support for two classification frameworks: (1) a land-cover, vegetation structure-based hierarchy developed by a scientific advisory council, and (2) a vegetation classification developed by [name]. It was decided that these two classifications could be reasonably crosswalked. A standard vegetation community classification will be developed from a review and modification of these existing classification frameworks. This community classification will reflect both vegetation structure and composition. This classification will be hierarchical in nature, describing general vegetative formations in the upper levels of the hierarchy and detailed, species-level associations in the lower hierarchical tiers.

Aerial photography will be interpreted by vegetation scientists and a photointerpreter to map vegetation communities. Black-and-white photos (date/scale) and color-infrared photos (date/scale) will be used in the interpretation. The primary data source for the photointerpretation will be the black-and-white photography, which exists for [site] in both film product and digital (scanned) formats. Vegetation communities delineated from the photointerpretation will be transferred onto a basemap of the same scale as the photos. The vegetation community polygons will be digitized into a GIS for analysis, refinement, and production of a preliminary map of vegetation communities.

Field visits will be scheduled to verify the preliminary map. All field observations will be precisely georeferenced using differentially corrected GPS locations. Final maps will incorporate revisions as identified during fieldwork. Products from this collaborative project will include:

Vegetation community classification and descriptions
Lists of flora and fauna by vegetation community
Characterization of species of conservation concern
Maps of vegetation community distributions
Final report
GIS data layers

4. Participating Organizations

5. Project Management

The project will be administered by [administrating institution], under the direction of [project director]. [Project manager] will manage [implementing institution's] project. An advisory council consisting of one member of each organization represented in the collaboration has been convened. This council will approve the scientific quality of the work undertaken in this initiative.

Box 2-1. A sample REA workplan. A workplan details the roles and responsibilities of the individuals and teams involved in an REA and establishes the basis and expectations for collaborative work.

6. Specific Activities and Task Assignments

Step 1: Classification Refinement and Development of Type Example Signatures.

The vegetation scientists will provide a document that details the classification system resulting from a crosswalk of the existing classifications. This document will contain written descriptions of the communities that are known or suspected to exist, and will form the basis of the photointerpretation work. The photointerpretation should be done only once, requiring an intense level of initial collaboration between the botanists and the photointerpreter. The botanists, after achieving consensus on the classification system, will then need to locate each community on a photo, which will represent the "typic example" of that community. The botanists will then work with the photointerpreter to deliver and describe the type examples and practice delineating these communities. The scientific committee should also review and approve the consensus classification. Responsible Individuals: [names].

Completion Date: xx/xx/xx

Step 2: Photointerpretation.

The photointerpreter will have been provided with the finalized classification and will have worked with the botanists. The photointerpreter will then interpret all photos onto acetate jackets with Rapidograph 000 pens. Preliminary work will result in the choice of a minimum mapping unit, which will be approved by the scientific committee. Responsible Individual: [name].

Completion Date: xx/xx/xx

Step 3: Transfer of Polygons to a Basemap.

The photointerpreter will send all interpreted photos and their jackets to [institution], where the polygons will be transferred onto a basemap printed out at the same scale as the photos. The basemap, with polygons, will then be sent to the botanists for their review. Responsible Individual: [name].

Completion Date: xx/xx/xx

Step 4: Review of Photointerpretation.

The photointerpreter will send all the interpreted photos to the botanists for their review and adjustment. The botanists will edit the maps and send the corrections back to the [institution]. Responsible Individuals: Botany Team

Completion Date: xx/xx/xx

Step 5: Development of Preliminary Vegetation Map for [site].

The [institution] will produce a preliminary vegetation map. Responsible Individual: [name].

Completion Date: xx/xx/xx

Step 6: Sampling Plan Development.

The Field Verification Team will study the preliminary vegetation community map and devise a sampling plan. Replicate examples of all mapped vegetation communities will be visited. Relatively unknown communities will be sampled more intensively than others. Responsible Individuals: Field Verification Team

Completion Date: xx/xx/xx

Step 7: Field Verification.

Field verification. Responsible Individuals: Field Verification Team.

Completion Date: xx/xx/xx

Step 8: Refinement and Production of Final Vegetation Map.

Refinement of vegetation map based on results from fieldwork. Responsible Individual: [name].

Completion Date: xx/xx/xx

(continues)

Step 9: Species Level Assessments.

All vegetation communities will be systematically sampled for faunal biodiversity at an appropriate level. Mapped vegetation communities will be characterized for species-level biodiversity using a combination of two approaches: (1) generation of species lists for each community using existing information, and (2) sampling exercises initiated in the context of this project. Disciplinary specialists will determine what, where, and how data should be collected. Sampling protocols for each taxa will be developed prior to sampling.

> Initiation Date: xx/xx/xx
> Completion Date: xx/xx/xx
> Requirements:

- Finalize taxonomic groups to work with.
- Identify zoology team.
- Compile and assess existing information regarding species composition for each described vegetation community type.
- Develop zoology sampling plan.
- Commence fieldwork.
- Define products.
- Write reports for each taxonomic group.

Step 10: Conduct a Biodiversity Threats Analysis.

Responsible Individuals: Disciplinary Specialists.

Step 11: Capture All Field-Generated Data into a Database Management System.

Responsible Individuals: [names].

Step 12: Write the Final Vegetation Classification and Mapping Report.

This report will also include a synthesis of the taxonomic analysis results, the threats analysis, and management recommendations. Responsible Individual: [name].

7. Agreement to Collaborate

8. Signatures

Box 2-1 (*continued*).

an REA in which vegetation community mapping is emphasized. The workplan is signed by all participants, affirming their commitment to the project. The workplan is not a contractual obligation, but it represents a clear statement of the intent to collaborate on a multifaceted, multi-institutional conservation initiative.

Sampling plans (chapter 1), which indicate the number and location of vegetation units (polygons) to sample are also developed in the planning workshop. The sampling plan represents a commitment on the part of the REA team to conduct sampling at a predetermined level of intensity and to document the results of that fieldwork according to agreed-upon deadlines. The development of the sampling plan is a joint effort between the vegetation and mapping teams (for vegetation type verification sampling) and includes the subsequent participation of the fauna team (for specific animal sampling requirements).

The planning workshop should be contemplated in the overall budget. For best management, the number of participants (implementors and observers) should not exceed forty individuals. Inviting observers is generally discouraged (but often politically necessary), unless they are likely to make a significant contribution to the process. Determination of the budget for the workshop should be relatively straightforward, based on the number of individuals invited and their funding requirements. Invitation of individuals with REA experience is encouraged.

An accomplished facilitator is essential for a successful planning workshop. The facilitator must have a clear vision for the structure and anticipated products of the workshop and must excel at crowd management. The facilitator must be prepared to exercise leadership, negotiate agreements, and resolve any conflicts that could undermine the smooth execution of the workshop. The facilitators primary language should be that of the assembled group. The facilitator requires the administrative support of an individual capable of capturing everything that is spoken during the course of the workshop in a word processor. Flip charts are indispensable, and overhead transparency or slide projection capability is also useful.

The Training Workshop

The training workshop is a meeting of REA scientists to receive instruction in specific sampling techniques and the use of field forms. The training workshop can be combined with the planning workshop if practical. The training workshop is an opportunity for technical training in the activities identified in the workplan. This type of training workshop usually involves practical instruction in field measurement activities—such as the use of global positioning systems (GPS) for geolocation—and establishing vegetation plots. Ideally, this type of training is provided in the actual study area during the commencement of fieldwork, using the actual maps and imagery for the area, but it can be provided elsewhere if necessary.

Specific sampling methodologies are described further in the following chapters. REA collaborators are often accomplished scientists, who "already know what to do" with respect to sampling techniques in their areas of expertise. In this respect, an REA "training" event is not a rigorous, formal, highly specific training activity. It is, rather, much more of a coming together of peers to share ideas and methodologies and to develop field protocols appropriate to the specific REA. Experience has shown that more strategizing occurs at these events than actual training, and the exchange of ideas is completely multidirectional.

Initiating Fieldwork

Once the workplan and sampling plan have been developed and the REA team assembled, fieldwork commences. For maximum concept retention and maintenance of initial levels of enthusiasm, fieldwork should begin as soon as possible after the planning and training workshops. The REA's greatest logistical effort is the initiation of fieldwork. The support of the Logistical Coordinator is necessary on a nearly full-time basis during this period to deal with transportation, accommodation, and meal coordination, as well as with equipment provision, financial disbursements, communications, and miscellaneous details. The Logistical Coordinator, however, should not have to guess or estimate anything related to preparations for fieldwork; all necessary details about the fieldwork (the number of people in the field, travel dates and times, equipment requirements, accommodation plans, and so on) should be contained in or easily interpreted from the workplan and sampling plan.

Planning for Safety

Another important planning dimension, safety also improves REA efficiency. REA fieldwork can be dangerous, and a few simple precautions can contribute to an incident-free REA. These precautions include the following:

- Travel lightly (with minimum field equipment) in the field.
- Always travel and work with a partner.
- Mark your way properly using marking or flagging tape and note major natural landmark references to aid navigation.
- Stay on predetermined trail routes wherever possible.
- Avoid the temptation of taking shortcuts, especially along rivers, because terrain changes rapidly and cliffs are encountered frequently. Travel with a light rope, if weight permits.
- Travel with maps, compasses, and GPS receivers, and know how to use them.
- Carry a first-aid kit that contains a snakebite kit; know how to use it.
- Always carry plenty of water to prevent dehydration.
- For remote work, carry an EPIRB (emergency repeater beacon broadcasting device) and know how to use it.

Project Leaders should develop appropriate safety guidelines for the area and discuss these guidelines with team members prior to commencing fieldwork.

Maintaining Focus

Maintaining focus is essential to ensuring successful project outcomes because the REA process is complex, often new to implementors, usually logistically difficult to engineer, and always demanding of staff and financial resources. Typically, the complex nature of REAs results in a tendency to get caught up in the process, sometimes losing sight of the overall vision of the effort. Substantial reflection on the objectives is necessary throughout the effort, or accomplishing the REA methodology can become the perceived objective of the REA. The managers and team leaders need to focus constantly on grounding the initiative in its conservation objectives.

Post-Fieldwork Management

Once field sampling has been initiated, the focus changes from how to get the REA started to how to complete the REA; at this point, a stronger management emphasis becomes necessary. At this stage, the REA has been conceptualized, characterized in detail in several collaboration agreements, and initiated. An active and proactive management approach ensures a smooth implementation of the fieldwork and subsequent steps. The management details of the subsequent REA process steps will be discussed in greater detail in the following chapters.

PART II

IN THE LAB: MAPPING TOOLS AND APPROACHES

Chapter 3

Mapping Technologies: New Tools for Conservation

Roger Sayre

The REA methodology has evolved continuously from its inception in the mid-1980s. One of the most significant advances in the REA approach has been related to the concurrent evolution of computer tools, which permit intensive numerical processing of large datasets and the display and analysis of geographic information. This spatial information processing capability has resulted in a considerable sophistication in the digital mapping aspects of REAs. This chapter describes the important spatial information concepts, tools, and applications for REA mapping.

The first edition of the REA manual, while well-grounded in the mapping emphasis associated with all REAs, did not include a characterization of the role and importance of digital mapping technologies in the REA process, primarily because these technologies were relatively new and cost prohibitive at that time. Today, however, these technologies have proliferated widely and are less expensive to obtain and easier to use. One primary reason for developing a new version of the REA manual is to highlight the use of these new mapping technologies in the REA process. Whereas the first version of the REA manual tended to emphasize techniques that could be applied with a minimum of equipment and trained personnel, this version advocates using spatial technologies as necessary for the adequate characterization of biodiversity distribution.

Spatial Technologies

REA depends on the use and integration of spatial technologies, which include geographic information systems (GIS), remote sensing (RS), and global positioning systems (GPS). This emphasis on spatial technology distinguishes REAs from other expert-based inventories and biodiversity assessment methodologies. These spatial technologies are a relatively new group of computer-based analytical tools that use spatially explicit, or georeferenced, information. GIS, RS, and GPS are modern spatial technologies that complement traditional geographic tools, such as cartography and surveying, to provide sophisticated techniques for the geographic characterization of biodiversity. These technologies will be discussed in detail in subsequent sections of this chapter.

The power of spatial technologies has allowed significant improvement in our ability to characterize the distribution, abundance, and condition of biodiversity as it exists on the landscape. Spatial technologies have revolutionized the way information is organized and processed for many disciplines and pursuits, particularly biology, creating new emphases on the precise georeferencing of collected data and the accurate geolocation of landscape and biological features.

Analysis of Spatial Information

At its most fundamental level, an REA involves the collection and characterization of spatial information about biodiversity. Biodiversity can be described at different levels of biological organization ranging from microcellular units (e.g., genetic codes) to landscape units (e.g., plant communities). REAs characterize biodiversity primarily at the landscape level, targeting the spatial distribution on the landscape of the unit of biodiversity under investigation. These units, or elements, of biodiversity exist on the landscape in spatial configurations that can be geographically represented as point features (e.g., locations of individuals), line features (e.g., a stream reach), or polygon features (e.g., vegetation types).

Although REAs accommodate multiple disciplines (e.g., botany, zoology, ecology, and sociology), all data that result from a REA have an intrinsically spatial character and can therefore be visualized and spatially analyzed with an appropriate spatial technology. This fact underscores the importance of spatial technologies in the REA process as an integration mechanism. The integrating nature of the spatial technologies is one of the keys to achieving the truly multidisciplinary character of an REA.

Basic Geographic Concepts

Mapping biodiversity requires an understanding of several basic geographic and cartographic principles, particularly the concepts of earth geometry, datums, projections, coordinate systems, scale, accuracy, and minimum mapping units. An understanding of these concepts by the REA mapping team is required for accuracy in geolocation and spatial analysis, and for producing accurate and high-quality map output. The concepts of minimum mapping unit and scale are fundamental to the proper implementation of any REA, and they need to be understood by the entire REA team. General sources of information about basic geographic concepts and technologies, from which much of this material is derived, include the following: Paine, 1981; Burrough, 1986; Snyder, 1987; Star and Estes, 1990; ESRI, 1990; ERDAS, 1991; Maguire et al., 1991; and Lillesand and Kiefer, 1994. Moreover, the National Center for Geographic Information and Analysis (NCGIA) provides detailed educational materials about geographic concepts and spatial information technologies over the Internet (http://www.ncgia.ucsb.edu/).

Earth Geometry and Map Projections

The Earth is not a perfect sphere, but it is like a sphere and has been modeled by geometricians as an oblate ellipsoid. Differing models of the geometry of the ellipsoid Earth give rise to different projection systems in which the Earth can be represented in maps. It is impossible to portray features on the Earth's surface (three dimensional) on a flat map (two dimensional) without introducing spatial distortion. Over the years, cartographers have developed several different projections for representing Earth features on maps with minimal spatial distortion. A map projection is a mathematical technique for "projecting" a portion of the Earth's curved surface onto a flat, or planar, surface. There are many different types of projections, each of which is designed to reduce spatial distortion in either distance, area, or angular dimension. Although there are many projections, only a handful are used regularly (e.g., UTM, Lambert, Albers, and State Plane).

Coordinate Systems

Geographic locations on the sphere-like Earth are described in geographic coordinates, which are referred to as latitude and longitude. Planar representations of the Earth's surface resulting from projections are associated with planar, or Cartesian, coordinate systems (figure 3-1). Latitude and longitude are angular measurements of degrees, minutes, and seconds. Longitude measurements depict the angular distance to the east or west of a standard meridian (zero degrees longitude) running through Greenwich, England. Latitude measurements depict the angular distance north or south of the Earth's equator (zero degrees latitude). Measurement units for planar coordinate grid systems are usually metric (meters), and the Earth is generally divided into a number of north-to-south zones that encircle the Earth along the equator.

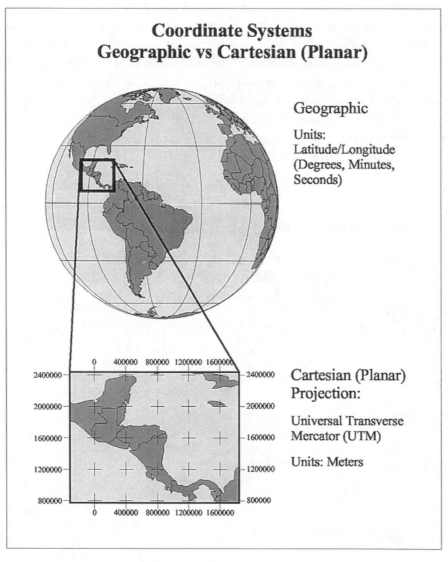

Figure 3-1. Representing locations on the Earth with geographic (latitude degrees, longitude degrees) and planar (x meters, y meters) coordinates.

Datums

For a particular region or area of the Earth, a datum—a model of the Earth's surface at sea level—is used as a reference for making controlled measurements on the ground. A datum has a smooth surface, unlike the topographically irregular surface of the Earth. Most places on the Earth have one or more datums (often older and revised calculations) describing the local ground measurement reference system.

Most good maps of the Earth contain information, usually recorded somewhere in the margins of the map, about the ellipsoid, the datum, and the projection. Although a deep understanding of these concepts is generally unnecessary, the information about the Earth model must be retained for geographic accuracy in computer-supported mapping and analysis. WGS 84 is a global datum used as a standard in many GPS technologies.

Scale

The concept of scale is fundamentally important to an REA. Scale refers to the ratio of a unit of distance on a map or image, and the corresponding ground distance. A scale of 1:50,000, therefore, means that one centimeter on the map corresponds to 50,000 centimeters on the ground. A large-scale map represents a relatively small area on the ground, whereas a small-scale map depicts a larger ground area. Large-scale maps are therefore more detailed than small-scale maps. Scales such as 1:10,000, 1:24,000, and 1:50,000 are generally referred to as large-scale maps, whereas scales of 1:100,000, 1:250,000, 1:500,000, and 1:1,000,000 are generally acknowledged as small-scale maps. A "working scale" for an REA that will yield satisfactory information detail should be determined. For most REAs, the working scale is typically 1:50,000, although for large areas scales of 1:100,000 or even 1:250,000 are necessary. Decreasing the working scale always results in data generalization. The concept of scale is graphically depicted in figure 3-2. Scale will be considered as it relates to GIS later.

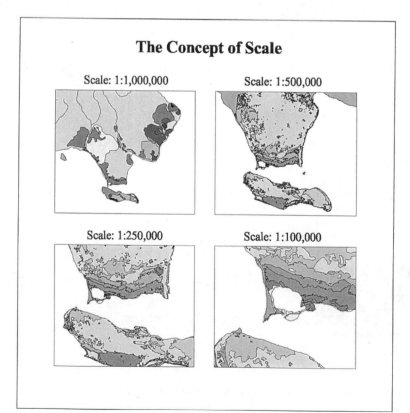

Figure 3-2. The representation of features on the Earth in relation to scale. The higher the number, the smaller the scale. At small scales, larger areas are portrayed, with lesser detail. At large scales, smaller areas are portrayed, with finer detail.

Accuracy

Geographic accuracy is another fundamental concept important to REA mapping. Geographic accuracy refers to how close the representation of a mapped object is to its true location and spatial extent on the Earth. Accuracy is not necessarily related to scale, but large-scale mapping is often more accurate than small-scale mapping. Poor accuracy degrades the quality of maps and may affect their utility. Accuracy sometimes refers to how well a measurement of some property conforms to a standard. In mapping, accuracy refers to the percentage of mapped points or polygons that are within a tolerable distance of their true location. As a rule of thumb for REA mapping, inaccuracies of up to 10 meters are generally acceptable for 1:50,000 scale work, 10 to 100 meters for 1:100,000 work, and up to a kilometer for 1:250,000 scale mapping.

Minimum Mapping Unit

The minimum mapping unit (MMU) is the smallest uniform area that will be delineated during photo or image interpretation and is determined from inspection of the image source. The MMU is another mapping parameter that varies with scale. It is not necessarily the smallest uniform area that can be perceived by the human eye. The larger the MMU, the less interpretation work is necessary. The size of the MMU may have a management dimension (e.g., only natural areas greater than a hectare will be delineated). Some common MMUs for a variety of common working scales are graphically represented in table 3-1. Some photointerpreters use a practical rule of thumb for developing an MMU: the MMU is the size of the smallest polygon into which a label can be drawn by hand.

Table 3-1. Suggested minimum mapping units (MMUs) for different working scales. These MMUs are typically employed in REAs; the actual MMU may have a management basis (e.g., a minimum size for a protected area) or a practical basis (e.g., the smallest polygon within which a polygon label can be drawn by the interpreter).

Working Scale	Typical MMU
1:1,000,000	1 km^2
1:500,000	64 ha
1:250,000	16 ha
1:100,000	4 ha
1:50,000	1 ha

Geographic Information Systems

Geographic information systems (GISs) are computer-based systems that permit the capture, maintenance, retrieval, integration, visualization, and analysis of georeferenced data, which are data with a geographic quality, locational framework, or intrinsic locational characteristic. Georeferenced data are most often described as data that are spatial, or "mappable." A GIS utilizes georeferenced data. While GIS is commonly understood to be a software package, a GIS is really a combination of the hardware (computer equipment), software, and human resources necessary to effectively display and analyze spatial data.

Data Organization in a GIS

GIS information is organized as a collection of single-theme data layers. While a hard-copy map may represent many themes (e.g., roads, rivers, villages, and vegetation classes) on one map, these themes constitute individual layers in a GIS (Figure 3-3). This organization of data in separate layers enables the selective display or analysis of one or more layers, as well as the creation of new data layers from existing layers. GISs can contain a few or many component layers, depending on the application. While there is no definitive or minimum set of layers to be included in a GIS for an REA (and most conservation applications), there are several "standard" biophysical and socioeconomic data layers that are commonly developed for REA-based GISs. These layers include geology, soils, climate variables (e.g., precipitation or temperature),

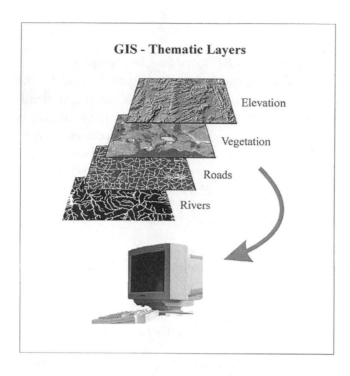

Figure 3-3. The multiple thematic layers of a GIS. A GIS is an integrating tool because it permits any thematic layer and data to be analyzed in the context of other layers.

land use and land cover, surface hydrography, elevation, protected areas, study area limits, political/administrative units, transportation networks, population centers, infrastructure, and land tenure.

GIS as a Database Management System

GIS software is actually a powerful database management system (DBMS) with a sophisticated data visualization and spatial analysis capability. Familiarity with basic database management concepts usually enables rapid acquisition of GIS concepts because a DBMS is the software engine for any true GIS. The GIS is useful for displaying and analyzing georeferenced information, such as numerical attributes of a geographic feature or pixel. As such, the GIS is not an appropriate DBMS for management of extensive, textual information (essay or memo fields), which generally lack georeferencing.

Raster and Vector GIS

There are two fundamentally different types of GIS softwares: raster-based and vector-based. Raster GIS employs a grid-based system for representing themes. Landscapes are subdivided into grid cells—commonly referred to as pixels—and each grid cell contains a numerical or character value that describes the data theme at that location. Satellite image data, where each pixel has a value representing spectral reflectance in that grid cell, are an example of raster data. The size of the grid cells in a raster-based GIS data layer is determined by the analyst.

Vector-based GIS differs from raster-based GIS in that the surface of the Earth is not gridded. Rather, features on the surface of the Earth (e.g., roads, villages, and lakes) are spatially described using a point/line/area geometry. These features become objects (information records) in a DBMS, in which both the geographic information about the feature (spatial data), as well as the descriptive characteristics (attribute data) about the feature, is maintained. In a vector-based GIS, for example, a forest stand is a feature and is represented spatially as a polygon. The dominant species, soil type, and road access are all attribute data about the stand, and they can all be represented visually in a displayed or hard-copy map and spatially analyzed. Raster and vector GIS models are depicted in figure 3-4.

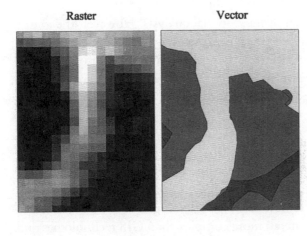

Figure 3-4. Raster and vector GIS approaches to representing landscape features. In vector GIS, all features on the Earth are represented as points, lines, or polygons, with associated attribute data. Raster GIS employs a grid-based data model with cells of a fixed spatial resolution that have a single value representing the theme.

Choosing GIS Software

Choosing GIS software involves making decisions about both the type of GIS to purchase (raster or vector) and the brand of software. Because most REAs strongly emphasize characterizing landscapes and mapping the location and extent of habitats, vector-based systems are generally preferred. The determining factor behind the brand of GIS (or any software) to purchase should be whether the software (1) represents the industry standard and (2) is a commercial, off-the-shelf technology. Functionality is obviously a primary consideration, but if the technology is regarded as the industry standard, the software is likely to be fully functional. The industry standard and most widely used GIS tools for conservation are the ArcInfo® and ArcView® products from ESRI. These products offer the full range of GIS functionality (including raster-based modules with higher-end packages) with user-friendly graphical interfaces.

The REA implementor will need to use a GIS to manage and analyze REA data and make map products. Many of the most logical candidates for REA implementation agencies already have GISs in place, and there is no reason to acquire another GIS system if an existing system can satisfy REA data management needs. Other vector-based and raster-based GIS systems may be suitable for REA purposes. A thorough comparison of data management needs with GIS software functionality should be conducted before adopting alternative systems.

Scale in a GIS

GIS data are maintained in a geographic, locationally accurate framework that is independent of scale. Although the quality of the data in the GIS is in part a function of the scale of the source data (scale-bound), a GIS is capable of producing map output at any scale. This independence of scale from the digital GIS data permits the spatial combinations and query of multiple data layers of variable source scales.

Although GISs are conceptually and mechanistically without scale, the data layers can generally be described as having a scale of development. A data layer of roads and trails digitized from a 1:50,000-scale topographic map has a 1:50,000 development scale and cannot be considered accurate if printed out at a larger scale, even though the GIS permits such an output. A typical analysis with a GIS involves combining or analyzing data layers derived from map sources with different scales. As such, the general accuracy of a multilayered GIS is often said to be only as good as the accuracy (or development scale) of the least-resolved data layer.

Topology

A vector-based GIS that maintains information about both depicted objects and their spatial relationships with neighboring objects is said to be topological. Topology is an advanced mathematical construct, and a comprehensive understanding of topology is not required of most spatial analysts. However, the ability of the GIS to create and maintain topological relationships is critical because many basic spatial query and analysis functions depend on topology. Some software packages (typically raster and computer-aided design [CAD] softwares) allow the digital capture of vector information, but these vectors are described as nontopological vectors and cannot be used to construct polygon topology.

Remote Sensing

Remotely sensed imagery in the form of satellite images, aerial photographs, or aerial videography constitutes the primary data source for all REAs. Remote sensing is a spatial technology based on the interpretation and analysis of remotely sensed imagery. Satellite remote sensing technologies are often referred to as image processing systems. These technologies are, in general, more complex than GIS technologies and are more computer intensive. The use of remote sensing technologies requires a basic understanding of spectral reflectances. In most REAs, satellite imagery is acquired, subsetted or mosaicked, rectified, interpreted (classified), and output as hard-copy imagery products.

Spectral Reflectance

Remotely sensed imagery is obtained by sensing devices carried on satellites or aircraft that record the spectral properties of objects on the Earth. These spectral properties—or signatures—are a result of the interaction between an object on the surface of the Earth and electromagnetic radiation from the sun and are generally categorized as reflectance. The wavelengths of electromagnetic radiation reflected from objects depends on the composition of the object; different objects reflect different wavelengths. Sensors have different bands, which can sense electromagnetic radiation of differing wavelengths (e.g., allowing for the separation of different vegetation types in satellite imagery). Grasslands reflect differently from closed-canopy forests, wetlands reflect differently from deserts, and so on.

Satellite Imagery

Most REAs integrate imagery from satellites (generally referred to as low-resolution imagery) with higher-resolution imagery (aerial photographs). Satellite imagery is sensed directly to digital media and is transmitted to receiving stations on the Earth. There are a variety of remote sensing satellites in space, and many more are anticipated to be launched in the future. The sensors on these platforms sense in different wavelengths and at different spatial resolutions. A variety of satellite imagery with differing spectral and spatial resolutions are available commercially (table 3-2). Spectral resolution is a property of the sensor that refers to the number and range of bands (wavelengths) recorded, whereas spatial resolution refers to the size of the image pixels (smallest area sensed). Landsat TM (Thematic Mapper) imagery, for example, has a 30-meter by 30-meter spatial resolution, and a seven-band spectral resolution of visible, near-infrared, far-infrared, and thermal wavelengths. SPOT XS (Multispectral) has a 20-meter by 20-meter spatial resolution and a three-band spectral resolution.

Radar imagery is a nonoptical type of imagery that is increasingly available. While optical sensors are

Table 3-2. Differences in spatial and spectral resolutions of typical satellite imagery data used for REAs.

Satellite	Spatial Resolution	Spectral Resolution
Landsat TM	30 m	7 bands
IRS	23 m	5 bands
Spot PAN (Panchromatic)	10 m	1 band
Spot XS (Multispectral)	20 m	3 bands
AVHRR	1 km	4 bands
RadarSat	9–28 m	1 band

passive, radar sensors record the backscatter of radar beams directed toward the ground. This active nature of radar makes it appropriate for chronically cloud-covered areas because radar is unaffected by clouds. Both high- and low-resolution radar is available.

Satellite Image Processing

Image processing refers to the preparation and use of imagery data. Digital imagery is sold as "scenes" of varying size, depending on the type of imagery data. In general, digital imagery is acquired, mosaicked (stitched) with neighboring scenes if necessary, georeferenced, enhanced, classified, output in hard copy, and exported to a GIS. Image processing is either a completely digital, computer-intensive exercise, or a semidigital, human-intensive activity. The former relies on the ability of the computer to discriminate fine differences in spectral variation in a scene, whereas the latter draws on the integrative experience and advanced pattern recognition capability of a human image interpreter. REAs have tended to emphasize the latter.

Hardware and Software Considerations for Image Processing

Because imagery files are relatively large (they may easily exceed several hundred megabytes) and complex, working with digital imagery requires substantial processing power. Digital image processing has traditionally been undertaken in a UNIX workstation or mainframe computing environment due to the relatively high storage requirements and processing capability necessary to manipulate large, multiband datasets. The acquisition of a UNIX-based workstation platform requires a substantial investment in financial and staff resources and is not generally advised for organizations whose primary function is not spatial data analysis. Fortunately, however, the rapid trend toward the development of powerful PC-based systems with high storage capacity may allow for an expansion of image processing into PC platforms. This trend is a welcome evolution that brings an "appropriate technology" dimension to a previously exclusively high-tech discipline and set of tools.

To accomplish image processing on a PC system, the configuration should include several gigabytes of storage capacity, maximum amounts of memory (RAM) and video memory (VRAM), a high-resolution video display and graphics capability, large monitors, a CD-ROM drive, and a powerful multifunctional Windows-based operating system. The industry-standard image processing software is ERDAS Imagine.®

Image Acquisition

Acquiring imagery is a relatively straightforward process that involves contacting the vendor of the imagery and providing information about the area of interest and the desired time and quality of the image. This information pertains to the location for which imagery is desired (usually the coordinates of a minimum bounding rectangle around the study area are provided), the acceptable age of the imagery (e.g., recent, up to five years old, up to 15 years old), the month or span of months (if seasonality is a consideration), the amount of cloud cover that can be tolerated, the desired product (i.e., digital data, hard copy, or both) and the level of preprocessing desired (ranging from none to extensive). The vendor then executes a search of the imagery database and generates a list of candidate scenes to be sent to the purchaser. This list of scenes provides a scene-I.D. number, the path and row of the image (using a gridded framework that organizes the globe into north/south paths and east/west rows), the date of image acquisition, and cloud cover scores. It is sometimes possible to shift scenes from their original path/row position to avoid having to buy multiple scenes; this possibility needs to be discussed with the vendor. The cloud cover scores are provided for each of the four quadrants in the scene. It is now common for the imagery purchaser to perform image searches on the Internet without the assistance of a vendor representative. Imagery is also increasingly available on the Internet at no, or a substantially reduced, cost.

Commercial satellite imagery continues to be expensive ($3,000 to $5,000 per scene) and, in certain instances, cost prohibitive. At such high cost, determining whether a satellite image is appropriate, and if so, ensuring that a high-quality image is purchased, is important. The appropriateness of image acquisition depends generally on the size of the area for which an REA is to be implemented. Purchasing satellite imagery for areas smaller than 10 square kilometers is usually not advised.

The quality of imagery is rarely discernible from the proofs and quick looks provided by the vendor. Smaller, dispersed "popcorn" clouds are usually present in imagery but are difficult or impossible to perceive in the resampled quick looks. Although rarely possible, an inspection of the actual image prior to purchase is preferred. Otherwise, it is fairly safe to buy an image with cloud scores of 0 percent in each quadrant (an essentially cloud-free day) or 0 percent in the quadrant of interest. Cloud scores of 10 percent or 20 percent may be acceptable; 30 percent or greater cloud cover is likely to prove unacceptable. Prior to purchasing any commercially available imagery, the buyer should discuss with the vendor the arrangements for returning or exchanging unsuitable imagery and obtain this information in writing.

Image Mosaicking

After purchase, the imagery must be downloaded from the distribution media (usually an 8-millimeter tape or a CD) and subsetted or mosaicked (when more than one scene is used). Raw data from one scene often need to be mosaicked (stitched) with data from an adjacent scene when the study area falls across two or more scenes. Stitching involves merging together two or more scenes by properly aligning corresponding rows and columns so that geographic integrity is maintained. Stitching requires that the original column and row numbers are known, and it is therefore generally unwise to stitch after subsetting due to the altered row and column numbers.

Image Rectification

Rectification of imagery is the process of georeferencing the imagery file so that the real geographic location of features in the imagery can be determined. Prior to rectification, the imagery has only a column and row referencing system (file position); rectification assigns the known geographic locations of features on the landscape to the same features discernible in the imagery. Rectification enables the query of imagery objects for their geographic location.

Typically, rectification involves using a hard-copy or digital map that already has georeferencing to provide the source locations for features discernible in the imagery. A hard-copy map is mounted on a digitizing table and registered. Map registration is a process in which the georeferencing system of a map is recorded by using a pointing device to point to the locations of control (known locations) points. The digitizing table usually contains an embedded, fine-resolution, accurately measured wire grid, which is used to transform digitizing table units (inches or centimeters) to real-world measurement units.

Image Enhancement

Image enhancement involves manipulating the original data to improve the visual aesthetics and clarity of the image. Spectral wavelengths detected by the sensor are known as the digital numbers (DNs), which generally range between 1 and 256. This range of numbers relates to information storage limits (bit constraints) of computer processing systems. Image enhancement involves altering the range of DNs to improve image contrast, a process known as histogram stretching or histogram equalization.

Image Output

Image output involves producing hard-copy output of images. While imagery is usually composed of multiband data, only three bands can be displayed or used for hard-copy output. The choice of bands selected for output, and their assignment to the color guns used in video display and printer technology, determines the ultimate visual appearance of an image. For example, bands 4, 5, and 3 of a Landsat image (near-infrared, mid-infrared, and blue, respectively) projected through color guns red, green, and blue, respectively, produce what is commonly referred to as a color-infrared composite. This specific band combination and color channel assignment is generally used for terrestrial REAs involving vegetation community classification.

Manual Image Classification

Manual, or visual, classification refers to interpretation of photos or imagery by the human eye. Aerial photographs have been manually photointerpreted for decades, leading to the refinement of a distinct and very precise science called photogrammetry. Hard-copy printouts or film products of satellite images are also amenable to manual interpretation. Manual interpretation does not require a computer, but a computer is necessary for the subsetting, enhancement, rectification, and output of the digital imagery data.

Digital Image Classification

Digital image classification refers to the use of computers and mathematical clustering algorithms to classify the spectral signatures of an image into a number of classes. These classes represent areas of similar spectral reflectances and often represent distinct vegetation or ecological communities. Digital image classification is either unsupervised or supervised. In unsupervised classification, the computer classifies pixel values into a number of different classes based on an analysis of the spectral reflectances (DNs). The number of classes is usually supplied by the analyst and should approximate the number of ecological community types thought to occur in the area. In supervised classification, the analyst provides information about known vegetation communities from specific areas to assist the classification process. Specifically, the analyst provides a set of seed pixels that the classification algorithm then correlates with all the pixels in the image. The seed pixel information is obtained through field verification or prior knowledge of the distribution of communities.

Manual versus Digital Image Classification

Although digital image classification has certain distinct advantages over manual interpretation (the computer has a greater spectral discrimination ability, permitting the use of multiple bands of data), REAs almost always employ manual photointerpretation techniques. This emphasis on manual classification is related to considerations of appropriate technology. Photogrammetry is a standard and familiar discipline in virtually every country because of the common and historical development of topographic maps based on aerial photography; thus, photogrammetric expertise commonly exists. Photointerpretation of satellite imagery is relatively straightforward and does not involve a stereoscopic analysis.

Digital classification, on the other hand, requires substantial hardware, software, and expertise. As mentioned earlier, remote sensing analyses are resource intensive and are still uncommon in many countries. Where these systems exist, they are often used primarily to rectify, enhance, and print out scaled and gridded hard-copy imagery, which is then photointerpreted. Manual interpretation should be considered the preferred classification methodology in most REA circumstances. Where substantial computer resources exist, along with expertise in the use of digital classification algorithms, digital classification should be considered as an alternative to manual photointerpretation.

Digital Capture of Delineated Features

Once interpreted, delineated features are always digitized into a GIS. This allows for the development of digital GIS data layers, which are subsequently used for spatial analysis and map presentation. This digitization step involves adding identification labels to points, lines, and polygons.

This step returns the information content to a digital dimension. Image pixels (digital data) have been manually interpreted into feature classes (hard-copy, nondigital polygons), which are then captured back into digital entities (GIS objects). This type of manual interpretation followed by digital capture into a GIS has become known as the semidigital classification approach, and it is standard procedure for most REAs.

Aerial Photography

Aerial photographs are obtained from a mapping camera mounted in a camera port on the underside of a special aircraft. These vertical photographs are taken in a time-controlled sequence so that overlap between two successive photos is obtained. This overlap permits stereo viewing of the two overlapping photos (a stereo pair) with a stereoscope. Canopy height differences are distinguishable in stereo analysis and are the basis for discrimination between plant communities.

Aerial photographs are obtained in either natural color or color-infrared. Color-infrared photographs are generally more appropriate for delineating vegetation communities. Natural-color aerial photographs are generally more appropriate for discriminating near-shore marine communities. The height of the aircraft determines the scale of aerial photography, which can therefore be controlled at a constant value. Common scales are 1:24,000 and 1:50,000, although many scales are possible. In general, high-quality, appropriately scaled, color-infrared aerial photography is more appropriate, and should be obtained and photointerpreted whenever possible. Aerial photography is sometimes available from public agencies.

Photointerpretation

Photointerpretation of aerial photography involves interpreting stereopairs with a stereoscope. Features delineated from this interpretation are drawn (traced) onto acetate jackets. Features are delineated based on the visual properties of the photographic media, which includes color, tone, and texture, and on the features of objects captured in the photographs, such as crown size and shape, and canopy height difference.

After features have been interpreted, they are transferred onto a basemap, which is typically a satellite image basemap produced at the same scale of the photography, during the feature transfer step. Photointerpretation always involves a "mapping from" and "mapping to" dimension. It is common in REAs to map from aerial photography to satellite-image basemaps, but features can be mapped onto GIS-produced maps or topographic maps as well.

Scale changes during the feature transfer process are undesirable and discouraged. A zoom transferscope is a specialized piece of optical projection equipment that permits feature transfers with change of scale. Zoom transferscopes, however, are expensive and rarely available. If aerial photography is to be acquired for an REA, the choice of scale should include a consideration of avoiding scale changes during the feature transfer process.

Videography

Videography and digital photography represent relatively new types of imagery that can be used for REAs and other conservation applications. Videography is video shot from an aircraft with a special video camera. The camera, when mounted in a camera port, can acquire near-vertical imagery output as analog (nondigital) videotape, which can be viewed immediately after the flight and even during the flight itself. Technological advances now permit the integration of a GPS receiver with the video camera so that individual frames of the video are location-tagged.

The equipment for collecting this imagery is not widely and commercially available and is fairly expensive. Digitizing the videotape using frame-grabbing software is possible, but it requires special video player/recorders and considerable technical expertise. Creating a digital image of an area by digitally capturing individual video frames and then mosaicking them together is a complicated and expensive process and is not recommended. Videography therefore should not be considered as a source of imagery for large-area mapping and vegetation classification work.

Videography may, however, prove to be an excellent landscape-level monitoring tool because the same flight path (typically park limits) can be reflown at regular intervals. Although the resulting imagery is not digital and is not amenable to computer analysis, the videotape is nevertheless a permanent, visual record of landscape condition at the time of the flight. This is useful for detecting human penetration into parks, land use changes, road and trail developments, and so on. Digital videography is becoming more available.

Digital Photography

Digital cameras sense directly to disk and have become increasingly popular since their development in the late 1990s. They are useful for obtaining a digital record of landscape condition at the time of acquisition, but they are still not widely used for vegetation mapping. Mosaicking digital photos can result in an image of an area, but the image will likely not be photogrammetrically accurate. Standard aerial photos are photogrammetric because the plane is maintained at a constant height and tip and roll of the aircraft is relatively controlled, allowing for vertical photography. This level of aircraft control is absent on all but the most professional mapping mission flights.

Using digital cameras on overflights to acquire imagery at point locations is, however, very useful. The camera is focused in as near a vertical orientation as possible, and the photos are useful for subsequent photointerpretation of other imagery. Digital photography in the field of species and communities is extremely useful and lends itself well to publication of results in the final REA report. Digital still photos are also easy to archive as data records.

Global Positioning Systems

A global positioning system (GPS) is a geolocation technology in which the GPS operator uses a receiving device to obtain an accurate coordinate location anywhere on the Earth. GPS technology is based on a constellation of twenty to thirty satellites, which broadcast signals continuously. A handheld GPS receiver receives these signals and uses a mathematical triangulation approach to determine the position of the receiver. Positions (coordinate locations) generated by the receiver are stored in files; these data can then be transferred to a GIS.

GPS is an incredibly useful spatial technology and is the basis for geolocating all field- and overflight-collected data in an REA. Each team (vegetation, fauna, mapping) needs to have and use GPS receivers when recording any data in the field or in the air. In addition to geolocating where specimens are collected, or where observations are recorded, GPS can be used to establish geographic control points for rectifying imagery.

Operating a GPS

A GPS is relatively easy to understand and operate. A number of parameters (critical settings) are established prior to use, which relate to desired level of accuracy. The coordinate system and datum to be used are identified so that GPS positions obtained by the receiver can be related to the maps available for the area under survey. Position locations are collected when the receiver is turned on, and these positions are usually captured into a file for subsequent analysis and transfer to a GIS.

Sources of GPS Error

There are several sources of error in GPS data, including satellite clock errors, satellite orbit errors, atmospheric transmission delays, receiver noise, reflected signals, and selective availability (SA). SA is a United States Department of Defense program that intentionally introduces error in GPS signal transmissions to deny full GPS accuracy to unauthorized users. Most of these errors are correctable using a technique called differential correction. When not using differential correction, and for the type of GPS receivers that are generally used for REA fieldwork, errors typically range from 10 meters to 40 meters but can be substantially greater. With differential correction, the range of error is generally reduced to from 5 meters to 15 meters.

Differential Correction

Differential correction is a technique for markedly improving the accuracy of position data by using two GPS receivers at the same time. Differential correction involves collecting data from a GPS receiver at a known location (called a base station) at the same time that GPS data are collected in the field with another receiver (called a rover). Since the receiver at the base station is stationary and in a known location, the magnitude and direction of the SA error can be determined. This error is then subtracted from the rover GPS data.

The software issued with GPS receivers can perform the differential correction without substantial expertise on the part of the analyst. Special GPS base station hardware is available that simplifies the collection of base data, but this equipment is relatively expensive. Alternatively, most GPS receivers can operate in both base and rover mode. Operating a standard GPS receiver in base mode has a particular set of constraints, relating mainly to memory and battery limits. Small, handheld receivers can use different sources of battery power (i.e., size AAs, rechargeable video camera batteries, etc.), and battery life should be a planning consideration for fieldwork. The amount of memory available to store point location files in the receiver can also be limiting, which necessitates downloading files from the receiver to the computer to free up memory.

Conclusion

GIS, GPS, and Remote Sensing technologies are important tools for REA. Their use requires an understanding of some basic geographic concepts, particularly scale and MMU. The REA mapping process, which utilizes these tools and concepts, is described in detail in the following chapter.

Literature Cited

Burrough, P. A. 1986. *Principles of Geographical Information Systems for Land Resources Assessment.* Oxford, England: Oxford University Press.

ERDAS, 1991. *Field Guide.* Atlanta, Ga.: ERDAS Inc.

ESRI (Environmental Systems Research Institute). 1990. *Understanding GIS: The Arc/Info Method.* Redlands, Calif.: ESRI.

Lillesand, T. M., and R. W. Kiefer. 1994. *Remote Sensing and Image Interpretation.* New York: John Wiley and Sons.

Maguire, D. J., M. F. Goodchild, and D. W. Rhind. 1991. *Geographic Information Systems: Principles and Applications.* New York: John Wiley and Sons.

Paine, D. P. 1981. *Aerial Photography and Image Interpretation for Resource Management.* New York: John Wiley and Sons.

Snyder, J. P. 1987. *Map Projections—A Working Manual.* U.S. Geological Survey Professional Paper 1395. Washington, D.C.: USGS.

Star, J. L., and J. E. Estes. 1990. *Geographic Information Systems: An Introduction.* Englewood Cliffs, N.J.: Prentice-Hall.

Chapter 4

The REA Mapping Process

Roger Sayre and Stuart Sheppard

The previous chapter presented basic geographic concepts and their technological application to biodiversity conservation and REA. Spatial information technologies were defined from a functional and conceptual perspective. This chapter describes in greater detail how these spatial information technologies are used in the actual implementation of REAs. This chapter is intended primarily for mapping specialists, who will be charged with spatial analysis and mapmaking responsibilities. On another level, however, the chapter also describes a process that is fundamental to the REA concept. This process should be reviewed by anyone desiring a full understanding of REA.

We begin by characterizing the REA mapping process in general and describing the planning dimensions of the mapping effort. We then describe the development of imagery and GIS datasets, followed by a discussion of the Initial Landscape Characterization step and the sampling plan development. We conclude the discussion with a description of overflights and field operations, and the development of map products. At the end of the chapter we include a set of seventeen color maps, twelve of which present the sequential development of REA map products using a single REA case study from the Parque Nacional del Este (National Park of the East), Dominican Republic (The Nature Conservancy, 1997). The remaining five maps present examples of map products from different REAs.

Mapping an REA

In general, mapping an REA refers to a complex set of activities that include the following: acquisition of image data sources, planning and participating in overflights, interpreting imagery, designing sampling strategies, operating field geolocation equipment, training other team members in the use of geolocation equipment, developing study area maps for all team members, assisting in data analysis and interpretation, developing thematic maps of results, writing relevant sections of the REA report, and generating final presentation-quality and publication-quality map products. These activities are the responsibility of the spatial technology specialists (mappers) of the REA team. Undertaking these activities requires an overwhelming dedication of effort by the REA mappers, who are called upon to support the other REA teams in a variety of ways. The mapping of an REA is a discipline-integrating process, permitting the analysis of species data in a habitat context and in relation to other species data.

Planning for Mapping

Thoughtful planning of the mapping component of an REA is necessary to ensure that the quality and relevance of mapping efforts are high. Planning for mapping should involve project managers, the mapping team, and key representatives from the other disciplinary groups, who should be prepared to discuss any special mapping considerations pertinent to their taxa or study subjects. All members of the REA team must realize that, although the mapping team members are experts in how to map, they do not necessarily know what should be mapped. Disciplinary specialists commonly expect that the mapping team will map everything important, but in reality mappers need considerable direction in determining the thematic content of maps. A very serious mapping planning effort is necessary to enable the mapping initiative to proceed smoothly.

The Mapping Workplan

A mapping workplan that clearly details mapping activity requirements, task assignments, delivery dates, product expectations, and management structures should be developed. As in the taxonomic disciplinary groups, the mapping team should designate a leader. The mapping team will be working on behalf of the entire REA team and will be called on to support many activities, especially sampling location determination, overflight planning, GPS operation, spatial analysis, and map production. Due to this high degree of involvement, the mapping team must proactively collaborate with the other groups from the initial planning stages of the REA forward. The mapping workplan therefore will duplicate much of the activities and product developments outlined in the other disciplinary and project management teams.

Determining Scales

The scale of data development (working scale) and the scale of final map production products (presentation scale) should be decided upon very early in the planning process. The mapping team should have some influence on this decision because this group is the most familiar with scales of existing imagery and maps. The scale is often decided upon in the early planning stages and should be explicitly stated in the contract for the REA.

Mapping at the scale of the highest resolution topographic maps that exist is often desirable. For many areas, a coarse-resolution (commonly 1:250,000 or 1:500,000) and a fine-resolution (1:50,000 or 1:100,000) topographic series exists; mapping at 1:50,000 or 1:100,000 is often adequate, especially for large, relatively unknown areas. Ideally, vegetation communities should be mapped at a larger scale, such as 1:24,000 or better, because vegetation community discrimination is more accurate and detailed. Discernible, mappable units at a larger scale (e.g., 1:24,000) are often not discernible at a smaller scale. Mappable units at smaller scales are often aggregations and generalizations of features that were evident in the higher-resolution imagery.

The appropriate working scale is normally a function of the size of the area under investigation and the available resources. A small area, for example, can be mapped at a relatively larger scale. In general, the working scale should be large enough to permit feature classification (e.g., vegetation types) but small enough to be manageable.

The presentation scale is usually smaller than the working scale. It is usually best to print maps out at a scale that plots the whole study area while maximizing the width dimension of the plotting device. Single, large maps for presentation purposes are preferred over paneled maps if enough detail can be presented.

Map Requirements

Each REA contract and statement of work should have the map end product requirements clearly stated, and map work in the REA should be directed toward satisfying these obligations. It is possible, and often tempting, for REA mappers to produce a wide variety of maps due to the generation of vast quantities of data during an REA. While the production of some intermediate maps and data exploration maps is inevitable, REA mappers should largely be working toward the production of only those maps specified in the contract. Map production is expensive and time consuming, and REA scientists often tend to request a number of maps from the mapping team that are not required. Extra-contractual mapping is generally discouraged, except where necessary. The types of maps typically produced in REAs are described later in the chapter.

The exact number (copies), scale, size, colors, thematic content, georeferencing information, and other map elements should be specified in the contract. The contract should also clearly specify how credit should be provided with respect to data sources and which logos of participating and funding institutions should appear.

GIS Database Construction

For every REA, an extensive, multilayered GIS database is constructed, which permits both spatial analysis and map production. The GIS database is the master database for the REA and contains all the geographic and attribute data necessary for the display and spatial analysis of each important theme. The disciplinary specialists may decide to maintain their own databases as well, independent of the REA master database, in order to track more descriptive information that is generally not visualizable (e.g., large text strings or memo fields). Each individual layer should be constructed from the best available data source at the largest manageable spatial resolution. Many REA data layers will have to be generated by digitizing the information from hard-copy maps. Other data layers will be obtainable in digital format. For vector mapping, each layer represents one biological, physical, or social theme. Every GIS layer should contain only one theme; different themes (e.g., roads and rivers) should never be mixed in the same data layer.

The list of thematic data layers typically captured and used as REA input includes the following:

- Study area boundary
- Regional location of study area
- Geological formations
- Soils
- Elevation contours
- Precipitation isohyets
- Rivers/Surface hydrography
- Roads/Trails
- Villages
- Land use/Land cover

- Political/Administrative units
- Existing zonation
- Land tenure

    Typical GIS layers resulting from REA implementation include the following:

- Sampling locations
- Vegetation communities
- Species encounters
- Critical areas for biodiversity conservation
- Proposed zonation
- Threats

The Project Logbook

A GIS/mapping project logbook, initiated during the early REA planning stages, maintains a documentation of the mapping activities, data dictionary, decision history, map citations, and other relevant information. The project logbook should be structured as follows: (1) REA Project Description and Mapping Perspectives, (2) Project Resources (personnel, equipment, software), (3) Data Dictionary, (4) Memos and Correspondence, (5) Contacts, and (6) Maps. The data dictionary is the most important part of the logbook. It is organized by layers and should provide the following information: (1) Name/Theme, (2) Date Created, (3) Responsible Individual, (4) Scale of Development, (5) Source Information (origin, date, primary source, projection, datum, grid system, series number, and so on), (6) Item/Variable Definitions and Values, (7) Layer Creation Sequence, (8) Map Registration Errors, and (9) Notes.

    Diligence in maintaining the mapping logbook is recommended because the logbook is invariably and frequently consulted during and after the project. The logbook should be duplicated at the close of the project and should be archived along with the maps, reports, and digital datasets.

Image Analysis

Following preliminary map planning, the development of a mapping workplan, and the initiation of a GIS/mapping project logbook, the mapping team is ready to begin image analysis in the Initial Landscape Characterization phase. Every REA is fundamentally based on an interpretation of vegetation types from imagery (either aerial photography or satellite imagery), which are subsequently mapped, field verified, and studied for community- and species-level biodiversity. This reliance on imagery discriminates REA from other rapid biodiversity assessments and places a priority on the delineation of vegetation types as management units.

    For satellite imagery, the prefieldwork REA image analysis process usually includes image acquisition, rectification, enhancement, interpretation, and output in hard-copy format. For aerial photography, the process includes acquisition, interpretation, and transfer of interpreted polygons to a basemap.

Image Acquisition

Acquiring imagery for an REA involves a thorough study of available imagery and a consideration of available resources. The previous chapter discussed image acquisition in general; what follows here are some practical tips for acquiring photographs or satellite imagery. Imagery should always be obtained from a professional supplier. Aerial photography not already available should be commissioned only from a reputable specialist. The REA team should not contemplate acquiring imagery themselves, even though there are a number of sensors available that permit the acquisition of data from airplanes. Unless the flight is planned and flown according to rigorous standards, the resulting photography will not be photogrammetric.

To commission an aerial overflight acquisition mission, the purchaser must contact the provider, provide a map of the area to be flown, specify the type of imagery (color-infrared, natural-color, or black-and-white), and specify the desired scale. The provider then prepares a bid or estimate on the job. Obtaining multiple bids is encouraged. If the provider has to travel significantly to the study area, especially for international travel, a mobilization fee will constitute part of the cost estimate. The mobilization fee is usually a significant expense, which is not refundable in a situation where inclement weather precludes obtaining satisfactory photos. A period of time is indicated on the bid and contract, usually ten days to two weeks, in which the provider will fly the mission or wait for better weather if grounded. At the end of this period, the provider may return to the place of origin, regardless of whether a full set of photos has been acquired. To return to the country, another mobilization fee may be assessed. This is standard operating procedure, but the providers may be willing to extend the time window or reduce or eliminate a second mobilization fee. Strong negotiation skills are useful in this discussion between purchaser and provider.

When the terms are agreed upon, the provider and the purchaser execute a contract. The contract should state clearly the specifications for the photography, as well as the disposition of the film (developed into negatives, nine-inch film products, etc.). A set of prints is always useful for both interpretation and archival purposes.

Satellite imagery is delivered on CDs or 8-millimeter tapes. The file size for single multiband scenes is typically large. Adequate mass storage must be available for manipulation of these files. Scene data are downloaded from the delivery medium onto the hard disk for subsequent analysis.

Image Rectification

Imagery sources are rarely delivered with a satisfactory level of geographic accuracy and generally need to be rectified. Hard-copy aerial photos have no georeferencing and are not rectified (although they can be scanned, rectified, and mosaicked using image processing software). Digital aerial photography is often available for purchase in the United States as digital ortho-photoquads, but this rectified photography is rarely available for many tropical or developing nations.

Rectification of satellite imagery requires a full set of good topographic maps, another similar image previously rectified, a digital elevation model (DEM), or a set of GPS-derived ground control points. Rectifying imagery to topographic maps is the most common REA procedure. The process involves registering the topographic map to the digitizer, displaying the image on screen, searching for control points (visible landmarks on both map and image), and establishing the location of the control point in the image using the known location of the point on the registered map. When the locations of several control points have been established in the image, a mathematical transformation is executed to apply locational information throughout the image. The image is then georeferenced, and any location in the image can be queried for geographic position.

Once the imagery has been georeferenced, it is normally printed and the hard-copy product is manually interpreted. Prior to printing the image, the bands that will be used are chosen. For terrestrial vegetation applications, natural-color band combinations (see map 1) are generally less suitable than color-infrared combinations (see map 2). For Landsat imagery, the bands chosen and the sequence of their display in the red, blue, and green color-channels are usually 4, 5, and 3. For SPOT multispectral imagery, the bands and sequence normally used are 3, 2, and 1. A number of commands in the image processing software then permit an enhancement of the image (contrast improvements) prior to printing. A georeferencing grid should always be applied prior to printing. The most appropriate grid to apply is often a one square kilometer UTM (Universal Transverse Mercator) grid in white or black. The grid is critical because it permits very accurate geolocation of field positions on the image.

Image Interpretation

Manual (visual) interpretation of the hard-copy image or aerial photographs is standard REA procedure because of the complexities of digital image classification, which requires both technology and expertise. For interpretation of aerial photography, a stereoscope is necessary. Aerial photographs are interpreted in stereopairs, which are adjacent photographs acquired in succession on the same flight line. One of the stereopairs is inserted in an acetate jacket, and vegetation units observed in stereo through the eyepieces are traced onto the acetate using a fine rapidograph pen. Vegetation types are discriminated from one another based on differences in canopy height (the primary discriminator), color, tone, texture, crown size, and crown shape (secondary discriminators).

Manually interpreting satellite imagery is similar to aerial-photo interpretation, but manual interpretation lacks a stereo dimension. Structural differences in vegetation community canopies therefore are not apparent, and spectral differences assume a greater importance for discrimination. An acetate or mylar sheet is affixed to the image, georeferencing points are marked, and communities visible in the image are traced onto the overlay using a thin rapidograph marker.

For either photos or satellite imagery, prior to drawing any polygons onto the overlay, the image should be looked at thoroughly to gain a general familiarity with the material. General landscape features, different spectral elements, topographic and hydrographic systems, and preliminary counts of unique natural communities or land cover systems should be noted. The quality of the interpretation is in many ways a function of familiarity with the imagery.

During this familiarization phase, the decision about the size of the minimum mapping unit (MMU) (also see chapter 3) should be made. This decision should consider practicality and management. It is often tempting to establish the MMU as the smallest interpretable area in the image, but doing so can be overly ambitious and time consuming, and can result in a level of detail that exceeds management requirements. The chosen MMU should be recorded in the project logbook, along with the criteria for making that decision and with a formula relating the area of the MMU on an image to the actual ground area (a simple scale conversion).

Implementing the Initial Landscape Characterization

The initial delineation of vegetation types from the imagery data source is called the Initial Landscape Characterization (ILC). The ILC, previously described in chapter 1, is implemented by the vegetation and mapping teams. It is the step in which the imagery is interpreted (usually manually) to produce the unknown polygon map (figure 1-1, maps 3 and 6). The maximum number of unique vegetation types is assessed by reviewing the imagery and noting examples of each different spectral or textural example. It is helpful to establish a running number class-I.D. system and to mark the case examples of each class on the image itself using semiadhesive notepad sheets for labeling. Alternatively, if two sets of imagery are available and one set can be destructively sacrificed, it is quite useful to establish a class-I.D. key by cutting (either digitally or manually) pure examples of the case type and pasting them into a key or legend along with the numerical class code.

Feature Delineation and Labeling

Once all unique polygon types have been established and coded, interpretation of the entire image (or relevant area of the image) begins. Interpretation should be implemented by one individual or a small group of individuals to ensure consistency. Lines depicting polygon boundaries should be drawn as thinly and solidly as possible to facilitate future digitizing efforts. Line intersections should be clean, and all polygons must close. Polygons smaller than the MMU should not be delineated, unless special circumstances warrant the capture of that information.

Every polygon must be labeled. Labels should be as simple as possible, but they can incorporate multiple types of information. For example, a five-digit label code could represent the following: the first number indicates the sampling region, the second and third numbers refer to the vegetation unit type, and the fourth and fifth numbers refer to the polygon identification. Using this labeling nomenclature, a polygon with a label-I.D. of 32715 would refer to the fifteenth example of class type 27 in sampling region 3. It is important to keep the labeling system simple and to avoid the temptation to pack as much descriptive information as possible into the label; this attribute information for each polygon is easily tracked in the GIS and does not need to be part of the labeling system.

The disciplinary teams should have many opportunities to observe and comment on the ILC activity while it is under way. The mapping team usually tends to overdiscriminate when delineating polygons (maximum class separation based on spectral and textural uniqueness), but the disciplinary teams often have had prior experience in the area and can provide information about the numbers and types of classes. Often the input of these experts results in a combining of classes to reduce the number of class types. Subsequent field verification also changes the number of class types; class combination is common, but class splitting also occurs.

Polygon boundaries should be captured with as much detail as possible; extensive generalization of boundaries is discouraged. Wanting to generalize features in the imagery to reduce the work effort is a common tendency, especially given the ecological reality that communities in nature are rarely separated by hard lines. However, it is always damaging to the credibility of the analysis when interpreted polygon boundaries do not match as closely as possible when the polygon GIS layer is overlaid on the image.

The polygons will eventually be digitized into a GIS following the completion of the ILC, but there still is usually a need to have a list in spreadsheet form of all of the polygons in the study area. While such a list can be produced from the GIS, this list is usually created by data entry for expediency and to enable discussions about the sampling plan before the GIS data layer is constructed.

The ILC work is very time consuming and can require several weeks. This work must be completed before the planning and training workshops. A sampling plan cannot be completed without the polygon map that results from the ILC.

Developing the Sampling Plan

The polygon map and spreadsheet list of individual polygons by vegetation type produced during the Initial Landscape Characterization are used by the vegetation/floristic and animal survey teams to develop the sampling plan. Usually the sampling plan is arrived at by group consensus, in which the participating teams are gathered around the polygon maps. A large table or clean, flat surface is necessary to display all of the polygon map sheets if several adjacent sheets were interpreted. The list of sampling locations is arrived at by visual inspection of these maps, not by a mathematical formula or a GIS selection routine.

As discussed in chapter 1, the sampling plan is developed by determining the number of replicate polygons in each vegetation type in each sampling region that needs to be sampled. At an absolute minimum, at least one example of each vegetation type from each sampling region should be visited. Accessibility is considered when choosing the sample units because more units can be sampled if they are easily accessible. It is unwise, however, to sample only sites that are close to roads. When resources are available to sample multiple examples (replicates) of the same vegetation type, vegetation units that are relatively dispersed throughout the sampling region, rather than highly clustered in one or two areas, should be chosen.

Vegetation Sampling

When choosing sample units, two levels of sampling intensity should be considered. The first level of sampling intensity relates to the units that will be sampled to identify or verify the vegetation type. This sampling is conducted by the vegetation team and improves the classification and mapping of the landscape units. The principle of the more units sampled, the higher the classification accuracy, guides this type of sampling. One result of this sampling philosophy is that the vegetation team typically wants to keep moving to new sample sites, which presents a problem for the fauna teams who typically desire to spend more time in fewer locations because of the need to set traps and so on.

Fauna Sampling

This difference in sampling requirements results in a second level of sampling—primarily for faunal inventory—at a subset of the units sampled by the vegetation specialists. The faunal surveys are time intensive, which limits the ability to have several replicate study sites within polygon classes. The faunal team must always, however, sample in units where the vegetation team has verified the vegetation community. This is necessary in order to relate species information from faunal surveys to vegetation types.

The distinction between the two levels of sampling should be understood and agreed upon by all the teams. On the spreadsheet-derived list of polygons, it is important to clearly indicate those polygons that will be sampled for classification work only, and those polygons that will be sampled for both classification verification and species information development. Working through the selection of sampling locations as a large group will help to avoid situations in which individual teams determine their own sampling locations, resulting in different sites being sampled by different groups. Every attempt should be made to ensure that all teams sample in the same units and that those units have been sampled for classification verification. Autonomy in deciding sampling locations is not advisable and generally reduces the overall quality of the REA.

Once a consensus is achieved regarding the polygons that will be sampled, a master list is provided to each group by the mapping team. Each group incorporates this list of sampling sites into its workplan, along with a list of sampling dates. Sampling dates also should be determined as a large group. Logistically, it is important to have a clear statement of when each team will be in the field. It is not necessary, but it is often most logistically appropriate, to have groups in the field at the same locations at the same time. The mapping team should elaborate the overall sampling plan document, which describes the decisions that were made and details the list of sampling units and proposed sampling times. This document should present basic descriptive statistics that detail the number and percentage of polygons in each vegetation type—for the entire study area as well as subsetted by sampling region—that will be sampled. This document should be as concise as possible.

The Overflight

Following the selection of sample polygons, but usually prior to initiating work in the field, an overflight is conducted. The purpose of the overflight is to provide a general familiarity with the study area and to collect valuable data about the number and locations of vegetation communities. Overflights reveal interesting characteristics of the study area that are not always discernible from the image interpretation. If the imagery is not current, overflights can also provide a sense of how the landscape has changed since the imagery was acquired. Information obtained from overflights often serves to improve the Initial Landscape Characterization, and it often results in a modification of the sampling plan.

Planning the Overflight

Overflights must be exceptionally well planned because they are highly orchestrated, short, and generally too expensive to repeat. Where possible, a rehearsal of the overflight is recommended to ensure that the communication and data collection roles of the flight team are understood. The overflight should not be regarded as simply a flyover, but rather as a serious data acquisition mission that will yield extremely important digital classification and mapping data.

Overflights usually consist of about six individuals who should be chosen carefully and who are often the team leaders (mapping expert, zoologist(s), vegetation scientist(s), and project leader). The mapping expert is responsible for the overflight planning, GPS operation, and incorporation of data into the GIS. The mapping expert manages the GPS that belongs to the overflight team, not the aircraft's GPS. The other individuals are responsible for making recorded observations, and one individual is responsible for making a photographic record of the flight. All observations and photographs are georeferenced using the GPS.

The aircraft is generally rented, but on occasion it is provided without charge by governments or the military. The credentials of the pilot should be requested and judged to be impeccable. Selecting an aircraft involves several considerations, but often cost and availability limit choice. Helicopters are excellent aircraft for overflights because of their ability to hover, but excessive noise and wind can be a problem for communication and recording observations. The use of headset radios for communication in helicopters adds a slightly increased level of complexity to the overflight but is necessary for communication. Practice in the use of these devices prior to takeoff, if possible, is encouraged.

Fixed-wing aircraft are more commonly available for hire to an REA team. For visibility purposes, aircraft with wings over the door are preferable to those with low wings. Single-engine and twin-engine aircraft are available. Twin-engine aircraft are often considered safer in the event of motor failure, but it has also been argued that the failure of an engine in a twin-engine plane causes an incredible disequilibrium shear force that is difficult to bring under control. Single-engine planes may be less capable of rapidly achieving sufficient altitude to clear high mountains. The plane should be inspected for obvious signs of disrepair or incomplete maintenance before being selected. Prior to takeoff, the plane's fuel level should be verified as full.

The flight path of the overflight should be predetermined by the overflight team using the polygon map and underlying image. The flight path should be developed so that a maximum number of different polygon classes are overflown. It should be drawn on the polygon map, and the coordinate locations of several segment endpoints along the path should be recorded on a list. This list of desired flyover points should be projected into latitude/longitude coordinates and presented to the pilot during the negotiation stage for the aircraft. The navigation system of the aircraft often includes a GPS; in this case, the desired flyover points can be programmed into the aircraft's navigation system. The pilot is then able to fly to these predetermined locations without assistance from the overflight team.

More commonly, however, the pilot's knowledge of the aircraft's GPS system is imprecise, and although the pilot can often program in an alpha point (one destination), he or she may not know how to program a route of segments. In this event, the mapping expert needs to advise the pilot on where to fly by constantly checking the overflight team's GPS, noting the aircraft position on the image, and directing the pilot where to proceed. Directing the flight en route, while recording GPS observations for the observers, is challenging.

Using a GPS on an overflight requires the use of an external GPS antenna. This antenna can be placed in the dashboard of the aircraft, which often is satisfactory to obtain position data. However, in the dashboard of the aircraft, the antenna is unable to receive signals from all the GPS satellites that may be available because of signal obstruction by the roof and body of the plane. Dashboard-mounted antennae can receive only from GPS satellites in the forward horizon. To improve signal reception and to optimize triangulation from the best satellite constellation, it helps to mount the external antenna somewhere on the top of the plane and find a safe and appropriate way to run the cable into the cabin. Custom-made threaded mounts that allow the antenna to be screwed on to some existing flange-like device on the top of the aircraft are generally secure.

Collecting Data

GPS data are collected on an overflight by opening a file and collecting position data into this file at an appropriate interval (every 5 seconds is generally adequate). A plot of these positions after the overflight is an exact depiction of the actual flight path during the mission. While the positions are being recorded automatically at regular intervals, the GPS operator also stores waypoint locations at the request of the observers. An observer notes something of interest and calls out for a waypoint. The operator stores the waypoint and calls the waypoint number back to the observer, who then takes notes that are location-tagged by waypoint number. An observer may prefer to use a voice recorder instead of taking notes, but the waypoint request and storing procedures are the same. The photographer also requests waypoints to geolocate photographs. If the photographer is continually shooting, waypoints that bracket rolls of film are recorded because it is not feasible to store waypoints for each individual photograph. However, in non-continuous photography, individual photographs are easily location-tagged with waypoints. Waypoints are embedded into the file, which is recording continuous position locations. An inset map of map 14 depicts the GPS-recorded flight path of an REA overflight.

After the flight, GPS data are downloaded onto a computer. If base station data are available for the time in which the overflight was conducted, these data are used to differentially correct the overflight data. It is highly recommended that overflight data be differentially corrected. This sometimes requires leaving a GPS receiver behind at the airstrip (in a known location if possible) operating in base mode during the flight. The corrected GPS points are then imported into the GIS environment and plotted for classification work.

Field Geolocation with GPS

After the overflight results have been discussed, and the classification system and sampling plan modified accordingly, the field survey phase begins. All field-collected data should be precisely georeferenced, and the mapping expert should accompany some of the field expeditions to ensure that field teams are able to properly locate their field positions on the imagery and properly record GPS coordinates at sampling locations. Each team must become proficient in the use of GPS.

Prior to beginning fieldwork, the imagery and polygon map should be prepared for field use. Both should be reproduced, if possible, to avoid using the original data sources in the field. The imagery, polygon map, and topographic series maps (if available) should be laminated to improve durability. Lamination can be purchased at most copy services, or clear plastic shelf-liner paper can be used. Ideally, one set of each of these three materials should be provided to each field team.

GPS Surveying

In the field, the GPS is used to determine actual position on the Earth. This coordinate location can easily be found on the image if the image has been properly rectified and printed with a fine resolution (1 square kilometer) grid. If the polygon map is overlaid on the image, ground location can also be identified on the polygon map in the same manner. Finding a ground position on a topographic map may prove more difficult if the topographic map lacks the same grid system.

Collecting GPS data at any point location in the field consists of opening a file, collecting positions automatically into that file, and closing the file. Storing waypoints in the field is generally unnecessary, unless a sampling point will need to be revisited during the expedition. The default file name is often a numerical time stamp that indicates when the file was initiated. Although the file name can generally be changed to a user-specified name, this practice is discouraged to avoid loss of information. The file should be left open long enough to collect, as a rule of thumb, thirty to fifty positions. GPS-obtained position data are transferred as files through a cable. These data are subsequently differentially corrected (where possible), and then averaged into one coordinate location. The data are then imported into a GIS for display and spatial analysis.

A photograph taken at the exact location of the GPS point is recommended. This photograph can be very useful for refining the vegetation community classification. Georeferenced photographs taken at every sampling location can be collected into an invaluable photographic inventory and baseline archive for the REA study site. Digital photography is easy to archive and can be included in reports and presentations.

Dense, tall forest canopy can prove difficult for satisfactory signal reception. Gaps in the canopy left by treefall are generally better sites for GPS operation. Although it is virtually impossible to emerge from tall rainforest canopies, elevating the external antenna above the understory canopy has dramatically improved signal reception in many REAs. The manufacturers of GPS devices sell telescopic range-poles for this purpose, but they are generally prohibitively expensive. For very little expense, a telescopic aluminum painting pole (for roller painting of two-story houses or buildings) can be rigged to take the screw mount of the external antenna. Fixing the external antenna to this pole, and elevating it three to four meters, usually places it above the understory and enables signal reception that was not satisfactory at ground (handheld) level.

Field navigation should be accomplished using a compass and topographic map. Navigating by GPS is not usually practical in most terrestrial REA situations, and it is much easier to calculate a distance and "shoot" an azimuth with a compass and a map. The GPS can then be used at intermediate or final destinations to check whether the sample point or desired destination has been reached.

Identifying and Verifying Vegetation Types

Field visits to predetermined locations within identified sampling polygons followed by the collection of data about vegetation structure and composition constitutes the vegetation type identification and verification step. In general, this step involves the establishment of point sampling locations and the identification of tree species, but it may also include vegetation measurements. GPS-aided geolocation is employed to ensure that the field team is actually at the predetermined location, or at least well inside the polygon to be sampled. Map 8 shows the delineation of sampling regions and the GPS-derived point sampling locations. Sampling for faunal groups is often conducted at these same locations. The amount and types of data collected to identify the vegetation types, and the approach to making this determination, are described in the following chapter.

Post-Fieldwork Classification

Subsequent to fieldwork, all the unsampled polygons are labeled with vegetation type names by correlating their spectral reflectances with the reflectances of known (visited) vegetation types. This process is commonly referred to as supervised classification and is accomplished by a classification algorithm in an image processing system (when working with the image) or a recoding algorithm in a GIS (when working only with vector polygons previously interpreted from the image). This activity results in every polygon being classified. The vegetation survey team should be present during this work because they will be familiar with the actual landscapes being classified, unlike the mappers who will have spent less time in the field. Some polygons will be misclassified by the assignment of two or more very different vegetation types with similar spectral reflectances into the same unit. Subsequent improvement in the classification accuracy can be achieved through additional fieldwork.

Producing Maps

Many maps are typically produced in REAs. These maps document sampling efforts, present results, and often prescribe management strategies.

The Map of Vegetation Types

The final map of vegetation types, derived from image interpretation and verified in the field, is perhaps the most important single product from the REA. This map is a comprehensive characterization of landscape-level biodiversity and is highly suitable for management planning. It should be produced in full color and in large format, and it should be circulated widely for review and refinement as soon as it is produced. Several of the color maps at the end of this chapter depict final vegetation type maps from different REAs (maps 9, 10, 13, 14, 16, and 17). All audiences should be informed that the classification accuracy of the vegetation type map is unknown because rigorous statistical classification techniques were not employed in the development of the product. A classification and map of vegetation types in the area are now available and can be subsequently refined as much as the demand for improvement requires and resources permit.

The map of vegetation types becomes the basis for the threats assessment, information integration, and formulation of recommendations stages that follow its elaboration. The vegetation types and their locations become the basis for reporting most species-level results as well. Sampling locations are frequently identified on the vegetation types map. Alternatively, a map showing only the sampling locations can be produced. This type of map conveys an immediate visual sense of the magnitude of the sampling effort.

Other Thematic Maps

Ancillary GIS data used in the Initial Landscape Characterization (e.g., elevation, roads, hydrography, and geology) should also be elaborated into a set of cartographically distinct map products. These maps will be used in the integration step (chapter 8) and should always be part of the final report (chapter 9) because they improve general understanding of the site. These maps also improve the visual presentation of the final report (for example, see map 7). The digital GIS files, or coverages, for these standard biophysical data layers should be archived with the satellite imagery and other GIS-derived layers.

Species of Conservation Concern Maps

Species of concern maps show at-risk species or exotics, and the locations and types of vegetation in which they were encountered. Intentional decisions to not show the actual locations where rare and endangered species were encountered, so that they are not put at greater risk, are common. A species of concern map (see map 10) has immediate management utility because it highlights specific areas and habitat types in sites where appropriate conservation strategies are essential to promote the persistence of species and communities of conservation concern. Rather than develop maps for each taxonomic group, mapping all the elements of concern onto a single map that has the final vegetation communities map as a backdrop is better. The different taxa are then represented with different symbols (see map 10).

Mapping Threats

Species and vegetation types have spatial footprints and lend themselves well to mapping. Threats to biodiversity, on the other hand, often do not have an intrinsic spatial dimension and are more difficult to represent on maps. The concept of threat involves the system being threatened, the stress to which the system is subject, and the source of the stress. Mapping threats may involve mapping human behavior, which may in turn involve mapping power and gender relationships in communities and perceptions that community members have about biodiversity.

Threats mapping is a pursuit that is likely to receive increasing attention in the conservation and human ecology communities in the near future. In the meantime, one of the more powerful ways to map threats is still symbologically (for example, see map 11), where threats are visualized and associated with particular areas where they may be prevalent but are not depicted as having spatial extent.

Zonation

Management recommendations from REAs frequently include proposals to zone or rezone the site; a proposed zonation map is a powerful REA product that can be used in the campaign for improved conservation at the site. Zonation maps should be simple maps with as few colors as possible (for example, see map 12) and should always highlight the proposed nature of the zoning recommendation to avoid offending authorities. Limiting the distribution of these zoning maps (and of many of the REA maps for that matter) to appropriate interested parties who solicit them in some official capacity is also wise. Good maps in the wrong hands can quickly become problematic.

Literature Cited

Nature Conservancy, The. 1997. *Evaluación Ecológica Integral: Parque Nacional del Este, República Dominicana. Tomo 1: Recursos terrestres.* Arlington, Va.: The Nature Conservancy.

Color Example Maps from REAs

The following seventeen full-color maps are examples of the type of cartographic output produced during REAs. The first twelve maps were produced for an REA of Parque Nacional del Este (National Park of the East) in the Dominican Republic. These twelve maps depict the typical mapping sequence and products of an REA and represent a pictorial case study of the REA from a spatial analysis perspective (see Appendix 1 for a textual description of this same case study REA). The maps were produced by staff from the Department of Inventory of Natural Resources (DIRENA) within the government's Secretariat of Agriculture, and modified for this book.

The remaining five maps were produced in other REAs and were included to illustrate the variety of mapping approaches and products that result from the REA process.

Although these maps are included here in 8.5 × 11-inch format, most were originally developed as larger and more detailed maps. They are included here for illustrative purposes only, and no claim to geographic or thematic accuracy of content is implied.

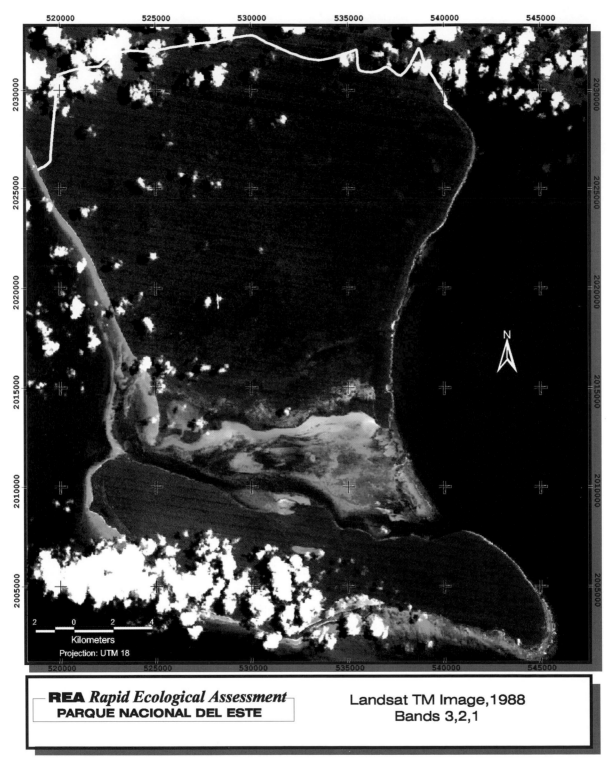

REA *Rapid Ecological Assessment*
PARQUE NACIONAL DEL ESTE

Landsat TM Image,1988
Bands 3,2,1

Map 1. Natural-color satellite image of Parque Nacional del Este, Dominican Republic. The northern boundary of the park has been mapped onto the image, along with a UTM grid. Extensive "popcorn" cloud cover and cloud shading masks a portion of the island and peninsula, a chronic problem for remote-sensing ecologists. Note the detail in reef development and other marine features; natural-color imagery and photography is generally superior for marine community mapping.

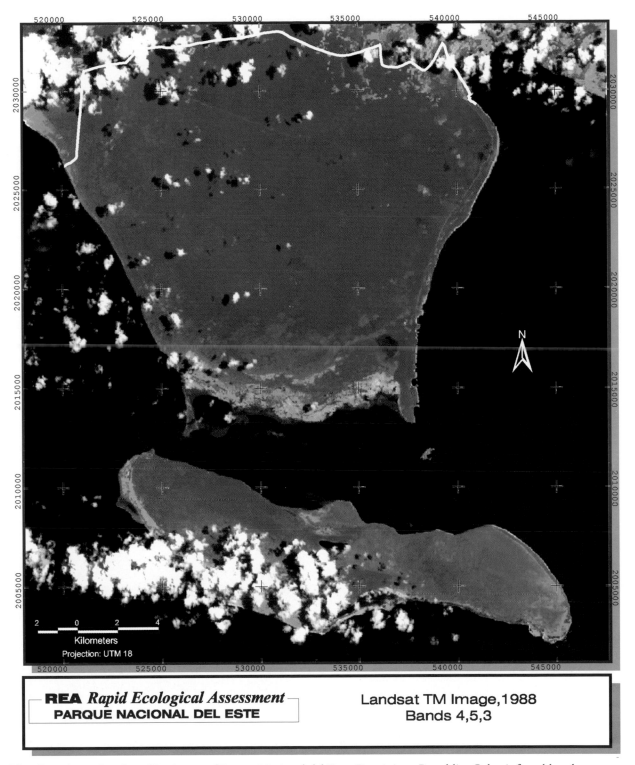

REA *Rapid Ecological Assessment*
PARQUE NACIONAL DEL ESTE

Landsat TM Image,1988
Bands 4,5,3

Map 2. Color-infrared satellite image of Parque Nacional del Este, Dominican Republic. Color-infrared band combinations are more suitable for terrestrial vegetation mapping. Note, for example, that mangroves (deepest red) are not discernable or are poorly discernible in the natural-color image (previous map) but are well separated from adjacent vegetation in this image. The detail in marine community delineation, however, has been sacrificed.

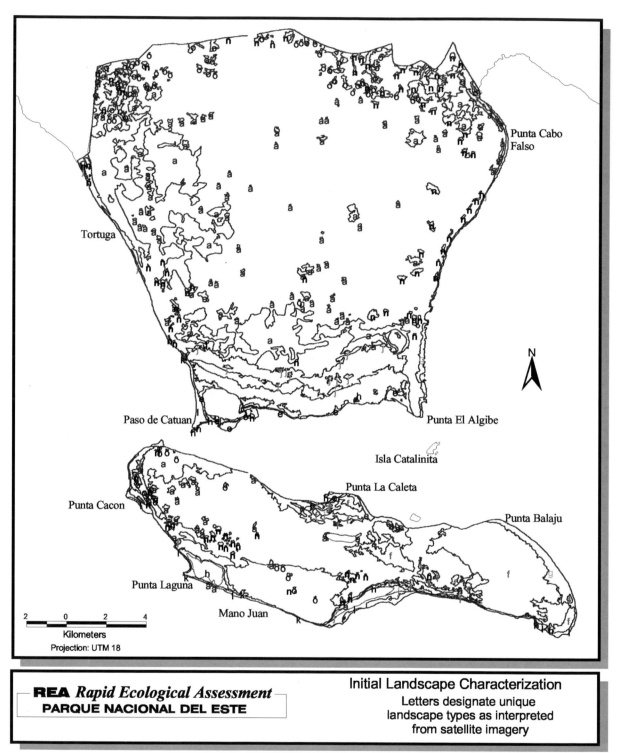

Map 3. Initial Landscape Characterization results from image interpretation. All spectrally unique areas have been assigned to classes and labeled. This working map is often called the unknown polygon map, but if vegetation ecologists participate in the interpretation, then actual preliminary vegetation class labels are assigned. If it is felt that the image interpretation does not sufficiently discriminate vegetation communities, and if resources permit, aerial photo acquisition should be considered.

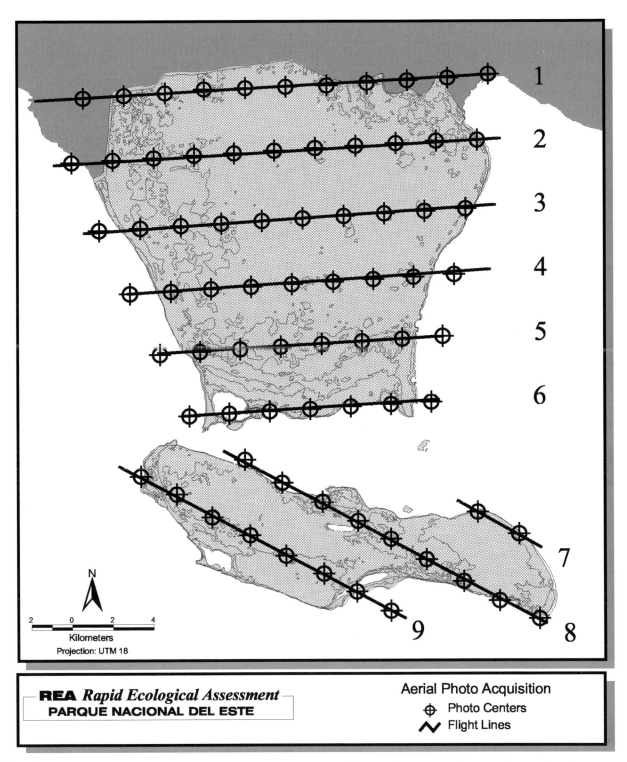

1
2
3
4
5
6
7
9
8

N

2   0   2   4
Kilometers
Projection: UTM 18

REA *Rapid Ecological Assessment*
PARQUE NACIONAL DEL ESTE

Aerial Photo Acquisition
⊕ Photo Centers
∿ Flight Lines

Map 4. Aerial photography acquisition mission. For most terrestrial vegetation community mapping applications, appropriately scaled (in this case, 1:24,000) color-infrared aerial photography is the most desirable data source. It can be interpreted in stereo, which enables the discrimination of differences in canopy height, usually indicative of changes in community structure and composition. This map shows the flight lines and photo centers from the aerial photo acquisition.

Map 5. Color-infrared aerial photography, Parque Nacional del Este, Dominican Republic. This photo of Bahia Calderas, in the southwest corner of the peninsula, shows the additional detail that is available for mapping with larger-scale aerial photography. The western edge of the landscape is a palm plantation; individual tree crowns are discernible. A tourist boat is about to exit the bay. At least seven vegetation communities or land cover classes are discernible in the photo.

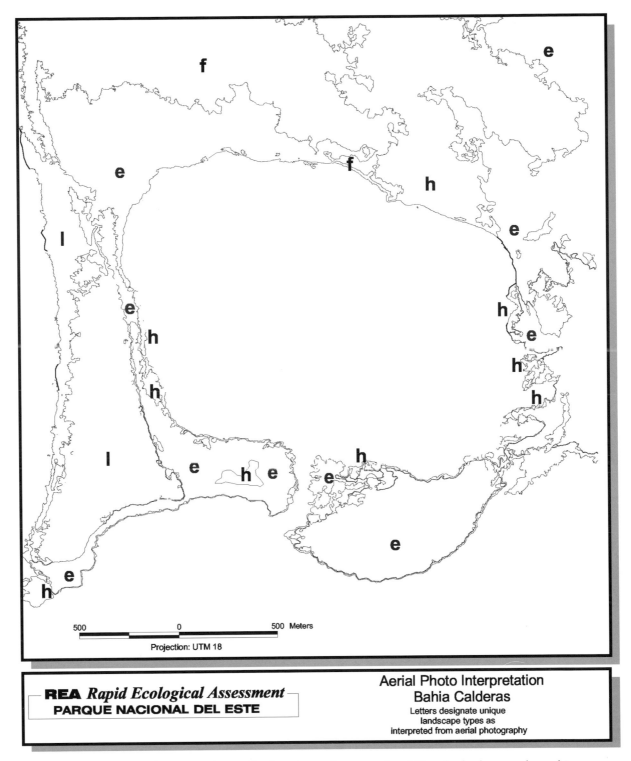

Map 6. Initial Landscape Characterization results from image interpretation. When both photography and imagery are available for the REA site, then the photos are interpreted and the mapped polygons are transferred to the image. The image may then be used to refine the photointerpretation, but more often it serves as a backdrop for subsequent mapping.

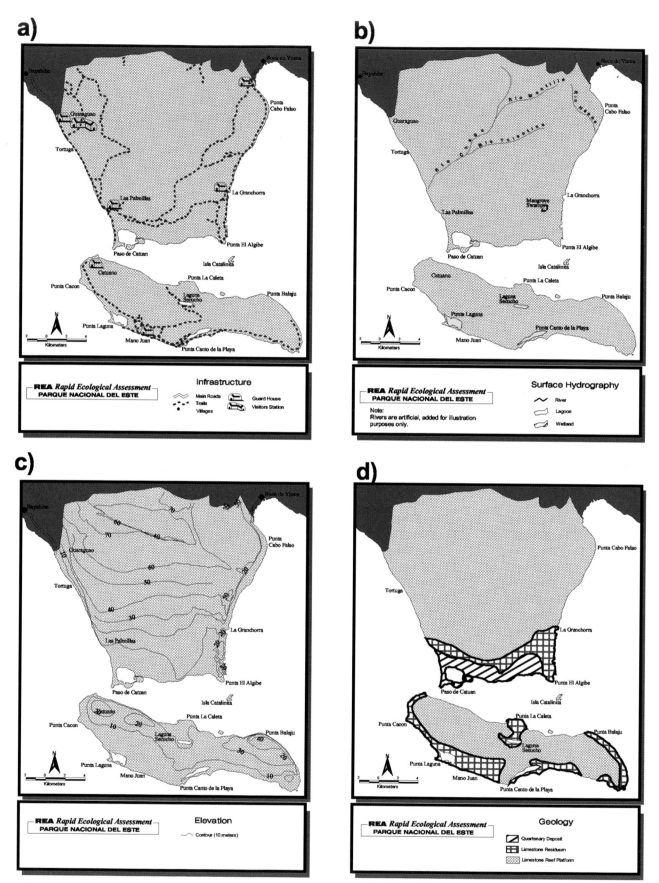

Map 7. Standard environmental GIS data layers used in the del Este Nacional Parque REA. Thematic data for roads, rivers, geology, elevation, and so on are digitized from existing hard-copy maps. These GIS layers are excellent ancillary data sources for the design of sampling strategies and for vegetation community classification and mapping.

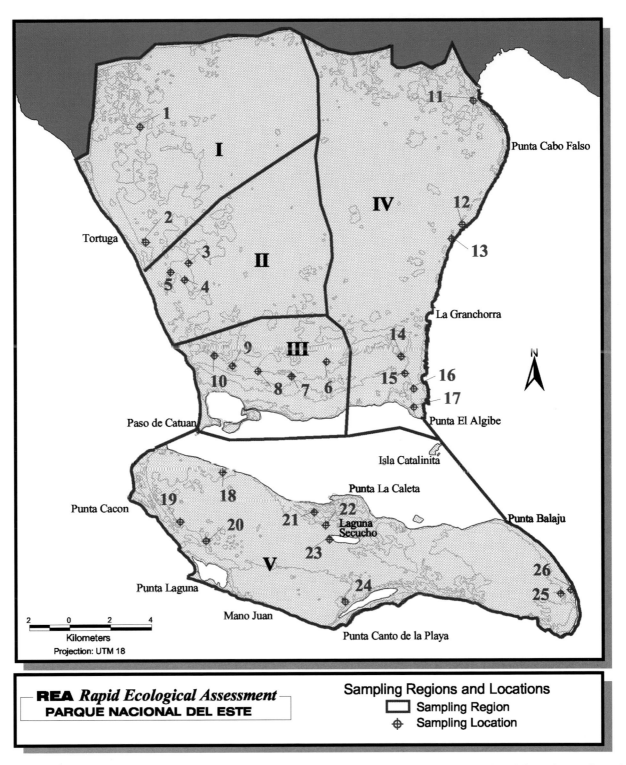

Map 8. Stratification of the site, and selection of sampling locations. Stratification can be employed for either ecological or logistical reasons. In this case, sample strata were chosen for logistical reasons related to site access and chronology of field sampling campaigns. Sampling locations within strata were chosen to ensure that replicate sampling (by strata) of all unique communities determined in the Initial Landscape Characterization was obtained.

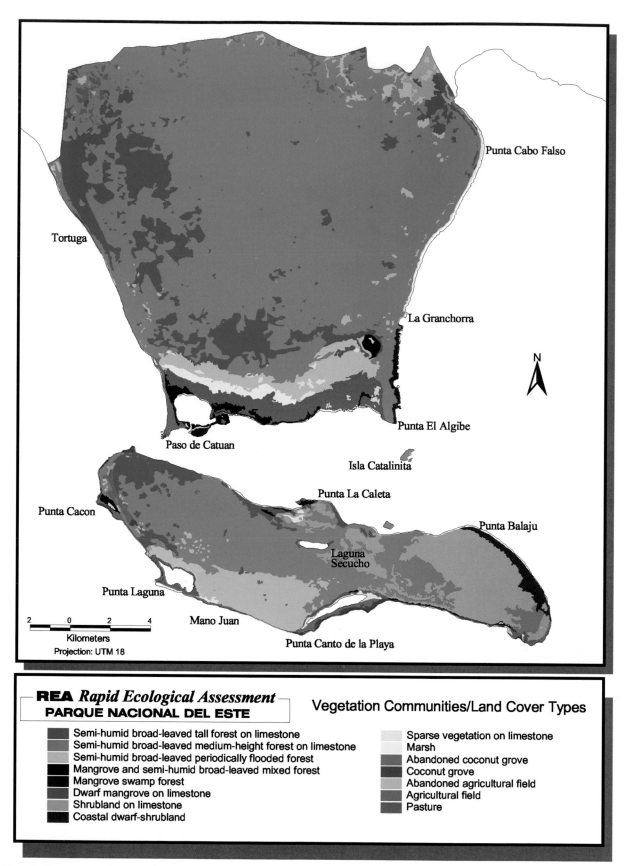

REA *Rapid Ecological Assessment*
PARQUE NACIONAL DEL ESTE

Vegetation Communities/Land Cover Types

- Semi-humid broad-leaved tall forest on limestone
- Semi-humid broad-leaved medium-height forest on limestone
- Semi-humid broad-leaved periodically flooded forest
- Mangrove and semi-humid broad-leaved mixed forest
- Mangrove swamp forest
- Dwarf mangrove on limestone
- Shrubland on limestone
- Coastal dwarf-shrubland

- Sparse vegetation on limestone
- Marsh
- Abandoned coconut grove
- Coconut grove
- Abandoned agricultural field
- Agricultural field
- Pasture

Map 9. Final map of vegetation communities, after field verification. This map represents one of the major products from the REA because it completes the characterization of landscape-level biodiversity and is immediately useful for conservation management planning. In this case, ten natural communities were characterized and mapped, along with five human-influenced cover classes.

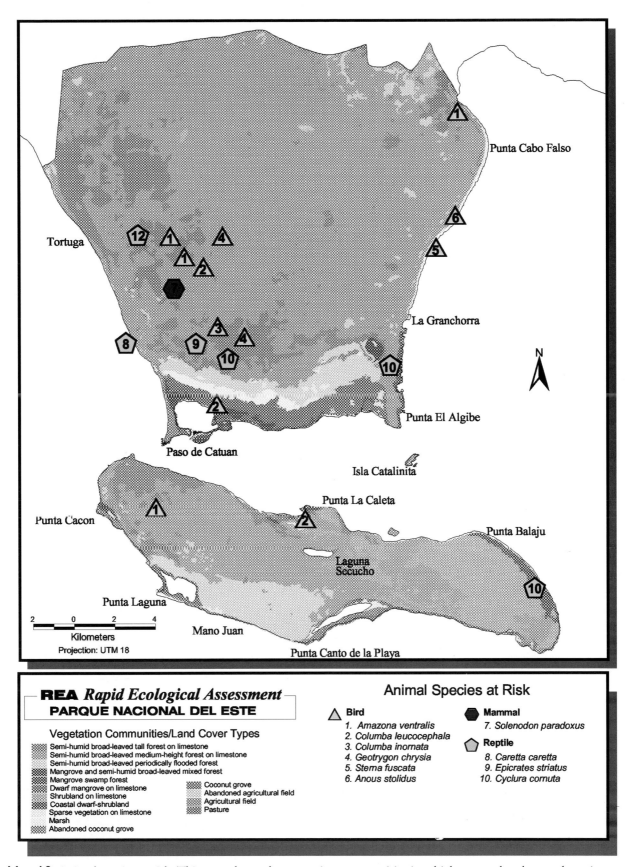

Map 10. Animal species at risk. This map shows the vegetation communities in which rare and endangered species were encountered during the REA. It is possible that these species of concern exhibit specific affinities for these habitats, but an REA does not typically attempt to characterize habitat affinities.

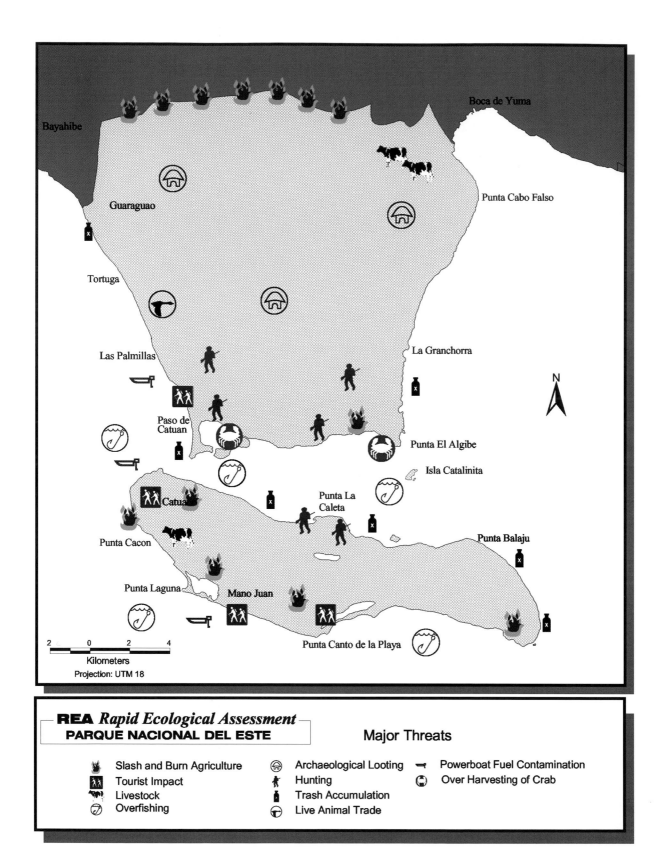

Bayahibe

Boca de Yuma

Guaraguao

Punta Cabo Falso

Tortuga

La Granchorra

Las Palmillas

Paso de Catuan

Punta El Algibe

Isla Catalinita

Punta La Caleta

Catuan

Punta Cacon

Punta Balaju

Punta Laguna

Mano Juan

Punta Canto de la Playa

2 0 2 4
Kilometers
Projection: UTM 18

REA *Rapid Ecological Assessment*
PARQUE NACIONAL DEL ESTE

Major Threats

Slash and Burn Agriculture

Tourist Impact

Livestock

Overfishing

Archaeological Looting

Hunting

Trash Accumulation

Live Animal Trade

Powerboat Fuel Contamination

Over Harvesting of Crab

Map 11. Major threats to biodiversity in the park, and areas where those threats are most pronounced. Establishing a spatial footprint for threats is difficult; in most REAs, threats are identified and sometimes, as here, cartographically symbolized, but they are rarely mapped. REA threats mapping is an area of experimentation and growth.

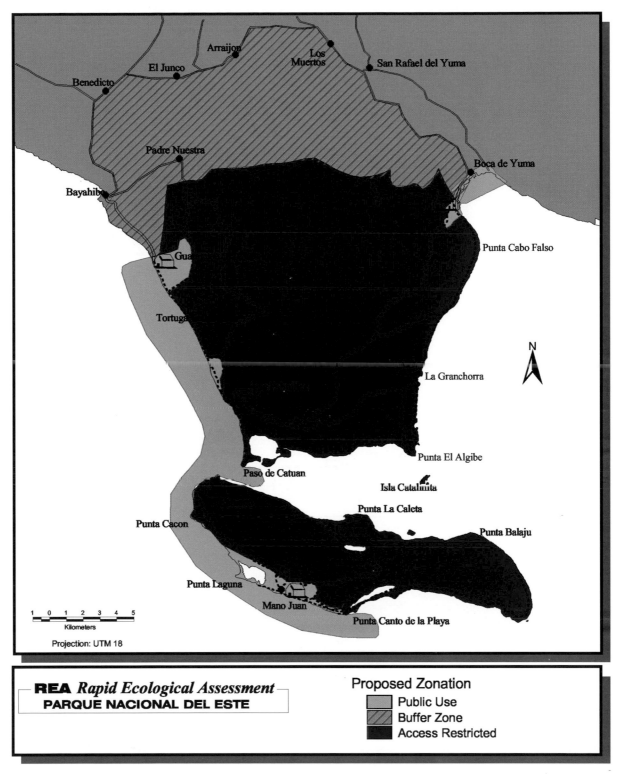

REA *Rapid Ecological Assessment*
PARQUE NACIONAL DEL ESTE

Proposed Zonation
Public Use
Buffer Zone
Access Restricted

Map 12. Proposed zonation scheme for conservation-oriented management of the park. Proposing new or improved zonation of the REA site is a common result of the REA process.

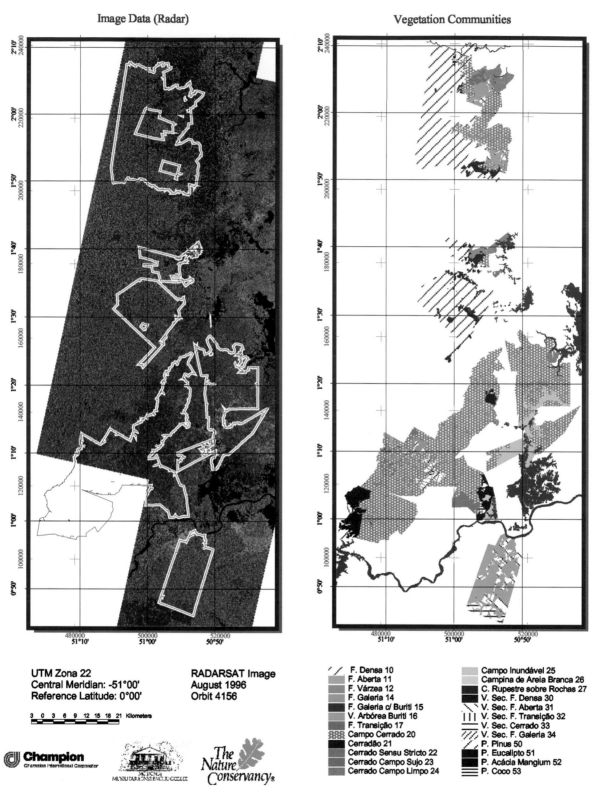

Image Data (Radar)

Vegetation Communities

UTM Zona 22
Central Meridian: -51°00'
Reference Latitude: 0°00'

RADARSAT Image
August 1996
Orbit 4156

3 0 3 6 9 12 15 18 21 Kilometers

Champion
Champion International Corporation

MINISTÉRIO PARA INSTITUCIÓN CCCLIX

The Nature Conservancy®

F. Densa 10
F. Aberta 11
F. Várzea 12
F. Galeria 14
F. Galeria c/ Buriti 15
V. Arbórea Buriti 16
F. Transição 17
Campo Cerrado 20
Cerradão 21
Cerrado Sensu Stricto 22
Cerrado Campo Sujo 23
Cerrado Campo Limpo 24

Campo Inundável 25
Campina de Areia Branca 26
C. Rupestre sobre Rochas 27
V. Sec. F. Densa 30
V. Sec. F. Aberta 31
V. Sec. F. Transição 32
V. Sec. Cerrado 33
V. Sec. F. Galeria 34
P. Pinus 50
P. Eucalipto 51
P. Acácia Mangium 52
P. Coco 53

Map 13. Map of imagery data source and final vegetation community map from an REA of Champion International Corporation's lands in Amapá, Brazil. Radar imagery was used for the landscape characterization process because cloud-free optical imagery was not available. This REA was conducted to determine the biodiversity importance of these lands to assist in the planning of a plantation forestry project.

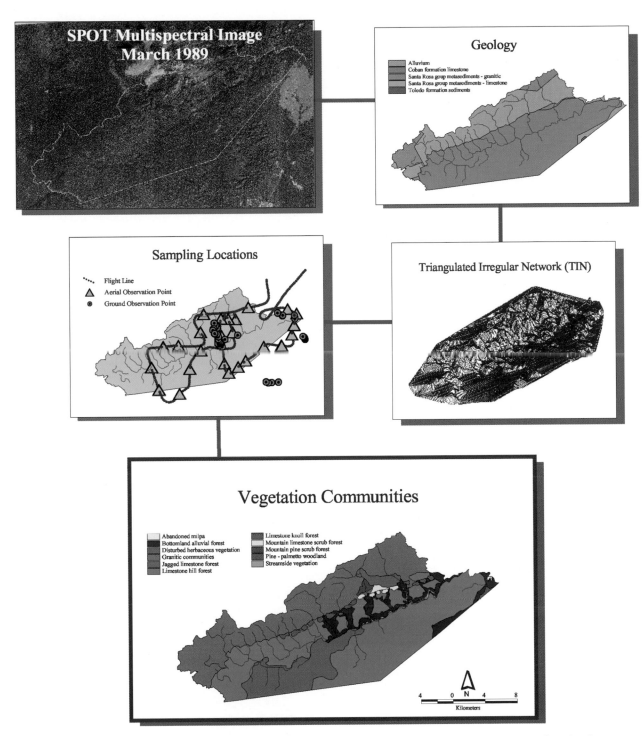

Map 14. Maps characterizing the Bladen Nature Reserve, Belize. Spot multispectral imagery was used as the data source for this REA. A geology data layer and map were developed, as was a data layer of elevation contours that was converted to a quasi–three dimensional representation of topography. The sampling map details the locations where aerial reconnaissance and field sampling campaigns were conducted in support of the development of the final vegetation communities map.

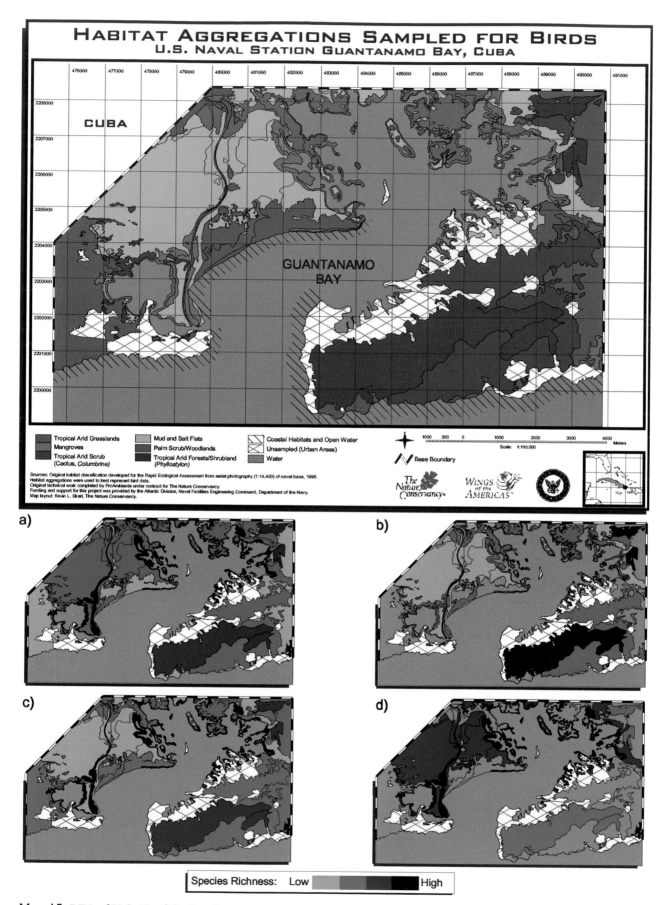

Map 15. REA of U.S. Naval Station Guantanomo Bay, Cuba: habitat aggregations sampled for birds. Bird species richness in habitats is presented for (a) all bird species, (b) species of conservation concern, (c) year-round residents, and (d) migratory birds.

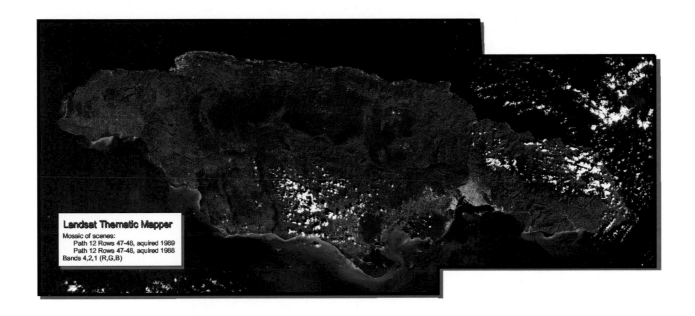

Landsat Thematic Mapper

Mosaic of scenes:
    Path 12 Rows 47-48, aquired 1989
    Path 12 Rows 47-48, aquired 1988
Bands 4,2,1 (R,G,B)

Image Classification

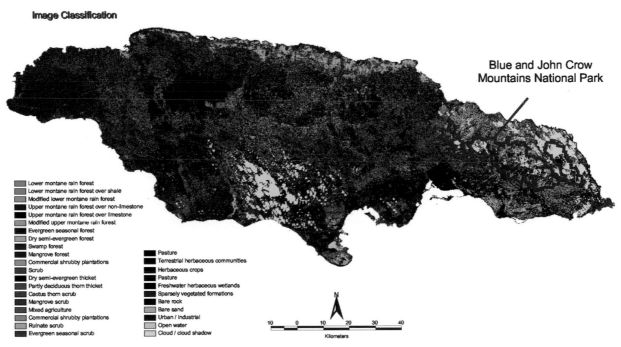

Blue and John Crow
Mountains National Park

Lower montane rain forest	
Lower montane rain forest over shale	
Modified lower montane rain forest	
Upper montane rain forest over non-limestone	
Upper montane rain forest over limestone	
Modified upper montane rain forest	
Evergreen seasonal forest	
Dry semi-evergreen forest	
Swamp forest	
Mangrove forest	Pasture
Commercial shrubby plantations	Terrestrial herbaceous communities
Scrub	Herbaceous crops
Dry semi-evergreen thicket	Pasture
Partly deciduous thorn thicket	Freshwater herbaceous wetlands
Cactus thorn scrub	Sparsely vegetated formations
Mangrove scrub	Bare rock
Mixed agriculture	Bare sand
Commercial shrubby plantations	Urban / Industrial
Ruinate scrub	Open water
Evergreen seasonal scrub	Cloud / cloud shadow

N

10 0 10 20 30 40
Kilometers

Map 16. Landsat imagery interpreted in an island-wide REA of Jamaica to develop a national-scale vegetation communities map. This regional-scale REA was followed by a site-scale REA in the Blue and John Crow Mountains National Park (see following map).

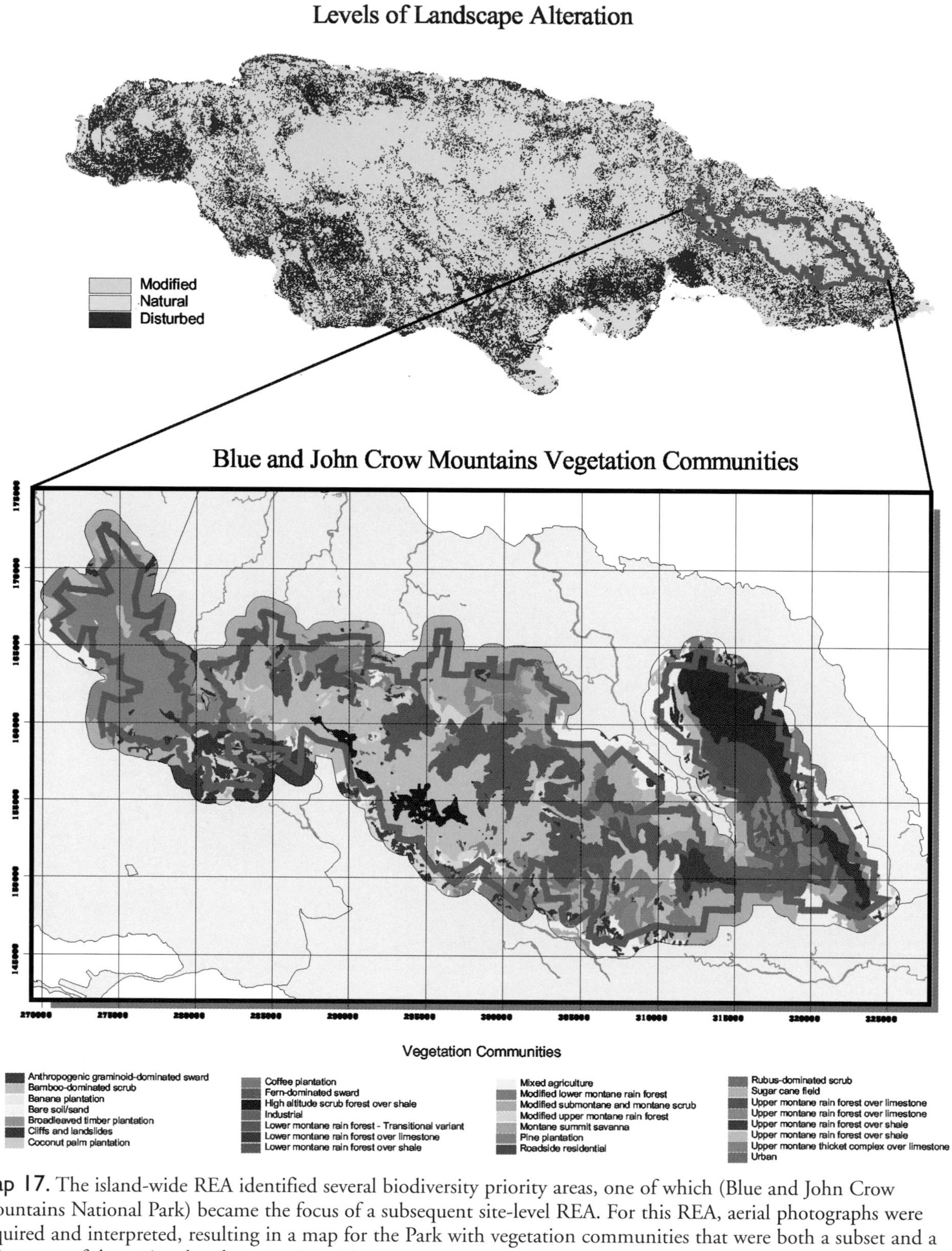

Levels of Landscape Alteration

Modified
Natural
Disturbed

Blue and John Crow Mountains Vegetation Communities

Vegetation Communities

Anthropogenic graminoid-dominated sward	Coffee plantation	Mixed agriculture	Rubus-dominated scrub
Bamboo-dominated scrub	Fern-dominated sward	Modified lower montane rain forest	Sugar cane field
Banana plantation	High altitude scrub forest over shale	Modified submontane and montane scrub	Upper montane rain forest over limestone
Bare soil/sand	Industrial	Modified upper montane rain forest	Upper montane rain forest over limestone
Broadleaved timber plantation	Lower montane rain forest - Transitional variant	Montane summit savanna	Upper montane rain forest over shale
Cliffs and landslides	Lower montane rain forest over limestone	Pine plantation	Upper montane rain forest over shale
Coconut palm plantation	Lower montane rain forest over shale	Roadside residential	Upper montane thicket complex over limestone
			Urban

Map 17. The island-wide REA identified several biodiversity priority areas, one of which (Blue and John Crow Mountains National Park) became the focus of a subsequent site-level REA. For this REA, aerial photographs were acquired and interpreted, resulting in a map for the Park with vegetation communities that were both a subset and a refinement of the national-scale vegetation units.

PART III

IN THE FIELD: SURVEYS AND THREATS ASSESSMENTS

Chapter 5

Vegetation and Plant Species Surveys

Shirley Keel, Roger Sayre, and
Gina Sedaghatkish

Vegetation surveys are a key component of every REA and focus on vegetation types. Plant species surveys focus on the distribution of species diversity across different vegetation types and identify target species for conservation management. These surveys are directed at characterizing, classifying, and mapping vegetation types, and at inventorying species of conservation concern (table 5-1). This chapter presents a vegetation science approach to characterizing plant diversity at both vegetation type and species levels.

We begin by discussing the responsibilities of the vegetation survey team and then describe the information resources they should consult in the planning stages. We then discuss the role of the vegetation specialists in the Initial Landscape Characterization and describe classification systems. The remainder of the chapter concerns fieldwork and data analysis.

The Vegetation and Flora Team

If possible, the REA vegetation and flora team should include both plant ecologists and botanists because being able to characterize plant communities in addition to identifying plant species during fieldwork is essential. As a minimum, the vegetation team should be composed of three participants (table 5-2). An experienced botanist or plant ecologist who knows the local flora well enough to identify sterile material in situ is essential. The lead vegetation specialist must be familiar with the flora of the area and should be able to identify a large percentage of the species or genera by visual recognition. This specialist is usually the team leader and is responsible for maintaining the rigor and rapid pace of the survey. Having the most respected expert on the flora of the survey area on the team, if possible, is recommended. Another botanist

Table 5-1. The major components of REA vegetation surveys.

Component	Activity
Vegetation Type Classification	Selection of the most appropriate classification system.
Vegetation Type Mapping	Mapping of the vegetation types for the study site, using available remotely sensed data. Verification in the field and map adjustment.
Vegetation Type Characterization	Field verification of image-derived vegetation types, identification of dominant species to characterize vegetation types, and identification of biotic/abiotic parameters that influence vegetation type distribution.
Summarizing Vegetation Data	In collaboration with fauna team, identification of vegetation types of conservation concern, including those that are • unique, • threatened, • habitats for plant and animal species of conservation concern, and • intact representative examples of communities occurring within the site.

Table 5-2. The vegetation and flora team, and qualifications and responsibilities of team members.

Team Members	Qualifications	Responsibilities
Vegetation Ecologist(s)	• Familiar with methods of vegetation analysis. • Knowledge of the study site's vegetation types. • Experience with photo-interpretation for vegetation type identification is helpful.	• Classify and characterize vegetation types. • Contribute to identification of vegetation types of high ecological importance and conservation value. • Integrate flora and fauna information for identification of critical areas for biodiversity.
Botanist(s)	• Strong knowledge of area's flora for rapid species identification. • Experience in photo-interpretation. • Experience in vegetation analysis.	• Conduct species surveys. • Characterize vegetation types. • Identify species of high conservation value. • Maintain quality in species identification and adhere to REA process and objectives. • Maintain and process voucher specimens. • Supervise field assistants. • Coordinate with herbarium.
Field Assistant(s)	• Botanical training. • Capable of labor-intensive fieldwork.	• Carry out tasks related to fieldwork, including setting up study plots collecting and processing specimens.

should be placed in charge of collecting and processing voucher specimens. This individual should contact local herbaria prior to field study to arrange assistance with the identification and administration of voucher specimens collected during an REA. Finally, a field assistant with botanical training is necessary for sharing the labor-intensive aspects of fieldwork, such as setting up study plots, collecting specimens, and climbing trees.

Sometimes it is possible to engage a botanist who is also a vegetation scientist (or vice versa) and can represent both the plant ecology and botany disciplines. If fieldwork is implemented without this expertise, an inordinate amount of time is spent identifying plants, collecting and preparing specimens, and contacting experts for assistance. It also helps if a member of the vegetation and flora team (hereafter referred to simply as "the vegetation team") has experience in aerial photography and satellite imagery interpretation; leadership by the vegetation team in the Initial Landscape Characterization step (see chapters 1 and 3) is critical. Whenever possible, multiple assistants are encouraged because the plot and plant identification work can be substantial.

Preliminary Information Gathering

The vegetation team must collect and review as much previously existing information about the vegetation of the study area as possible. REA floristic assessments are principally designed for projects in areas with little or no botanical information, but an attempt should be made to identify previous studies, management plans, and national and regional floras because this information is always useful. In some cases, floristic information is already available, but species information needs to be organized by floristic groups or vegetation units to refine an existing vegetation classification or to develop a classification. A thorough knowledge of available information enables a more efficient identification of field survey requirements, as well as facilitates data analysis and interpretation. An REA is rarely implemented in a location that has already been well characterized. Some information usually exists about the area, but it may be coarse, out of date, or of suspicious quality. The statement that "there isn't any information at all" is not usually true and is often just a pretext for an unwillingness to look for the information.

Knowing where certain types of data can be obtained will encourage and expedite preliminary information gathering. Data sources that are useful for vegetation surveys are listed in order of importance and availability at the end of this chapter. Published books and articles on phytogeography and vegetation classification are the most important sources for vegetation surveys. Monographs, herbarium specimens, and databases are useful for learning about the distribution and conservation status of individual species.

Although complete floristic information from a particular site may not be available, vegetation classifications and lists of species of conservation concern at national or regional scales may exist. General vegetation descriptions in the form of naturalists' travel notes or forest inventories tend to be available for most regions or countries. Such information, published or unpublished, will usually be found in institutions charged with the study of botany or forestry, such as universities or the government's forest service. Moreover, these institutions are usually good sources of local botanical experts. Information on plant species of conservation concern can best be obtained from government forest services, CITES in-country scientific authorities, and Conservation Data Centers.

Initial Landscape Characterization—The Role of Vegetation Specialists

The REA vegetation team should lead the Initial Landscape Characterization step to provide guidance to the mapping team in the interpretation of imagery. This participation is necessary because the vegetation specialists can contribute their knowledge to the delineation of vegetation types in the imagery. The mapping team is responsible for delineating features from imagery based on properties of the image (color, texture, tone, canopy height, etc.). This photo-interpretation results in a map of polygons that are classified by identifiable characteristics. These polygons are essentially unknown, however, with respect to the vegetation types they represent. The vegetation specialists are often able to name, or preclassify, these unknown polygons based on their knowledge and experience, enabling the fieldwork component of the REA to have more of a verification function instead of an information development function.

Vegetation sampling locations are determined in the Initial Landscape Characterization and include multiple examples of all unique vegetation types that have been delineated. Generally, fieldwork will concentrate on natural vegetation, which is usually easily distinguishable in satellite imagery and aerial photographs. At least one site in each vegetation type needs to be surveyed.

Selection of the Classification System

The vegetation team chooses the appropriate classification system to use, which should be as standardized as possible and based on a consideration of both vegetation structure and floristic composition. A commonly used local classification system usually exists and is studied by the vegetation team during the preliminary information review. This classification system is evaluated for its strength and utility, and a decision is made to adopt it, adopt it with modification, or reject it and develop a new classification. Modifying an existing classification system is the most common approach. The classification system then needs to be reconciled to the vegetation polygon map that results from the Initial Landscape Characterization. Mapping the classification system can be difficult, and it requires the full participation of the vegetation specialists collaborating with the mapping team.

Vegetation Fieldwork

Fieldwork for the vegetation survey involves visiting representative samples of all the polygon classes (vegetation types) identified from the Initial Landscape Characterization, establishing sampling locations, establishing plots, and collecting information. Pre-established sampling locations, identified in the sampling plan, are precisely geolocated with GPS technologies. The vegetation survey of any REA usually requires several months, along with considerable organization and methodological rigor. Organizational activities include developing sampling plans, workplans, and chronograms; conducting training workshops; and assigning responsibilities (e.g., data collection, data analysis, and report writing) to individual team members. The methodological principles involve characterizing plant diversity at both landscape and species scales, with a progressively narrower focus from identification of plant formations using imagery to identifying individual species in the field. The major challenge of the vegetation fieldwork is to visit as many replicate polygons as possible in all unique vegetation types recognizable at a given scale, in all sampling regions, while respecting budget and time constraints. This keep-moving approach can be especially difficult to coordinate with the fauna survey team, which generally prefers a more sedentary sampling approach.

Sampling Intensity and Sampling Location Prioritization

Sampling intensity above a minimum sampling requirement (at least one representative example of each unique vegetation type) will depend on the availability of resources. Resources rarely permit an intensive level of sampling, and prioritization of sampling sites is necessary. Rare and complex vegetation types are usually prioritized, and they merit a higher level of sampling effort (plot studies). More common and better understood vegetation types may be adequately sampled by general observation techniques. A set of general considerations relating to establishment of site sampling priorities follows:

1. Establish conservation priorities of the different vegetation types by a ranking process that may include considerations of diversity, endemism, representativeness, degree of fragmentation, and so on.

2. Choose at least one relatively large and accessible polygon for each vegetation type, regardless of conservation priority.

3. Select replicate polygons in priority vegetation types as resources permit.

Sampling intensity varies depending on the objectives of the REA as well. If the objective is to characterize the vegetation types of a large area in a limited amount of time, direct observations in many sampling locations is more efficient and productive than establishing plots in a few sampling locations. A point sampling location with a 20-meter sampling reach in all directions around the point is equivalent to a sampled area of 1256 square meters and is adequate for characterizing a 50-hectare forest. Sampling at these locations involves identifying dominant floristic groups and filling out a single field form (form 2 of appendix 2); this type of sampling is relatively straightforward and rapid.

However, if the objective is to characterize a single vegetation type of high conservation priority and quantitative data on species richness is desired, then plot studies are necessary. Plots of equivalent size and shape are necessary for comparing similar vegetation types at different sampling locations.

Survey Techniques, Field Forms, and Equipment

To verify vegetation types, analyze floristic composition, and measure vegetation diversity, the vegetation team uses a variety of sampling techniques, field forms, and equipment. In general, the team will establish sampling locations, which may or may not include plot-based work at the location. At least one sampling location in each vegetation type identified in the Initial Landscape Characterization should be established.

For the collection of vegetation and plant species data, several examples of field forms have been developed (see appendix 2). Form 1 is used to describe the study site in general. Form 2 is used to characterize vegetation structure and to record physiognomic information and environmental parameters useful for vegetation classification. Form 3 is used to record detailed species-level measurements from sampling locations. The plot-sampling field form (Form 5) records vegetation data collected from detailed plot-based sampling efforts. Form 6 allows for the documentation of opportunistic (not derived from sampling locations or plots) vegetation information. Finally, Form 8 allows for the documentation of species of conservation concern. These sample field forms were designed for general use. For specific data needs in an REA, fields may be modified or added.

Vegetation survey equipment includes the following:

- Aluminum nails and aluminum tags
- Binoculars
- Camera and slide film (several rolls)
- Compass
- Collecting poles
- Field forms (1, 2, 3, 5, 6, 8—appendix 2)
- Clipboard
- Flagging tape (multicolored and biodegradable)
- GPS
- Hammer
- Hand pruners
- Machete
- Maps (topographic maps, polygon map, imagery)
- Marking pens
- Measuring tapes (50 meter (2); 30 meter (2), DBH tape)
- Newspaper
- Plastic bags (self-sealing; large and small)
- Plant press
- Pocket magnifier or field lens
- Surveyor's step stakes (to mark plot corners)
- Waterproof field notebook

Verifying Vegetation Types

Verification and labeling of vegetation types is accomplished by comparing field-derived information with characteristic, standardized descriptions of vegetation types as presented in published classifications or as developed for the REA. Frequently, the verification work is relatively straightforward and nonquantitative, especially when unique vegetation types are discriminated largely on the basis of physiognomy and dominant floristic group. The existence of relatively sharp environmental gradients often results in well-separated, easily discerned vegetation types. In these instances, verification of vegetation type is usually accomplished by noting and documenting the presence of dominant species. For example, if in the field the vegetation scientist is sampling in a riparian palm thicket that is dominated by Buriti *(Mauritia flexuosa),* and the vegetation classification being followed defines a Buritizal as a "periodically inundated palm thicket characterized by the presence of Buriti," the scientist can with confidence label the community type as Buritizal. This kind of verification is easily accomplished without the need for any kind of numerical quantification.

If, however, the site is relatively homogenous and environmental gradients are not strongly expressed, discriminating vegetation types by dominant species can be more difficult. In this case, plot studies will be necessary to quantify dominance. DBH (diameter at breast height) measurements need to be converted into basal areas for species, which are then compared among sampling locations. Sampling at this level to identify subtle differences in species composition and dominance is not typically undertaken in an REA because of resource and time constraints. Moreover, the spectral reflectance signatures of vegetation types, which differ only slightly in composition and dominance, may be very similar. Separating these subtly varying vegetation types during image interpretation can be difficult, which would preclude their identification as unique vegetation types during image interpretation.

Estimating Plant Diversity

In addition to verifying vegetation types, many vegetation surveys include an estimation of plant diversity by utilizing data from plot survey techniques. Establishing plots and quantifying diversity inside these plots is a time-consuming operation. In general, plots should be established only in high-priority sampling locations. The size of sample plots and the kinds of data collected will depend on the objectives of the vegetation survey. For measuring and comparing diversity, the sampling focus is usually on vascular plants or the major life forms of a vegetation community (e.g., woody species of forests and shrublands or herbaceous species of grasslands). Nonvascular plants are rarely surveyed in REAs because less is known about this group and specialists are not always available.

Plots for this type of work vary in size and number surveyed. As a general rule, 20-meter by 20-meter plots are adequate for forests, and 10-meter by 10-meter plots are adequate for shrublands and grasslands. Data from plot studies can be used to develop species/area curves, but recent work (Condit et al., 1995) has shown that diversity measurements are more consistent when based on stem numbers rather than on plot size.

Dallmeier Method

The Dallmeier method (20-meter by 20-meter plot size) is commonly employed in REA vegetation surveys, and the number of sampled stems normally ranges between 100 and 1000. Dallmeier (1992) maintains that forest plots up to two hectares in size and containing 1200 to 1400 trees of DBH (10 centimeters will yield reliable diversity estimates and allow relatively quick and accurate characterizations of a given forest. In a comparison of the species diversity of three forests in India, Panama, and Malaysia determined using 50-hectare permanent plots, Condit et al. (1995) reported no improvement in diversity estimates after the stem number exceeded 1000 stems. We therefore conclude, consistent with Dallmeier, that a 2-hectare forest plot will be sufficient for measuring plant diversity. However, resource constraints in most REAs usually preclude the establishment of 2-hectare plots in all representative community types. Condit (pers. comm., 1995) recommends sampling at least 100 stems before any useful estimate of diversity can be developed. The vegetation survey team probably should sample no fewer than 100 stems, and no more than 1000 stems, in any area for which plant diversity estimates are desired.

The most detailed description of a 20-meter by 20-meter plot sampling approach is presented in Dallmeier (1992). Predetermined plots are sampled, and new plots adjacent to the original are added and sampled until an acceptable number of stems is sampled. Woody species with DBH ≥ 10 centimeters in forests and DBH ≥ 2.5 centimeters in shrublands are identified and measured in order to characterize the vegetation type and estimate plant diversity and abundance of major life forms. This method generally requires three botanists working for three days to survey a 1200-square meter area. For herbaceous communities, the percentage cover of individual species within a 10-meter by 10-meter plot should be measured. The most rapid assessment of the species diversity of a vegetation community is accomplished by counting the number of species that can be identified by the botanists within the sample plots. For plants unfamiliar to botanists, specimens are collected for subsequent identification.

Gentry Method

Another commonly used plot method for estimating diversity is Gentry's 0.1-hectare "exploded" transect method, which is a rapid survey technique that provides the quickest preliminary understanding of diversity patterns in forest or shrubland communities. The Gentry method (Gentry, 1986; Keel et al., 1993) samples a 0.1-hectare area consisting of ten 2-meter by 50-meter subplots, which can be surveyed by three botanists in two days when stems ≥ 2.5 centimeter are measured. Although Gentry's narrow rectangular plots yield 15 percent more species than square plots of equal size (Condit, pers. comm., 1995), this method is not as conducive to sampling larger trees. This technique requires that subplots are adjacent and stem numbers within the plots are accurately recorded. For measuring diversity, Gentry's exploded transect techniques are an appropriate and rapid survey methodology. Other plot and plotless survey methods are available (Braun-Blanquet, 1932; Cain and de Oliveira Castro, 1959; Campbell and Hammond, 1989; Cox, 1985; Mueller-Dombois and Ellenberg, 1974; Kent and Coker, 1992), but for most REA applications the Dallmeier and Gentry methods are most commonly used.

Inventory of Individual Species

An REA is not a complete floristic inventory; thus it is not necessary to identify every plant to the species level. Certain plants, however, should always be identified to the species level. The vegetation team leader should identify, to the extent possible, these species prior to beginning fieldwork by using research articles, museum studies, endangered species lists, and so on. These species include:

1. Species for characterizing vegetation types, such as canopy species, dominant and codominant species, and indicator species
2. Species of conservation concern, such as endemic species, and rare or endangered species
3. Species of management concern, such as exotics or economic plants

Whenever these species are observed in a plot, sampling location, or opportunistically, their habitats, phenology, population size, and economic uses should be recorded. A sample field form (Form 8) is provided for this purpose in appendix 2.

Classifying Vegetation

The vegetation classification procedure involves compiling information from the field forms, determining vegetation classes, assigning classified names to identified units, and quantifying relative dominance levels of species. The vegetation team must work closely with the mapping team in the assignment of vegetation class labels to the unknown polygons developed during the REA. The vegetation classification involves the following steps:

1. Gathering together all the field forms that contain vegetation information
2. Organizing the forms by sampling locations within sampling regions
3. Developing plant lists for sampling locations
4. Considering the criteria and parameters for vegetation classification, and applying these on a location-by-location basis
5. Relating field observations to the unknown polygon map to extrapolate vegetation type labels established for sampled polygons to all unsampled polygons

Subjectivity in Vegetation Classification

Vegetation classification is highly subjective. Vegetation types usually are not discrete and easily defined units (in the way that species are discrete because of genetic barriers to reproduction). The boundaries between vegetation types are often diffuse. Although imagery may suggest obvious, discrete boundaries, field observations may reveal that these suggestions were false impressions.

Standardized Naming of Vegetation Types

Locally employed vegetation classifications should be integrated into standardized, regional, hierarchical systems whenever possible. The classification system used for the verification of vegetation types is normally the one that is being used locally and may have many popular terms and local naming conventions. For the sake of scientific standardization, and to be able to compare vegetation types from other areas, the local classification should always be crosswalked into a standardized, regional classification system such as the UNESCO-TNC system (FGDC, 1996; Grossman et al., 1998). Crosswalking means assigning a vegetation unit from one classification system (the local classification) into an appropriate level and position in another classification (the standard). For example, *Quebrachal* is a local name for a vegetation community dominated by *Aspidosperma quebracho-blanco*. This community's major life form is trees over 10 meters in height, and over 50 percent of the species are deciduous. In the UNESCO-TNC classification, this community would be described with highly standardized classification conventions, such as the following: "Lowland, subtropical, semideciduous, xeromorphic, closed-canopy, *Aspidosperma quebracho-blanco* forest." Each of these descriptors provides information about the various taxonomic units used in the UNESCO-TNC classification, which is based on a hierarchy of the following:

Order

    Class

        Subclass

            Group

                Formation

                    Alliance

                        Community Association

The criteria for defining these different hierarchical levels is presented in FGDC (1996).

Rhizophora mangle Tidally Flooded Forest

A community found on the cays at Cuba's Granadillo Bay and along the coast north of Punta Caracoles, where the substrate between the water and the limestone terraces is more consolidated. This community is dominated by short red mangroves (*R. mangle*) under 5 meters in height. A 10-meter to 15-meter wide external band of red mangroves that are 3 to 4 meter tall surrounds the cay. This band decreases toward the center of the cay with trees decreasing in height, diameter, and prop roots. Trees at the internal border growing in 40 to 50 percent salinity are less than 1.5 meters tall. Inland, the red mangrove belt is substituted by a band of black mangroves (*Avicennia germinans*) with disperse trees of the white mangrove (*Laguncularia racemosa*) and bottonwood (*Conocarpus erecta*). The canopy of this last band can reach up to 4 meter. In some cays, where the salinity at the center can reach more than 1000 ppm (parts per million), there is a denuded area surrounded by dwarf black mangroves.

Stenocereus peruvianus Cactus Scrub

This community occurs in hills with gradients greater than 5 percent and a substrate of coarse debris derived from shale. True soil exists only in small pockets. Canopy height is less than 5 meters. The dominant species in this community varies with topography, soil depth, and exposure to wind. In steep places with very little soil, the dominant species are the cactus *Stenocereus peruvianus,* and trees *Plumeria tuberculata, Neea shaferi, Capparis ferruginea, C. flexuosa,* and *Jacquinia sp.* In flatter areas with soils of greater depth, the dominant species are the cactus *Pilosocereus* and the tree *Colubrina elliptica.*

Box 5-1. Example descriptions of vegetation types surveyed in U.S. Naval Station Guantanamo Bay, Cuba (Sedaghatkish and Roca, 1999).

REAs normally involve classification down to the Formation level, sometimes lower, depending on the spatial resolution of the imagery data source.

Summarizing Vegetation Data

An accurate description of the vegetation types mapped in an REA is important for conservation management purposes and is developed from a summary of observations from several sampling locations. These descriptions should include information about location, key environmental factors, canopy height, vegetation strata, major life forms, dominant and codominant species, indicator species, and variations in structure and composition. Box 5-1 presents two examples of vegetation type descriptions from an REA of Guantanamo Bay, Cuba (Sedaghatkish and Roca, 1999).

Compiling Data and Presenting Results

Species data from literature and field surveys are organized and presented for each vegetation type in the site, with an emphasis on species of conservation concern. These data summaries by vegetation types are immediately useful for highlighting vegetation types with higher plant diversity and greater numbers of species of concern. Tables 5-3, 5-4, and 5-5 illustrate some typical tabular summaries from vegetation surveys. Table 5-3 summarizes numbers of target plant species by vegetation types from an REA in Panama (ANCON and The Nature Conservancy, 1996). Table 5-4 characterizes some example plant species of conservation concern from an REA in Guantanamo Bay, Cuba (Sedaghatkish and Roca, 1999), and table 5-5 presents examples of target vegetation types from the same REA.

Table 5-3. Numbers of plant species of conservation concern by vegetation type recorded during an REA in the Panama Canal Zone (ANCON and The Nature Conservancy, 1996).

Vegetation Type	Total Area (acres)	No. of Plant Species Identified	No. of Species at Risk Globally
Evergreen seasonal tall forest	501	145	8
Evergreen seasonal mixed forest	8305	179	11
Evergreen seasonal low forest	1279	108	7
Semideciduous mixed forest	1058	14	5
Semideciduous low forest	834	121	6
Deciduous forest	282	46	2
Flooded cativo forest	2548	106	1
Flooded palm forest	558	61	2
Mangrove swamp forest	209	26	0
Flooded shrubland	131	10	0
Marsh	242	8	0
Seminatural flooded grassland	360	8	0

Table 5-4. Plant target species for conservation and the vegetation communities in which they were encountered during an REA of U.S. Naval Station Guantanamo Bay, Cuba (Sedaghatkish and Roca, 1999).

Species of Global Conservation Concern	Vegetation Type or Habitat	*Sampling Location (UTM)	Reasons for Concern
Caribea littoralis	Coastal rock pavement	454000,2199.500	Very rare; restricted to only a few localities in southeastern Cuba.
Dendrocereus nudiflorus	*Phyllostylon brasiliensis* forest alliance	489500,2208.200	Population in decline; few juveniles or seedlings remaining. The site harbors the largest populations of this species.
Melocactus harlowii	Rock outcrops of cactus scrub and thorn scrub	482250,2200.250/ 488900,2202.200	Rare endemics; small populations restricted to rock outcrops; subject to collecting pressure for house plants.
Opuntia militaris	Beach and limestone terraces	485000,2199.600	Rare; found only in the site and surrounding area.
Gochnatia microcephala	Cactus scrub, thorn scrub, *Croton-Coccothrinax* scrub	482250,2200.250/ 488900,2202.200/ 482900,2208.000	Rare; found only in the site and surrounding area.

*Location data approximate to protect actual species locations.

Table 5-5. Target vegetation types for conservation in U.S. Naval Station Guantanamo Bay, Cuba (Sedaghatkish and Roca, 1999).

Vegetation Types	Conservation Importance
Coccothrinax scrub	Few occurrences; narrow distribution; habitat of endemic birds species.
Bucida woodland	Restricted distribution.
Phyllostylon cactus forest	Few quality examples remaining; most disturbed or destroyed.
Colubrina scrub	Highest plant species diversity in the site; habitat of two rare endemics *Gochnatia microcephala* and *Spirotecoma guantanamensis*.

Species of Conservation Concern

For rare or endangered species or exotic species encountered in an REA, team members should record information on population size, viability, habitat conditions, and use by humans. The location of these elements of special concern should be precisely recorded using GPS technologies. Management recommendations for the site should include a consideration of approaches that promote the persistence of these species of concern. It should also be noted that in some areas, entire plant genera can be considered conservation targets because of their endemicity. For example, in the Guantanamo Bay REA, two genera were encountered that were endemic to Cuba (*Caribea* and *Dendrocereus*). These two genera clearly should be considered genera of conservation concern, especially if highly threatened.

Threats Analysis

The vegetation team should characterize, to the extent possible, the overall level of threat to the integrity and persistence of all vegetation types in the study area. An imagery-based assessment of land uses within the study area that impact vegetation types provides useful information on land-conversion threats to natural systems. During fieldwork, land use information is also noted on field forms, and this information is incorporated into the threats analysis. The vegetation team characterizes the degree of threat to the different vegetation types, documents these threats in the final vegetation report, and participates in the larger, integrated threats assessment for the study site (see chapter 7).

Management Recommendations

REA vegetation surveys usually identify plants that are of conservation concern because they are at risk (rare and endangered) or are exotics. Species with small or declining populations are considered at risk, and enhancement of existing populations and habitat restoration to provide suitable sites for re-establishment are sensible management approaches. Management often depends on the condition and vigor of extant populations in the wild. Valuable discussions on the management of rare and endangered plants can be found in Elias (1987), Falk (1987), and Falk and McMahan (1988). Small reserves providing a wide choice of habitats can play an important role in conserving rare or endangered plants (Reznicek, 1987). Research on both life histories and the distribution of genetic variation in populations of rare plants is sometimes required prior to implementing appropriate management strategies for individual species. The discovery of economically useful plants and their wild relatives in the site may lead to an additional focus on in situ germplasm conservation, which will increase the site's overall conservation value.

Information on exotic species can also affect management considerations (Temple, 1990; Coblentz, 1991). Eradicating exotics may be the most important conservation strategy at a site. Eradication of invasive exotics can be a difficult and costly undertaking; good scientific information on the type, condition, and location of those exotics is necessary for strategizing their removal. REAs can provide this type of information, especially if an objective of the REA is the characterization of exotics at the site.

Conclusion

The vegetation survey team identifies and maps vegetation types, produces estimates of plant diversity, and characterizes species of concern. This information can be used to prioritize sites and inform conservation-based management planning. The vegetation survey work also contributes to understanding of the conservation status and biological importance of plants and vegetation types.

Literature Cited

ANCON (Asociación Nacional para la Conservación de la Naturaleza) and The Nature Conservancy. 1996. *Ecological Survey of U.S. Department of Defense Lands in Panama. Phase IV: Fort Sherman, Pina Range and Naval Security Group Activity; Galeta Island.* Arlington, Va.: The Nature Conservancy.

Braun-Blanquet, L. 1932. *Plant Sociology: The Study of Plant Communities.* New York: McGraw-Hill.

Cain, S. A., and G. M. de Oliveira Castro. 1959. *Manual of Vegetation Analysis.* New York: Harper & Brothers.

Campbell, D. G., and H. D. Hammond, eds. 1989. *Floristic Inventory of Tropical Countries.* New York: The New York Botanical Garden.

Coblentz, B. E. 1991. A response to Temple and Lugo. *Conservation Biology* 5:5–6.

Condit, R. 1995. Personal Communication. Panama City, Panama.

Condit, R., R. B. Foster, S. P. Hubbell, R. Sukumar, E. G. Leigh, N. Manokaran, and S. Loo de Lao. 1995. Assessing forest diversity from small plots: Calibration using species-individual curves from 50 ha plots. In *Measuring and Monitoring Forest Biological Diversity: The International Network of Biodiversity Plots.* International Symposium, 23–25 May in Washington, D.C.

Cox, G. W. 1985. *Laboratory Manual of General Ecology.* Dubuque, Iowa: W. C. Brown Publishers.

Dallmeier, F., ed. 1992. Long-term monitoring of biological diversity in tropical forest areas: Methods for establishment and inventory of permanent plots. *MAB Digest* 11. Paris: UNESCO.

Elias, T., ed. 1987. *Conservation and Management of Rare and Endangered Plants.* Sacramento, Calif.: California Native Plant Society.

FGDC (Federal Geographic Data Committee). 1996. *Vegetation Classification and Information Standards.* Reston, Va.: FGDC Secretariat.

Falk, D. A. 1987. Integrated conservation strategies for endangered plants. *Natural Areas Journal* 7(3):118–123.

Falk, D. A., and L. R. McMahan. 1988. Endangered plant conservation: Managing for diversity. *Natural Areas Journal* 8(2):91–99.

Gentry, A. H. 1986. Species richness and floristic composition of Chocó region plant communities. *Caldasia* 15: 71–91.

Grossman, D. H., D. Faber-Langendoen, A. S. Weakley, M. Anderson, P. Bourgeron, R. Craword, K. Goodin, S. Landaal, K. Metlzer, K. Patterson, M. Pyne, M. Reid, and L. Sneddon. 1998. *International Classification of Ecological Communities: Terrestrial Vegetation of the United States.* Vol. 1. The National Vegetation Classification System: Development, Status, and Applications. Arlington, Va.: The Nature Conservancy.

Keel, S., A. H. Gentry, and L. Spinzi. 1993. Using vegetation analysis to facilitate the selection of conservation sites in eastern Paraguay. *Conservation Biology* 7(1):66–75.

Kent, M., and P. Coker. 1992. *Vegetation Description and Analysis.* Ann Arbor, Mich.: CRC Press.

Mueller-Dombois, D., and H. Ellenberg. 1974. *Aims and Methods of Vegetation Ecology.* New York: John Wiley and Sons.

Reznicek, A. A. 1987. Are small reserves worthwhile for plants? *Endangered Species Update* 5(2):1–3.

Sedaghatkish, G., and E. Roca. 1999. *Rapid Ecological Assessment: U.S. Naval Station Guantanamo Bay, Cuba.* Arlington, Va.: The Nature Conservancy.

Temple, S. A. 1990. The nasty necessity: Eradicating exotics. *Conservation Biology* 5:113–115.

Vegetation and Plant Survey Information Sources

The following sources of information are useful for understanding the distribution and biological importance of plant species and vegetation types that may be encountered during REA.

VEGETATION

- Publications on phytogeography, vegetation classification, vegetation ecology, local flora/florula, travel notes, and vegetation studies, such as *Floristic Inventory of Tropical Countries* and *Flora of Peru.*

- National or international botanical or ecological journals, such as, *Annals of Missouri Botanical Garden* and *Biotropica.*

SPECIES

- *Species descriptions:* monographs of local flora, national or international botanical journal.

- *Species checklist:* such as, *CITES Cactaceae Checklist* and *Checklist of Flora of Panama.*

- *List of species of conservation concern:* CITES Appendix I, II, and III, *1997 IUCN Red List of Threatened Plants,* list of commercial timber species, and the Biological and Conservation Data (BCD) System of The Nature Conservancy and Conservation Data Centers. Select rare plant species of Latin America and the Caribbean can be found on the Conservancy's website at www.tnc.org.

- *Species distribution:* herbarium specimens or museum collections, botanical experts (including indigenous experts), BCD, and other (e.g., botanical garden) databases.

- *Conservation status:* BCD, other databases, and botanical experts.

Chapter 6

Fauna Surveys

Bruce Young, Gina Sedaghatkish,
and Roberto Roca

In addition to characterizing and mapping vegetation types, REAs usually incorporate surveys of selected animal taxa. REAs offer a valuable opportunity to survey animal communities in diverse habitats at sites of potential conservation importance. Without information on where animal biodiversity is distributed on the landscape, drafting intelligent conservation policies and management plans and monitoring projects in these areas is not feasible. Obtaining preliminary knowledge of the species that occur in a site and their spatial distribution is therefore fundamental to achieving the objectives of most REAs.

This chapter discusses how to decide which taxa to survey and in what depth, and the issues central to planning and executing the animal survey component of an REA. These issues include how these surveys fit into the larger project, selecting and organizing the fauna team, and the advantages and disadvantages of different survey techniques. The chapter concludes with a series of tips on data management, report preparation, and data interpretation. This chapter draws from past REAs and similar surveys to illustrate key points and to provide ideas for future REAs.

Careful planning is essential to ensure that the data collected in animal surveys are relevant to the objectives of an REA. REA fauna specialists should participate in all aspects of the REA, from formulation of objectives to production of the final report. Although the fauna team will sample in predetermined locations necessary for the verification of the preliminary vegetation classification, it is to the team's advantage to participate in the sample point selection process because the members can bring valuable zoological perspectives to these decisions. For example, after studying site maps and imagery, a zoologist may identify specific areas that should be sampled for fauna based on suspected diversity or endemism. These areas may not, however, have been selected as ground truthing points for the vegetation mapping verification.

Planning the fauna survey also involves identifying target species, determining which fauna to sample and how to sample them, assembling the fauna team, and developing fieldwork and postfieldwork analysis and reporting strategies. Planning a fauna survey so that available resources are best matched with activities necessary to satisfy REA objectives requires considerable effort.

The Decision to Conduct Fauna Surveys

Although fauna surveys are typically incorporated as fundamental components of an REA, their inclusion is not automatic, and REA team leaders should be able to justify including animal surveys in the REA. Nonbiologists may entertain the notion that REAs will describe the patterns of distribution and interactions of all of the animal communities in the targeted site. Unfortunately, even intensive studies do not produce this information. For example, despite decades of in-depth studies on the rodent communities in the species-poor deserts of the southwestern United States, ecologists still do not fully understand species interactions and they continue to record new species (Heske et al., 1994). The best an REA can do is produce an incomplete species list of target taxa and an approximate understanding of where these species occur at the site.

To help in deciding whether to perform fauna surveys, the fundamental constraint on information generated by REAs should be considered. By definition, REAs are short-term projects employing limited sampling techniques over a limited amount of time. Producing a nearly complete fauna list for any taxon at a site requires years of sampling and a great variety of techniques. For example, the list of mammal species at the well-known La Selva Biological Station in lowland humid forest in Costa Rica continues to increase even after thirty years of study (Timm, 1994). To map the distributions of birds inhabiting a tiny 97-hectare plot of Amazonian floodplain forest, scientists employed six different census techniques (Terborgh et al., 1990). Thus the species lists produced on an REA will include most of the common species and only a few of the rare species. Groups of species that inhabit the site on a seasonal basis will be missed altogether unless sampling occurs when they happen to be present. However, management efforts are often directed toward at-risk species, which tend to be rare or wary and therefore unlikely to be detected in brief surveys. If the species of primary conservation interest that are thought to occur at a site are not detected during surveys, then the REA may not be particularly successful in accomplishing its species-oriented objectives.

Fauna surveys *should* be considered when any of the following are true:

- *Resources are available.* Sending teams of zoologists to the field is expensive, including the costs of staff time, transportation, room and board, and equipment. If enough resources are available to support a team in the field for enough time to collect a significant amount of information, then fauna surveys should be attempted if they can provide information relevant to the objectives of the REA.

- *Rough estimates of diversity are desired.* During any fauna survey, new species are rapidly accumulated at first and then become increasingly difficult to detect. Brief surveys of the type usually performed on REAs capture the geometric-increase portion of a species-accumulation curve and therefore can record a majority of the species present. Recent theoretical work has shown that even fairly incomplete surveys can allow for robust estimates of the total species diversity at a site (Colwell and Coddington, 1994).

- *Target species are conspicuous.* The presence and abundance of some typically threatened species can sometimes be readily determined because the species are easily detected, often by sampling at a key time of day or using a specific technique. Examples include parrots and macaws that call loudly at dawn and dusk, caimans that are detectable at night in flashlight beams, and large mammals that congregate at water holes during dry seasons and leave footprints.

- *The survey site is on an island.* Islands, especially those located great distances from the nearest mainland, have depauperate faunas that can be reasonably well surveyed in a short period of time.

- *The survey site is in an area that is poorly known by zoologists.* In regions of high endemism, such as the Andean cordillera or Atlantic forest in Brazil, many vertebrate species have yet to be discovered and named. Also, the ranges of most described species in such areas are usually not well known. Any amount of effort invested in surveying fauna will almost certainly produce valuable information to scientists about species ranges and may uncover undescribed species.

- *Species lists are needed.* The position of conservationists lobbying for the protection of a site or of development officers trying to raise funds is strengthened by being able to present a list of animals (especially charismatics) that occur there.

Fauna surveys should *not* be attempted when any of the following are true:

- *Resources are very limited.* If funds are limited, spreading them too thin across mapping activities, vegetation analysis, and fauna surveys may result in a product that fails to satisfy REA objectives. This result is especially true when the land area is very large compared to the funds available for survey work. In these situations, a team leader may wisely decide that an accurate vegetation map of a site may be the most useful product of the REA on which to base management decisions.

- *Target species are rare or hard to detect.* If the target species include Maned Wolves, Harpy Eagles, or other hard-to-detect species, an REA-style survey may not be intensive enough to detect these species even though they actually occur at the site. In fact, an REA that detects no target species could even erode support for a proposed or existing protected area by casting doubt on the value of the site for protecting these species. Considerable discussion on target species is presented in a subsequent section.

If field surveys are not feasible, faunal information can still be incorporated into a study. Previous studies may be available for the site in question or for a nearby site with similar vegetation types from which general information about the fauna can be obtained. In addition, specimens collected from the site may be housed in local or international museums. Inquiries at local universities, museums, and other local institutions often produce valuable information. If sufficiently detailed, this information can take the place of a field survey.

Deciding Which Fauna to Survey

The decision to survey is followed by the selection of taxa that will be sampled. To fulfill the objectives of many REAs to provide preliminary survey lists, surveys of the major vertebrate taxa and even a few invertebrate taxa are necessary. If funds are limited, an REA may concentrate on only one or a few taxa. Moreover, background information may indicate that only one taxon at the site includes species of interest. For example, an REA of the Blue and John Crow Mountains National Park in Jamaica (Muchoney et al., 1994) included only birds in its faunal component because of a lack of resources and an interest in endemic species. In general, birds are among the easiest taxa to survey. Species announce themselves dependably with vocalizations, and fairly complete lists are possible in short periods of time if talented observers are available. Mammal surveys can be time consuming because of the need to use traps, nets, and low-reward visual surveys. Herpetofauna can be difficult to find. On the other hand, conservation target species may include large mammals, economically important fish, or endangered turtles or crocodilians. In these cases, surveys of taxonomic groups that include target species are necessary.

When deciding which taxa to survey, consider the value of the data to the overall goals of the REA, the availability of qualified field personnel, and the cost of performing the surveys. Taxonomic keys and field guides are lacking for some taxa. To assist in the decision of which taxa to include, the following advantages and disadvantages of surveying each taxon along with realistic views of expected REA results are offered:

1. *Birds.* As mentioned, birds can often be rapidly surveyed. Observers familiar with the fauna at a site can often detect over two hundred species in low- or mid-elevation rainforest in just a few days. Many avian species are good indicators of the presence of hunting or poaching of live ani-

mals for sale in the pet trade. A good bird list for a protected area is valuable for managers to help promote ecotourism. Many species are mobile, however, and migrate locally or over long distances. Thus the community of birds one finds at a site may reflect the conditions somewhere else as much as it does those at the site itself. To the extent that local movements are unknown, bird communities can present perplexing questions of why some species are or are not present.

2. *Mammals.* Mammals are also good indicators of hunting and poaching. Essentially nonvocal and exhibiting a wide range of natural histories, mammals require a number of survey techniques. Even if all of these techniques can be used, the time available for surveys in most REAs will be inadequate to produce a list that includes even half of the total species present. Many species are nocturnal and arboreal and therefore are very difficult to detect despite their abundance. Some bat species routinely fly only at canopy height or above and thus are virtually impossible to capture in standard nets. Nevertheless, even an incomplete list of mammals can be valuable for guiding management decisions because populations of especially large mammals are often in the greatest need of management.

3. *Reptiles.* As with mammals, reptiles can be difficult to survey exhaustively in a short period of time. Most snakes and arboreal lizards are rarely seen and therefore are unlikely to be detected by an REA survey. Again, several survey techniques are required to sample the different groups of reptiles. Many reptile species have more limited ranges than either birds or mammals and are potentially at greater risk of extinction. These species may be stronger candidates for surveying.

4. *Amphibians.* Amphibians can be easier to survey than reptiles if the species at a site breed in aggregations at water sources during predictable times of the year. Surveys during these peak reproductive cycles can produce good lists of species for a site that would be next to impossible to survey successfully during other times of the year. If, however, scheduling constraints prevent surveys during the peak breeding season (often occurring at the onset of rain after a dry season), then amphibian surveys can be very unproductive. One exception is humid forests, where searches of leaf litter plots can turn up many species of amphibians at almost any time of year. Almost all amphibian survey techniques also detect reptiles, so the two taxa can be surveyed in concert. Finally, recent reports of mysterious, catastrophic declines of amphibian populations in montane areas in Central and South America and Australia underscore the need for baseline information about global amphibian populations (Laurence et al., 1996, Pounds et al., 1997, Lips, 1998).

5. *Fish.* Methods for surveying fish are straightforward and can produce useful species lists in short periods of time. Like birds and some mammals, many fish are migratory and therefore only inhabit a given reach of a river during specific seasons. In high-elevation sites, fish fauna may be depauperate or even absent. In these situations, fish surveys may not be worthwhile. Many fish species are economically important and therefore in need of management to prevent the decimation of stocks. If an REA takes place at a site with one or more large rivers, understanding the fish fauna may be very important to managers. However, the depth of information that will be produced in an REA probably will not be sufficient on its own to form the basis of fisheries regulation. REA data can point to areas where more intensive study is needed to adequately inform decision makers.

6. *Invertebrates.* Invertebrate surveys are not commonly conducted in REAs because of a lack of resources and the astonishing diversity of invertebrates at virtually every terrestrial locality on the planet. Most of the invertebrate biodiversity will probably be preserved if management efforts successfully protect populations of all of the vertebrates at a site (Balmford and Long, 1995; Lombard, 1995). Important exceptions to this rule include aquatic invertebrates, which may be vulnerable if no other attention is directed to aquatic habitats at a site, or *Lepidoptera,* which may have special habitat needs for certain life stages (Gilbert, 1980). Invertebrate surveys may be difficult because zoologists familiar with the taxa may not be available. Whereas only a handful of

herpetologists in a country may be capable of identifying the herpetofauna, probably only a handful of zoologists in the world are capable of species-level identification for most invertebrate taxa. Thus, invertebrate surveys should be attempted on targeted taxa only if a need exists for the information and sufficient expertise is available for the survey.

Target Species

Both the decision to conduct a fauna survey and the decision about which fauna to survey should also incorporate a serious consideration of target species. Target species are species that managers are particularly interested in understanding, especially at the level of presence or absence, distribution, abundance, and movements. Using target species to focus efforts in an REA can increase sampling efficiency. Two categories of target species exist: species at risk and invasive exotics. Populations of target species may be at risk because they are rare, threatened or endangered, important to local cultures, or otherwise vulnerable to local or global extirpation. Target species may also be of interest because their presence, absence, or abundance provides information about ecological processes taking place at the site. For example, the presence of some species may indicate considerable habitat disturbance. Exotic species may also be considered targets because their presence may be alarming and important in directing management efforts.

Threatened or endangered (or at-risk) species cause concern because their population size at a site may be too low. The term threatened and endangered is used here in a local context. Because of low population sizes, these species are considered threatened and endangered at a particular site even though they may be abundant elsewhere in their range. The goal of management is to increase their population sizes

These species can be threatened or endangered at a site for a variety of reasons, including habitat destruction, competition with or predation by other species, exploitation by hunters, or capture for the pet trade. In addition, a species may be endemic to a small geographic area and thus may be threatened with extinction even though its population has not been reduced in historic times.

Invasive or exotic species are another category of conservation targets. These are species that are (or are potentially) too abundant at a site. These species can directly threaten at-risk species or merely indicate that a beneficial ecosystem process is not functioning satisfactorily. The goal of management is to decrease their population sizes or eliminate them through either direct action or altering ecosystem processes (e.g., suppressing or promoting fire, or increasing or decreasing water flow).

Invasive or exotic species can proliferate at a site to the detriment of native species. On islands, exotic species that evolved in species-rich mainland habitats often outcompete native species. Exotic species (including those introduced intentionally or unintentionally by humans) can also prey on native species to the point of eradicating them. Sometimes the introduction of agricultural species, such as African grasses, can promote the spread of invasive species, such as rodents, that in turn cause declines in the native fauna. In general, invasive or exotic species are more of a problem on island than on mainland sites.

Identifying Conservation Targets

The identification of target species takes place before fauna surveys are initiated. This identification is based on conservation value, environmental indicator value, ecosystem value, and detectability (species at risk), or on conservation threat, environmental indicator value, and detectability (invasives and exotics). Prior knowledge of the REA site is essential when selecting targets. Target species may be identified because historical records indicate their presence in the vicinity of the site or because they occur in a habitat type that is known or thought to be found at the site. An exotic species also may be chosen because it is known to be affecting a similar or nearby site. One way to identify target species based on conservation value is to consult a list of threatened and endangered species for a country (table 6-1) and select those species that potentially could occur at the site.

Table 6-1. Lists of globally threatened and endangered species. These lists provide the international justifications for determining the conservation status of species. References for these lists are provided in the Information Sources section at the end of this chapter.

List	Advantages	Disadvantages
Breeding Bird Survey	Comprehensive coverage of most birds that breed in the United States and southern Canada. Provides population trend information.	Limited to bird species that breed in North America.
CITES (Convention on International Trade in Endangered Species of Wild Flora and Fauna)	Has international legal authority. Covers all taxa.	Treats only species that are typically traded across national boundaries.
IUCN (International Union for the Conservation of Nature) Red Lists	Comprehensive coverage of birds and mammals.	Variable coverage of vertebrates other than birds and mammals. Lists only the most threatened species.
National Endangered Species Lists	May have legal authority in country of origin.	Variable from country to country. Most lists treat only large-bodied vertebrates.
The Nature Conservancy/ Natural Heritage Program Global Ranks	Excellent coverage for species that occur in the United States. Considers all known species.	Variable coverage for taxa in Latin America or the Caribbean. Information not easily accessible.
Partners in Flight	Comprehensive coverage for birds that migrate to and from North America.	Limited species coverage. Difficult to find actual scores for specific species.
U.S. Endangered Species Act	Has legal authority in United States. Covers all taxonomic groups, including invertebrates.	Only treats species on U.S. soil or territories. Species listing can be subject to political pressure.

Alternatively, an REA project might begin without identified target species. After general surveys are performed, the species lists generated are compared with lists of threatened and endangered species to identify the most important taxa detected in the study. *A priori* identification of target taxa is helpful because sampling can be aimed at these species. If little is known about a site, however, prior designation of target species may be impossible.

When selecting target threatened or endangered species at an REA site, the following considerations are helpful:

1. *Conservation value.* Why is the species important? Is it threatened globally? Is it important to local cultures? Is it a local endemic? Is it hunted in some areas to the extent that its abundance at the site will provide a metric to the level of hunting currently occurring there?

2. *Environmental indicator value.* Is it susceptible to some environmental influence (such as water levels, fire, or availability of year-round food resources) and therefore indicates factors perturbing the local ecosystem?

3. *Ecosystem value.* Does the species provide a key ecosystem function (such as seed dispersal, pollination, or predation)?

4. *Detectability.* Will the sampling effort available for the REA be realistically sufficient to survey the distribution and abundance of the target species adequately?

When selecting invasive or exotic species as targets, the following considerations are important:

1. *Conservation threat.* Does the presence of the species threaten or potentially threaten the population of a desirable species?

2. *Environmental indicator value.* Does the presence of the species indicate that some undesirable environmental change is in process? Does the presence of the species cause fundamentally important ecosystem processes to be disrupted?

3. *Detectability.* Can the species be surveyed efficiently?

Instead of target species, an REA might focus on higher-level taxa, such as families, orders, or even classes. This strategy is useful when the individual species that occur at the site are unknown and the presence or absence of species of the entire taxon all provide important ecological or conservation information. For example, psittacids (parrots, macaws, and parakeets) or cracids (guans and curassows) are two families for which most species are vulnerable to hunting or exploitation in the pet trade. Species in the mammalian order *Carnivora* all play important predatory roles in ecological communities; therefore, this order may be a useful target taxon. Many amphibian populations are in decline worldwide (Pounds, 1997; Lips, 1998); this vertebrate class may be an appropriate target taxon as well.

Forming and Organizing the Team

A well-coordinated team that understands the objectives of the project and what is expected of them will collect the most valuable faunal information for the REA. Consideration of project goals should precede and guide the assembly of the fauna team and the design of the fieldwork plan. Once the scope of zoological survey work has been determined, the REA coordinator can recruit members of the fauna team. The size of the budget allocated to fauna surveys will dictate the size of the team. In general, at least a specialist and an assistant are desirable for each taxon surveyed. Considerations for team member candidacy include (1) expertise in the discipline, (2) familiarity with the fauna likely to be found at the site, (3) time available to devote to the project, (4) likelihood of managing data in an organized fashion and turning in data summaries on time, and (5) ancillary benefits of collaborating with the individual's host institution. One of the team members should be designated the fauna team leader. This person will (1) serve as the liaison between the fauna team and the REA coordinator, (2) ensure the quality of the data collected, (3) oversee expedition logistics, (4) be responsible for decisions made in the field to modify sampling effort or methods, and (5) guarantee the timely reporting of results to the REA coordinator.

At the first meeting of the fauna team, which is likely to occur at the planning workshop (see chapter 3), members should discuss the REA proposal, begin selection of survey methods, identify equipment purchase needs and permit requirements, outline goals of a literature review, and plan a training session. Getting acquainted with the official REA proposal is a fundamental step of the REA process. All team members should understand all of the project objectives as well as the expected products, which may include maps, species lists, and management recommendations. Particular attention should be paid to target species. If, for example, black caiman are identified as a target species, then the herpetologists should plan to spend some of their time sampling at the times of day when black caiman are active and in the habitats where black caiman occur.

Fauna Survey Methods

Different sampling methods are available for fauna surveys; the technique chosen will reflect objectives, resource constraints, and preferences of the fauna experts. Descriptions of fauna survey methods are found in many texts (see the Information Sources section at the end of this chapter); our goal here is to provide an overview of the advantages and disadvantages of different standard methods for sampling the major taxa. We assume that the taxon specialists hired to perform the sampling are competent at employing the various techniques for their taxa. Our summary (table 6-2) presents the most commonly used options available and is designed to help nonspecialists (including REA coordinators) to understand why some methods may be better than others in providing the information needed for management.

Table 6-2. Survey methods for vertebrates. References for survey methods are listed in the Information Sources section at the end of this chapter.

Technique	Brief Description	Advantages	Disadvantages	Other Considerations	Equipment Needs
BIRDS					
Point count	Count of all birds seen or heard during set time periods (e.g., 3–10 min.) at points separated by 100–200 m.	Rapid, efficient detection of species; sampling in discrete units; can estimate population densities if fixed radius is used.	No statistical treatment of species detected between points and not during counts; can only be performed in early morning when birds are vocal.	Requires observer who is familiar with local avifauna.	Binoculars, tape recorder to record unfamiliar vocalizations for posterior analysis by expert.
Transect Survey	Count of all birds seen or heard along a transect (usually a trail).	Very efficient at detecting most species in the area covered; can estimate population densities if transect width is fixed.	Sampling not in discrete units—need to divide in 10–60 min. samples for statistical analysis.	Requires observer who is familiar with local avifauna; must keep track of hours censused or kilometer walked; can be performed at night to detect nocturnal species.	Binoculars (headlamp at night), tape recorder to record unfamiliar vocalizations for posterior analysis by expert.
Mist Net	Capture of birds in nets; release after identification.	Species identification usually more reliable than observational methods; allows handling of birds for measurement, banding, or other purposes.	Time consuming for number of species detected; only samples small, understory birds; does not estimate density; samples small area; nets are expensive.	Requires well-trained technician to remove birds from net; observer need not be familiar with local avifauna if identification guide is available.	Nets, poles, cloth handling bags; other equipment depends on data to be collected from captured birds.
MAMMALS					
Sherman, Tomahawk Trap	Capture of small- and medium-sized, nonvolant mammals in traps set overnight; release after identification.	Virtually the only method to sample small- and medium-sized mammals; simple and efficient.	Density estimate not possible in short-term study; lowland rainforest mammals have low capture rate.	Traps can be placed high in vegetation to capture arboreal species.	Traps; bait; cloth handling bags; leather gloves.
Transect Survey	Count of all mammals seen or heard along a transect (usually a trail).	Allows study of large mammals, especially primates; can provide density estimate.	Time consuming for number of individuals detected; difficult in dense vegetation.	Requires observer who is familiar with local mammals; must keep track of hours censused or kilometers walked; can be performed at night to detect nocturnal species.	Binoculars (headlamp at night).
Mist Net	Capture of bats in nets at night; release after identification.	Virtually the only method to survey bats if roost sites are not known. Allows handling of bats for measurement, banding, or other purposes.	Does not estimate density; nets are expensive; capture rate is low on moonlit nights.	Requires well-trained technician to remove bats from net; set nets along corridors in the forest to capture individuals from a wide area.	Nets, poles, cloth handling bags, gloves, headlamps; other equipment depends on data to be collected from captured bats.
Survey of local populace	Interview of local hunters and woodsmen about large mammals that occur at the site.	Possibly the quickest method to determine presence/absence of rare, shy, large mammals; involves community in survey.	Does not estimate density; information can be unreliable if not corroborated by others.	Use of pictures of potentially occurring species can be useful.	None, except perhaps a local guide to serve as ambassador to community.

Method	Description	Advantages	Disadvantages	Comments	Equipment
Targeted Survey	Depends on target species; can include surveys of caves for bats, surveys of watercourses for evidence of manatees or otters, watches at water holes for large mammals.	Can be only technique available to survey certain species.	Can be too time intensive; negative data equivocal (target species may be present but too rare or shy to be detected in survey).	Requires good knowledge of natural history of target species.	Depends on method.
HERPETOFAUNA Transect Survey	Count of all reptiles and amphibians seen along a transect (usually a trail or watercourse); may need to turn over logs, rocks, and other resting sites.	Can be the only technique available to survey certain species.	Can be difficult in dense vegetation; does not estimate density.	Requires observer who is familiar with herps; must keep track of hours censused or kilometers walked; can be performed at night to detect nocturnal species or sleeping individuals.	Snake stick, noose, plastic bags, and notebook (headlamp at night).
Leaf Litter Plot	Careful search of leaf litter in 3 x 3-meter to 10 x 10-meter plots.	Estimates density; detects species that are otherwise hidden.	Time consuming, covers small area; useful in habitats where leaf litter occurs.	Requires observer who is familiar with herps; can be dangerous if poisonous snakes are present.	Measuring tape, gloves, plastic bags, and notebook.
Pitfall Trap with Drift Fences	Placement of bucket in hole; erection of low fences leading toward the pit from opposite directions (can also be placed in form of a funnel); periodic return to area to check trap.	Can be efficient way to catch wide-ranging lizards, especially in open habitats.	Can be time consuming; only samples subset of herpetofauna.	Can also capture salamanders and shrews (which will need food to survive the night).	Buckets, fencing material, tools for digging hole and erecting fence.
Surveys of Breeding Amphibian Aggregations	Survey pools, marshes, swamps, ponds, or other aggregations of breeding amphibians.	Many frog species are only detectable when breeding; can use vocalizations to identify species.	Only useful during episodic breeding, which may be an unpredictable event; does not estimate density.	Headlamps, plastic bags, protection from biting flies, leeches, or cold water, tapes of vocalizations, if available.	Different species may appear at different times of night and on different days during breeding episode.
FISH Dip Net	Dipping of net in small stream to capture fish.	Captures small species inhabiting small bodies of water.	Does not estimate density; limited to small species in small bodies of water.		Nets, bucket.
Seine Net	Walking with seine in water and drawing net up to examine fish captured.	Efficient method of capturing small- to medium-sized species inhabiting shallow water.	Limited to shallow-water habitats; does not estimate density; does not capture large species.		Seine, bucket, foot protection.
Cast Net	Throwing the net into water and drawing up to examine fish captured.	Allows sampling fish in deep water.	Can be inefficient; does not sample large species; does not estimate density.		Nets, bucket, boat if needed.
Gill Net	Setting of vertical, linear net in water over a period of time; withdrawal of net to examine fish captured.	Samples open water species; can sample large species.	Usually kills fish; does not estimate density; does not sample small species.	May require special permit to use; can be set to sample different levels of water column; different mesh sizes sample different fish sizes.	Net, floats, boat.

One method to highlight is the surveying of local community members to determine the presence and distribution of animals hunted for game or captured for the pet trade. Research zoologists accustomed to in-depth surveys may instinctively opt for an encounter survey to study their taxa, but rare and wary game species may be very hard to detect in the short periods of field time available in most REAs. Information about game species may be more efficiently gathered by interviewing local hunters who may have a far better understanding of these species than a Ph.D. mammalogist could garner in a week in the field.

When selecting survey methods, we emphasize the importance of matching methods with information needs while staying within the bounds of the agreed-upon budget. If an objective of an REA is to list the long-distance migratory birds that occur at a site, there is no need to survey using a technique that provides density information. If the only survey technique available to satisfy a goal of an REA is too expensive, then the goal needs to be re-examined and perhaps modified.

Fauna Survey Design Considerations

The type of survey method, location of sampling areas, and manner of data collection should be decided during development of the sampling plan (see chapter 2), should be integrated with and complementary to the vegetation sampling efforts, and should be consistent with REA goals for generating faunal information. Box 6-1 illustrates how sampling intensity varied according to the goals of two REAs. Typical

---

Blue and John Crow Mountains National Park, Jamaica

This national park encompasses 79,666 hectare of the Blue and John Crow Mountains chain. The chief objective of the REA was to provide natural community data for conservation planning, zoning, and management, along with training in REA methodologies. Because adequate biodiversity information was already available for some areas in the park, the REA concentrated six weeks of surveys in the lesser-known regions of the park. A natural community classification and detailed maps of important ecological information were defined products. Financial, as well as time and logistical, constraints focused the avifauna survey to one area of the park. During two days of sampling, a series of 10-minute point counts characterized the avian community at that location.

The survey resulted in a list of species recorded in one survey location in one time period. A significant finding was the observation of fifteen of the twenty-five endemic Jamaican bird species, underscoring the area's conservation value.

U.S. Naval Station Guantanamo Bay, Cuba

In contrast to the Jamaican park, the smaller area (11,655 hectares) of the U.S. Naval Station at Guantanamo Bay is dominated by cactus and thorn scrub rather than by dense rainforest. The goal of the REA there was a fairly complete inventory of vertebrates. Along with a detailed plant community classification, plant, mammal, bird, and herpetofauna surveys were conducted for several weeks in the major habitat types. The U.S. Navy had a special interest in the occurrence of Nearctic–Neotropical migratory birds due to the Department of Defense's involvement with the Partners in Flight conservation organization. Therefore, additional funding was secured for bird surveys in the fall, winter, and spring when migrants were present. Both point counts and mist nets were used to record bird species over several days in the various habitats.

These more intensive efforts resulted in the observation of 101 bird species, of which 62 were migrants. By sampling in several major vegetation types and across seasons, the REA was able to identify the most important habitats for both migratory and resident bird species.

Box 6-1. Sampling intensity in two REAs; Blue and John Crow Mountains National Park, Jamaica (Muchoney et al., 1994), and U.S. Naval Station Guantanamo Bay, Cuba (Sedaghatkish and Roca, 1999). The objectives of the REA will determine the sampling intensity for each taxa. These two examples illustrate low- (Jamaica) and high- (Cuba) intensity bird sampling survey efforts.

goals for acquiring fauna information in an REA, and associated survey design considerations, are presented as follows:

Goal 1: Associate animal communities with the vegetation types they inhabit. This common REA goal seeks to provide at least a first approximation of where different species occur at a site. Although it may seem obvious, this objective requires that all fauna observations take place at sampling locations where vegetation data are also being collected. Zoologists often have their own sixth sense about where animals are likely to be found and often desire to strike off for these habitats once they arrive in the field. To ensure the integration of information across disciplines, fauna team members should be careful to restrict their observations to the same points as the vegetation team.

Goal 2: Determine as completely as possible the diversity of target taxa of the site or different subregions of a site. The survey effort in an REA alone will never produce a complete species list for most sites. However, by keeping track of the total number of individuals of each species detected, a statistical technique can be used to calculate the approximate total number of species present in the area that was surveyed. Box 6-2 provides details on diversity estimators. Although statistical diversity estimators do not provide names for species lists, they do provide an approximation of the total diversity of the taxa surveyed at a site.

Goal 3: Compare diversity among different subregions of a site. Managers may be interested in which areas of a site have the greatest diversity and therefore require the most protection effort. All cross-site comparisons must control for sampling effort in order to be meaningful. For example, it is hard to interpret a result showing that a site that was sampled for five days has more species than a site that was sam-

---

The simplest, and remarkably one of the better, estimators for diverse taxonomic groups is the "Chao 1" estimate (S_1^*):

$$S_1^* = S_{obs} + \left(\frac{a^2}{2b}\right)$$

where S_{obs} is the number of species detected, a is the number of singletons, and b is the number of doubletons. Additional work has produced two additional refined estimators—the Abundance-based Coverage Estimator (ACE) and the Incidence-based Coverage Estimator (ICE)—both accounting for species recorded in ten or fewer samples. For more information, consult Colwell and Coddington (1994) and Chazdon et al. (1998). Colwell has produced a handy software package, EstimateS, to produce smoothed species accumulation curves and calculate these estimators. EstimateS is available free on the World Wide Web (http://viceroy.eeb.uconn.edu/estimates).

Example. The Chao 1 estimate was used to predict total species richness of birds at two elevations in the La Selva–Braulio Carrillo reserve complex in northern Costa Rica. Ten-minute point counts were used to sample bird diversity at two localities located at elevations of 1000 meters and 2000 meters (source: B. Young, unpublished data).

Measure	1000-m locality	2000-m locality
Number of Points Counted	19	25
Number of Species Detected	49	34
Number of Singletons	17	8
Number of Doubletons	9	5
Chao 1 Species Richness Estimate	65.05	40.4

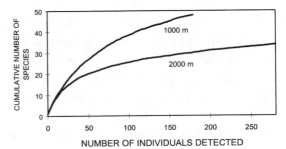

Species accumulation curve. A plot of these data reveals that, despite unequal sample sizes, the curves clearly show higher relative diversity at the 1000-meter locality.

Box 6-2. Diversity estimates for sampled taxa.

pled for three days. One method is to make sure the effort expended in sampling is equivalent in each subregion. However, due to inclement weather, scheduling constraints, and many unforeseen circumstances, equal intensity can rarely be accomplished in practice. The best way to compare sites is to keep track of effort (e.g., the number of traps set, the number of kilometers of trails surveyed, or the number of points counted) and make comparisons on a per-unit-of-effort basis. Variation in observer quality can also cause variation in the number of taxa detected at sites sampled by different biologists. Where possible, the same observer should collect all of the data for a taxon. A useful way to compare diversity among sites and control somewhat for observer variation is to compare species accumulation curves compiled for the different subregions. Species accumulation curves will be described in a subsequent section.

Given the time and effort restrictions of REA, *detailed* information about species distributions is hard to obtain. The coarse-level surveys of an REA may exhibit a wide margin of error for determining habitat affinities of the species detected. Nevertheless, sampling across the spectrum of habitats present increases the likelihood of detecting those species that are associated with particular habitat types. More detailed information about habitat affinities can sometimes be found in published scientific literature.

Goal 4: Characterize the communities of various animal taxa in the different vegetation types at a site, emphasizing the most common vegetation types. If a site consists primarily of one or a few types of vegetation but contains several other vegetation types in relatively small areas, a manager may be most interested in the species that inhabit the dominant vegetation type(s). This situation might arise, for example, if a protected area is established to preserve the dominant vegetation type, but other vegetation types are mixed in on the edges. In this case, sampling should be concentrated in the dominant vegetation classes. If some information about diversity in the nondominant vegetation types is desired, a scheme could be set up to vary the level of sampling effort in each vegetation type in proportion to its total area at the site.

Goal 5: Map the distribution of target species. Managers often need to know where endangered species are concentrated or where exotic species are infiltrating a reserve. A map is the most effective way to communicate this information; therefore, team members should record GPS locations wherever they locate a target species. Other sensitive conservation elements to map include nesting colonies of birds, bat roost caves, turtle or crocodilian nesting beaches or river banks, concentrating areas of migratory birds, and dens of large mammals.

Goal 6: Perform a survey to initiate a monitoring program. Sometimes an REA is performed to obtain baseline information for the initiation of a monitoring program. This situation requires great care to ensure that the REA data will be compatible with data collected in the future. The goals and methods of the monitoring program must all be established before sampling for the REA can begin. REAs provide a snapshot view of the populations of some of the species at a site, but they do not provide any sense of how these populations fluctuate over time either with or without anthropogenic influences.

Taxonomic Standards

Taxonomic standards should be agreed upon by all team members and used for consistent, standardized descriptions of organisms. One often-overlooked topic to discuss in the planning stages of any project involving biological inventories is taxonomic nomenclature and standards. A taxonomic standard allows all zoology team members and the readers of the report to be clear on the basis of the taxonomic names used in a report. Systematics is a science in flux; Latin binomials and even higher-level taxonomy change frequently. Each subdiscipline should be clear on what taxonomic standard will be followed when recording the data and summarizing results. Otherwise, the final REA report may include unpublished or out-of-date nomenclature, and readers will not know what biological entities are listed. Note that not every specimen must be identified to the species level. This level of identification may be impossible for some species, especially immatures. However, the taxonomic information associated with an observation should agree with the standard even if only the genus is listed (e.g., *"Empidonax* sp.").

Data Management

Fauna surveys can produce large quantities of data, so a data management strategy that details what information is collected, recorded, and analyzed is essential. Field forms are useful to remind team members of the sorts of data needed in the field. If planned strategically, field forms can also greatly streamline data entry. Different forms may be necessary to describe each hierarchical level of sampling location and possibly for each survey technique. Well-designed field forms are not useful if they are incompletely or incorrectly filled out. Thus the team leader should check over completed field forms from each team member after the first round of sampling to make sure everyone is filling them out satisfactorily. Sample field forms are provided in appendix 2.

The team also needs to assign responsibility for data entry. If the budget allows, a part-time data manager can free up the rest of the team to concentrate on sampling and data interpretation. Alternatively, each disciplinary team can be responsible for entering its own data. If conditions allow, laptop computers can be brought to the field to allow data entry at the campsites during times when sampling is not possible.

Proper documentation of the data, also known as *metadata* in recent parlance, is very important for interpreting the data. As time passes after sampling, researchers forget quickly how many traps they set, how many kilometers they walked, whether it rained the day they detected few bird species, what the symbols and codes in the data mean, and so forth. Thus, recording all of this information at the time of data capture and data entry is crucial. If each disciplinary team summarizes its own data, in addition to submitting a spreadsheet of species occurrence in the different points (or in whatever form it presents its data), it should also submit a complete set of metadata. The fauna team leader should be responsible for setting metadata standards for the team.

Equipment and Permits

Fauna surveys can require specialized equipment and permits, which can be difficult to obtain. These necessities should be acquired early in the REA planning process.

The zoology team should inventory all field equipment before beginning surveys to determine whether the necessary sampling tools are available. Aging equipment should be refurbished, recalibrated, or replaced if necessary. If equipment needs to be ordered, it should be done well before the anticipated start-up of fieldwork. Shipments of equipment from overseas distributors can be slow, and local customs agents can slow the process considerably and contribute additional costs.

Due to CITES regulations and the increased international trade of endangered species, some distributors regulate the sale of certain equipment. For example, purchasers of mist nets from U.S. distributors must hold a current banding permit issued by the U.S. Department of the Interior. Non-U.S. scientists should either identify U.S. colleagues to assist in purchasing regulated equipment or contact the distributor directly for special international instructions on how to purchase this equipment.

The application for research permits should be initiated well in advance of fieldwork. Most countries have a system for regulating research, especially when it entails capturing and handling wild animals. Fauna team members should have experience with the permit process from their prior research. Depending on how the permit process in a particular country is organized, the zoologists may want to team up with the botanists to submit a joint permit application for the entire ground portion of the REA.

Literature Review

Because time and money are often limiting factors to REA depth and implementation, duplicating past efforts should be avoided. Efficiency in obtaining information is always necessary. As a part of the planning process, information from all sources should be gathered. It should not be assumed that existing data will not be relevant to the particular REA objectives; any type of information about the fauna of a certain survey site or even a similar habitat in a different site is always useful. The REA proposal should already include a selected bibliography about the survey site and its fauna. In addition, zoology team members should search for information from other literature references and museum collections. Also, researchers who have worked previously at the site might have unpublished field notes that would be useful for compiling species lists. If, for example, the species that occur at the site are fairly well known, the REA can focus instead on the distribution of target species. Alternatively, one section of a site may have been studied, allowing the REA team to concentrate on other sections.

Training

Our experience to date has shown that training workshops conducted prior to the initiation of fieldwork are necessary for the success of an REA project, especially if a variety of taxa will be surveyed and the fauna team is larger than one or two people. During these workshops, team members review the methods that will be used to survey the fauna and how the data will be recorded in the field and later organized in a database. Team members must understand how the data they collect fit into the broader picture of the REA. With this understanding, field researchers will be less likely to make last-minute changes in survey protocol that could hinder overall interpretation of the data, such as sampling in an area with no vegetation data. The integrated nature of REAs requires a high level of coordination among team members; a well-presented training workshop helps ensure that this coordination happens.

At the training workshop, team members learn how data are recorded in a hierarchical fashion at sampling locations within different sampling regions throughout the site. They are introduced to the field forms that will be used for recording data, and they learn when to fill out the different forms. This workshop is also the opportunity to make final decisions about sampling schemes and protocols and to vet these plans with the entire fauna team. Strategies for interpreting the data and making comparisons among sites can also be finalized. In the end, a detailed, day-by-day schedule of fauna survey activities can be drawn up to help coordinate the logistics of the field survey and to inform nonzoological REA participants of the fauna team's activities.

The workshop may be more successful if it is facilitated by an outside zoologist with prior experience in REA projects. Often, team members have never participated in such a large project that integrates information across disciplines as rapidly as an REA does. Scaling up from individually motivated projects with which most team members have experience is not always straightforward. A seasoned REA zoologist can impart to the team wisdom learned from experiences and mistakes on previous REAs to improve communication, coordination, and logistics.

Workplan and Sampling Plan

Fauna survey workplans state the components of the project that need to be completed, by whom, and when. REAs by definition need to be completed rapidly. A detailed workplan will help team members focus on their work and avoid distractions that could cause delays. REA projects can languish if workplans are not strictly followed. Ideally, zoology workplans should be developed after completing and verifying a preliminary classification of the vegetation types. The workplan should list all tasks that must be accomplished to complete the project successfully, including logistics, data gathering, management, analysis, and report writing. Team members responsible for accomplishing each task should be identified, and the estimated dates of completion should be decided. All vegetation types to be surveyed and their respective sampling locations should be determined in close coordination with the botanists and detailed in the workplan. Because the botanists will have already verified the vegetation types, they can provide guidance in selecting sampling locations and determining the best access to the area.

In addition to the workplan, the zoology team should also develop a sampling plan, which is a detailed description of the day-to-day activities of the team while in the field. For example, the sampling plan might list which days a mammals team will be trapping, netting, and performing transect surveys. The same sampling plan might also list what the ornithology team is doing on those same days. Writing a sampling plan forces all team members to be realistic about the time available and the effort they will invest at each site. Table 6-3 provides an example of the fauna sampling plan developed for an REA that under way in the Chaco savanna of Paraguay at the time this book was being developed.

Table 6-3. Field schedule for fauna sampling in the Defensores del Chaco REA.

		Sampling Points			
Team	Date	Day OPs	Vegetation Class	Night OPs	Vegetation Class
All	12-Aug.	Travel to Madrejón			
Mastozoology	13	1–5	*Calycophyllum multiflorum* riverine forest	1–5	*Calycophyllum multiflorum* forest
Mastozoology	14	1–5	*Calycophyllum multiflorum* riverine forest	16–18	Closed Quebrachal
Mastozoology	15	16–17	*Aspidosperma quebracho-blanco* dense forest	54	Cerro León
Mastozoology	16	54	Cerro León	16–21	Closed Quebrachal
Herpetology	13	1–2	*Calycophyllum multiflorum* riverine forest	1	*Calycophyllum multiflorum* forest
Herpetology	14	3–4	*Calycophyllum multiflorum* riverine forest	16	Closed Quebrachal
Herpetology	15	16–17	*Aspidosperma quebracho-blanco* dense forest	54	Cerro León
Herpetology	16	54	Cerro León	2	*Calycophyllum multiflorum* forest
Ornithology	13	1	*Calycophyllum multiflorum* riverine forest		
Ornithology	14	2	*Calycophyllum multiflorum* riverine forest		
Ornithology	15	16	*Aspidosperma quebracho-blanco* dense forest		
Ornithology	16	54	Cerro León		
All	17	Travel to Asunción			
All	31-Aug.	Travel to Madrejón			
All	1–3-Sept.	6–9	*Aspidosperma quebracho-blanco* dense forest	6-9	Closed Quebrachal
All	4-Sept.	Travel to Cuatro de Mayo			
All	5–14	23, 26–27	*Aspidosperma quebracho-blanco* dense forest	23, 26–27	Closed Quebrachal
All		29	*Elionurus muticus* savanna	29	Espartillar
All		22, 24–25	*A. quebracho-blanco/C. multiform* transitional forest	22, 24–25	Quebrachal/Palo Blancal Transition Zone
All	15	Travel to Asunción			

(continues)

Table 6-3 (*continued*).

Team	Date	Sampling Points			
		Day OPs	Vegetation Class	Night OPs	Vegetation Class
All	30-Sept.	Travel to Lagerenza			
All	1–6Oct.	48, 49	*Aspidosperma pyrifolium* open forest/scrub transition	48,49	*Aspidosperma pyrifolium* open forest/scrub transition
All		50	Mixed Moist Forest	50	Mixed Moist Forest
All		36, 38	*Aspidosperma pyrifolium* open forest/scrub Transition	36, 38	*Aspidosperma pyrifolium* closed forest
All		37	*Elionurus muticus* savanna	37	Espartillar
All	7	Travel to Lagerenza			

An important lesson learned from past REAs is that flexibility is essential when designing sampling plans. Inclement weather, vehicle breakdowns, Africanized bee colonies newly established in latrines, and a host of other unknowns can conspire to throw a team off schedule. Realistic sampling plans therefore include contingency plans. The close coordination of activities among all members of the fauna team will guarantee that the workplan will be followed.

Field Logistics

Poorly coordinated trips usually result in poorly collected and deficient data. The fauna team leader and REA coordinator should carefully organize the transportation (of personnel and equipment), food, and other on-the-ground needs of the field team. Keys to backcountry shelters, maps of sampling locations, power sources, radio communications, and a host of other details all need to be addressed for the valuable (and expensive) field time to be used efficiently. Dedicated logistical coordination efforts should continue for the duration of the field campaigns, not just until the team arrives in the field.

A Note about Safety

Part of logistics coordination is planning for the safety of the team. Thus, to prevent accidents from happening, the zoology team leader should go over safety issues relevant to the study sites with the team before going to the field. This person should also ensure that a well-stocked first aid kit accompanies every expedition to the field and that team members know what to do in the event of an emergency. Injury, dehydration sickness, snakebite, and other medical emergencies not only throw a project off schedule but are also dangerous to victims, especially if first-aid contingencies are not planned. Take all actions possible to prevent emergencies and to know what to do in the event of the unexpected.

In the Field

Subsequent to planning the fauna survey, the team goes to the field and begins sampling in the manner agreed upon in prior meetings and workshops. Situations will inevitably arise that prevent sampling protocols from being followed precisely: a new landslide that blocks a trail, a week-long rainstorm, a new clearing at an observation point, or any one of countless other scenarios. REAs are characteristically flexible enough to accommodate these unplanned circumstances. When adjusting the schedule and sampling plan around these events, always keep the goals of the REA in mind to ensure that the data collected will still be useful to the project. Field researchers should consult with the zoology team leader if at all possible when they feel a need to alter the sampling scheme or schedule.

All team members should be familiar with the list of target species that has been developed. A target eagle may happen to fly over the herpetologists when the ornithology team is working on a different ridge. Alert herpetologists will take note and report the sighting to the ornithology team the next time they meet. With everyone on the lookout for target species, the team will produce a more comprehensive map of the distribution of target species than if every field worker concentrates on his or her designated taxon to the exclusion of others.

Collections

Although producing an extensive reference collection is not the primary goal of most REAs, specimen collection can play an important role in an REA. Species that cannot be identified in the field, and those for which occurrence at the site represents a range extension, should be collected if (1) the expertise for preparing the specimens is available, (2) the specimen preparer has the necessary time and materials on hand, and (3) the specimens can arrive at a suitable museum for curation before spoiling. If specimen collection is anticipated to take place, then the necessary preparation (including gathering collecting equipment and materials, arranging for a museum to receive the specimens, and securing permits) must be part of the planning stages of the project. Past REAs have collected specimens that have proven to be undescribed species, an undeniable benefit for conservation and a significant contribution to science in general.

Compiling Data and Interpreting Results

Producing meaningful information for managers and policymakers requires skillful compilation and analysis of large quantities of field data. If data management strategies were developed in the planning stages and the data and metadata have been digitized, work can now focus on analysis, not on locating missing data. The most efficient way to organize this work is to perform the following steps in order:

1. *Complete the data entry process.* If species identifications are still pending or if the data from an observation point are not yet available, gather this information before analyzing the data. Otherwise, similar analyses will need to be repeated as new data become available.

2. *Quality control the data.* Develop some preliminary graphs and analyses to make sure the data analysis approach is reasonable. If most point counts recorded 15 to 25 individuals per point, then one for which 197 individuals were recorded would be suspect and should be checked to make sure the number on the field form matches the number in the computer. Similarly, check for out-of-range species or any other irregularity that may represent human error and not a natural phenomenon. If a project is exceptionally well funded, double data entry may be considered; two individuals enter all of the data and then use quality control software to flag all instances in which the values entered by each are different.

3. *Produce summary tables and graphs.* Once the database is complete and accurate, analyses can be performed to provide overall results. Ideas for data summaries are listed below.

4. *Conduct more in-depth analyses.* If planned, species accumulation curves, diversity estimates, or other statistics should be calculated. If planned, maps of target species should also be produced.

5. *Decide what the major conclusions and recommendations will be.* Management actions that would be prudent in light of the suite of species inhabiting the site and their distribution relative to other geographic and anthropogenic features should be developed. Example recommendations are listed in a separate section below.

6. *Write the fauna survey report.* Once all analyses are complete and the conclusions are reached, the actual writing of the report begins. Writing should not start until all available information is gathered and analyzed. Important sections to include are an introduction (including the objectives of the study), the methods used to accomplish the objectives, a summary of the results, and a discussion of how the results relate back to the objectives of the project. To save time, the fauna leader should try to write in a manner that allows the REA coordinator to easily copy sections from the fauna report and paste them directly into the final REA report. The report should be written for a general audience, not in a style aimed at publication in a scientific journal. The simpler and clearer the writing, especially the figures and tables, the easier it will be for nonspecialist managers and policymakers to understand.

Data Summaries

Good data summaries, providing a quick overview of the major findings of a study, are essential. Examples of typical summaries of fauna surveys include the following:

1. *Taxonomic diversity by vegetation type.* An effective way to initiate the results section of a fauna survey report is to provide a simple table listing the number of species of each faunal taxon found in each vegetation type. Consider including the name of each vegetation type, its spatial extent in the site, and the effort invested in surveying each vegetation type, in addition to the number of species of birds, mammals, and other taxa. Table 6-4 contains an example of a data summary from an REA in Parque Nacional del Este, Dominican Republic (The Nature Conservancy, 1997). If total diversity was estimated for each vegetation type, this information could be included in the diversity summary or inserted in a separate table.

2. *List of target species.* A list of the target species found at the site is very useful for managers. The species can be identified by their conservation status, by the vegetation type where they occurred, or by the spatial subunit where they were found. If target species include both at-risk taxa and taxa that indicate conservation problems, such as edge or exotic species, separate the two groups in tables for clarity. Table 6-5 shows a sample list of target species from the REA of the Panama Canal Watershed (ANCON and The Nature Conservancy, 1996).

Table 6-4. Taxonomic diversity by vegetation type from an REA in Parque Nacional del Este, Dominican Republic (The Nature Conservancy, 1997). The objectives of this REA were to characterize the vegetation types within the park and survey the flora and fauna of each vegetation type.

Vegetation Types	Area (km²)	Vascular Plants	Mammals	Birds	Reptiles	Amphibians	Insects
Tall semimoist broad-leaved forest	49.9	40	6	24	14	1	18
Medium semimoist broad-leaved forest	277.26	36	7	26	7	3	16
Semimoist broad-leaved forest in rocky wetlands	11.95	11	—	—	7	—	2
Semimoist broad-leaved forest in salt water wetlands	2.71	6	—	6	1	—	—
Permanently inundated coastal mangrove forest	1.36	1	—	1	—	—	—
Shrubland on limestone	27.26	14	2	13	6	—	10
Coastal dwarf shrubland	3.60	27	—	6	7	—	—
Savanna on salt marsh	2.82	2	1	—	1	—	—
Scarce vegetation on bare rock	2.59	16	1	2	3	—	6
Abandoned cocoa plantations	3.25	20	—	18	—	—	—
Secondary vegetation	18.09	23	—	14	—	—	—

Table 6-5. List of target species encountered in a tall semideciduous forest at Semaphore Hill in the Panama Canal Watershed (ANCON and The Nature Conservancy, 1996). USESA = U.S. Endangered Species Act, LE=Listed Endangered; Panama Law = species protected by Panamanian legislation; Global and National ranks = conservation status per The Nature Conservancy/Heritage (on a 1–5 scale where G1/N1 represents the most endangered and G5/N5 represents the most secure); BBS = Breeding Bird Survey (figures represent percentage of change in North American populations per year over the last ten years).

Common Name	Scientific Name	USESA	Panama Law	Global Rank	National Rank	BBS
BIRDS						
Bay-breasted warbler	*Dendroica castanea*			G5		−10.2%
Gray-headed chachalaca	*Ortalis cinereiceps*		•	G5	N3	
Indigo bunting	*Passerina cyanea*			G5		−1.3%
Great tinamou	*Tinamus major*		•	G5	N4	
MAMMALS						
Howler monkey	*Alouatta palliata*	LE	•	G3	N5	
Capuchin monkey	*Cebus capucinus*		•	G4	N5	
Titi monkey	*Saguinus oedipus geoffroyi*	LE	•	G3	N3	
White-tailed deer	*Odocoileus virginianus*		•	G5	N5	
Paca	*Agouti paca*		•	G5	N3	
Coati	*Nasua narica*		•	G5	N5	
Agouti	*Dasyprocta punctata*		•	G5	N5	
Armadillo	*Dasypus novemcinctus*		•	G5	N5	
AMPHIBIANS						
Leaf litter toad	*Bufo typhonius*				N1	
Glass frog	*Centrolenella granulosa*				N1	
Frog	*Chiasmocleis panamensis*				N1	
Tink frog	*Eleutherodactylus diastema*				N2	
Tree frog	*Eleutherodactylus vocator*				N1	
REPTILES						
Green iguana	*Iguana iguana*				N3	

3. *Species lists.* A list of all identified species should be included in either the body or appendix. To provide more information for the reader, the species can be listed with the vegetation types where they were detected and with an indication of how common or rare they were. Nonspecialist managers and other readers appreciate common names as well as scientific names. Listing species together with their higher taxonomic status (family and order) also helps readers who are accustomed to a different taxonomic sequence of species or different taxonomic authorities.

Species Accumulation Curves

Species accumulation curves show how rapidly the number of species detected in a given locality increases with increased sampling effort. These curves generally increase steeply during the initial samples and then less steeply as all of the common species are detected. Used comparatively, species accumulation curves are helpful in contrasting species richness at more than one locality even though the sampling effort may have differed. Species accumulation curves themselves do not estimate total species richness in a locality. A species accumulation curve from a bird survey in Costa Rica is presented in box 6-2.

Species accumulation curves are most useful if they are smoothed by repeatedly randomizing the order in which the samples are added and then calculating an average number of species accumulated for each level of effort. In this way, variation in curve shape caused by sampling order is removed and curves are more directly comparable. The program EstimateS provides a simple tool to produce smoothed species accumulation curves (available free at http://viceroy.eeb.uconn.edu/estimates).

In some vertebrate studies, especially bird studies, the most convenient sampling unit is an individual animal detected (e.g., a bat captured in a net, a bird detected on a transect survey, or a reptile or amphibian captured in a pitfall trap) rather than a timed unit of sampling (e.g., a mist net hour or a survey hour). Using the individual as the sampling unit controls for temporal variability in detectability caused by some times of day being more productive than others for detecting animals. In this fashion, species accumulation curves can also partially control for observer variability, assuming that observers vary in their ability to find an animal but that they are equally able to identify the animal once it is detected.

Mapping Fauna Survey Results

Maps are a powerful way to present fauna survey data visually. To the extent that the mapping team of the REA is available to help, as much fauna data as possible should be presented in map format. Maps are more visually attractive than tables or text, and readers are therefore much more likely to pay attention to maps than to other information presented in the report. The harm that could come to a threatened species if its location were widely known should be considered. For example, locations of macaw nesting trees should be confidential to avoid giving the information to poachers. A solution used in some cases is to map locations of sensitive species with squares (for example, 0.5 kilometers on a side) that indicate the occurrence of the sensitive species somewhere in that vicinity without giving away the exact location. The square should not be centered exactly on the location of the element or the location will not be sufficiently vague. A randomization routine can be used to offset the center of the square from the true location.

The following are suggestions for mapping fauna data. Consult with the mapping team for details on projections, scale, and data needs.

1. *Locations of target species.* The spatial distribution of target species helps managers to determine different protection or usage categories for the different units of a site. When mapped along with political and geographic features, such as site boundaries, roads, trails, elevation contours, rivers, and population centers, the locations of target species are key to designing effective management plans. As with the summary tables, separate maps with target at-risk species and target species causing conservation problems may be clearer. If one problem species affects the population of an at-risk species, it might make sense to map the two elements together on the same map. A map showing the relationships between species at-risk and the habitats where they were found to occur is presented in chapter 4, map 10.

2. *Diversity.* If diversity was measured or estimated for different vegetation types or other subunits of the site, a map of the site can be produced showing the subunits with a different fill pattern or color indicating a scale of diversity. Separate maps can show overall diversity, diversity of the different taxonomic groups (e.g., separate maps for birds, mammals, etc.), and numbers of target species if appropriate.

3. *Locations of other important biological elements.* If the fauna team kept records of amphibian breeding ponds, concentrations of migrating or colonially breeding birds, bat roosts, nesting beaches, or other important biological phenomena, these can be mapped as well. Again, the spatial information provided will be invaluable for making management decisions and determining protection priorities.

Management Recommendations

To promote the long-term viability of the faunal diversity found in sites, management recommendations are formulated that flow from the analysis and consider the perspective of the target audience. It makes no sense to recommend actions for which the target audience has no power, authority, or ability to act. The recommendations should not represent preconceived notions that could have been made before any data were collected. By being objective and allowing the data to motivate recommendations, the suggestions will carry more weight and authority. Examples of typical management recommendations follow:

1. *Suggestions on how to zone a site for mixed uses.* The mapping exercise may show where at-risk species are concentrated. These areas should be earmarked for a higher level of protection or for less-intensive human use than areas where target species do not occur. Be careful not to mistake the absence of target species for a lack of survey effort. If an area of the map has no target species, this absence may result from a true absence of the species or from a lack of survey effort in that area.

2. *Suggestions for active management action.* Concentrations of exotic or edge species can spell trouble for a protected area. These areas might be targeted for intensive management programs to ameliorate these threats.

3. *Consideration of watershed issues.* Consider the watershed implications of mixed-use management of a site. For example, a selective logging program may harm the integrity of a swamp or pond downstream where amphibians breed.

4. *Directions for future land acquisition.* If a site is targeted for future expansion, suggestions of where that expansion should occur are appropriate. For example, an REA of the Pantanal National Park in Brazil (FPCN, 1992) discovered that the national park contained mostly seasonally flooded savannas. Most terrestrial vertebrates migrated between the savannas in the dry season and the upland forests during the wet season; thus the existing park did not provide protection of the wet season refugia of these species. The REA identified where these refugia existed near the park, and two of these areas were later purchased to form private preserves.

5. *Suggestions on hunting controls.* The REA may provide information on game densities useful in determining whether hunting should be controlled or even stopped altogether at the site.

6. *Identification of major threats to the fauna.* By being on the ground at a site during the surveys, the fauna team may form a good impression of the principal threats to the fauna. These threats may include hunting for meat or the pet trade, mining, habitat destruction, fires, lack of fires, water quality, water volume, or a host of other possibilities. Any evidence the team can marshall toward identifying threats will be useful for managers. Threats assessment is treated more rigorously in chapter 7.

7. *Monitoring needs.* The fauna team may discover that the populations of one or more species are vulnerable and require monitoring to determine whether management intervention is warranted.

8. *Priorities for future research.* REAs barely scratch the surface of faunal community dynamics. More information, including information about animal movements, seasonality, natural history, or human influence, may be necessary before wise management decisions can be developed. Details about these research priorities should also be presented in REA reports.

Conclusion

Fauna surveys are integral components of most REAs. These surveys provide initial road maps to biodiversity at important sites. With careful consideration of the objectives of the REA and with careful choice of the appropriate survey techniques, the fauna team can provide much valuable information for management decisions. The key to the success of the fauna team is prudent planning before the surveys begin and coordination throughout the project.

Literature Cited

ANCON (Asociación Nacional para la Conservación de la Naturaleza) and The Nature Conservancy. 1996. *Ecological Survey of U.S. Department of Defense Lands in Panama. Phase II: Albrook Air Force Station, Corozal, Fort Clayton, Fort Amador, Quarry Heights, Semaphore Hill, Summit Radio Station.* Arlington, Va.: The Nature Conservancy.

Balmford, A., and A. Long. 1995. Across-country-analyses of biodiversity congruence and current conservation effort in the tropics. *Conservation Biology* 9:1539–1547.

Chazdon, R. L., R. K. Colwell, J. S. Denslow, and M. R. Guariguata. 1998. Statistical methods for estimating species richness of woody regeneration in primary and secondary rain forests of NE Costa Rica. In *Forest Biodiversity Research, Monitoring and Modeling: Conceptual Background and Old World Case Studies,* edited by F. Dallmeier and J. A. Comiskey. Paris, France: Parthenon Publishing.

Colwell, R. K., and J. A. Coddington. 1994. Estimating terrestrial biodiversity through extrapolation. *Philosophical Transactions of the Royal Society* (Series B) 345:101–118.

FPCN (Fundação para a Conservação da Natureza). 1992. *Pantanal Avaliação Ecológica Rápida.* Unpublished report. Brasilia, Brazil: FPCN.

Gilbert, L. E. 1980. Food web organization and conservation of Neotropical diversity. In *Conservation Biology,* edited by M. E. Soulé and B. A. Wilcox. Sunderland, Mass.: Sinauer Associates.

Heske, E. J., J. H. Brown, and S. Mistry. 1994. Long-term experimental study of a desert rodent community: 13 years of competition. *Ecology* 75:438–445.

Laurence, W. F., K. R. McDonald, and R. Speare. 1996. Epidemic disease and the catastrophic decline of Australian rain forest frogs. *Conservation Biology* 10:406–413.

Lips, K. R. 1998. Decline of a tropical montane amphibian fauna. *Conservation Biology* 12:106–117.

Lombard, A. T. 1995. The problems with multi-species conservation: Do hotspots, ideal reserves and existing reserves coincide? *South African Journal of Zoology* 30:145–163.

Muchoney, D. M., S. Iremonger, and R. Wright. 1994. *Blue and John Crow Mountains National Park, Jamaica.* Arlington, Va.: The Nature Conservancy.

Pounds, J. A., M. P. L. Fogden, J. M. Savage, and G. C. Gorman. 1997. Tests of null models for amphibian declines on a tropical mountain. *Conservation Biology* 11:1307–1322.

Sedaghatkish, G., and E. Roca. 1999. *Rapid Ecological Assessment: U.S. Naval Station Guantanamo Bay, Cuba.* Arlington, Va.: The Nature Conservancy.

Terborgh, J., S. K. Robinson, T. A. Parker III, C. A. Munn, and N. Pierpont. 1990. Structure and organization of an Amazonian forest bird community. *Ecological Monographs* 60:213–238.

The Nature Conservancy. 1997. *Evaluación Ecológica Integral: Parque Nacional del Este, República Dominicana. Tomo 1: Recursos terrestres.* Arlington, Va.: The Nature Conservancy.

Timm, R. M. 1994. The mammal fauna. In *La Selva: Ecology and Natural History of a Neotropical Rain Forest,* edited by L. A. McDade, K. S. Bawa, H. A. Hespenheide, and G. S. Hartshorn. Chicago: University of Chicago Press.

Taxonomic Standard References

American Ornithologist's Union. 1998. *Check-list of North American Birds.* 7th ed. Lawrence, Kans.: Allen Press. Covers all bird species of North America, Central America, and the Caribbean.

Frost, D. R. 1985. *Amphibian Species of the World: A Taxonomic and Geographic Reference.* Lawrence, Kans.: Allen Press and Association of Systematics Collections. Now somewhat out of date, but it provides the only comprehensive list of amphibians. See supplement published in 1993 (Duellman, W. E. *Amphibian Species of the World: Additions and Corrections.* Lawrence, Kans.: University of Kansas, Museum of Natural History Special Publication.)

King, W. F., and R. L. Burke. 1989. *Crocodilian, Tuatara, and Turtle Species of the World.* Lawrence, Kans.: Association of Systematics Collections. Comprehensive for taxa covered.

Schwartz, A., and R. W. Henderson. 1988. *West Indian Amphibians and Reptiles: A Check-list.* Milwaukee Public Museum, Contributions in Biology and Geology No. 74:1–264. Very useful for West Indies.

Sibley, C. G., and B. L. Monroe, Jr. 1990. *Distribution and Taxonomy of the Birds of the World.* New Haven, Conn.: Yale University Press. Most recent and widely accepted standard that covers South American birds.

Wilson, D. E., and D. M. Reeder, eds. 1993. *Mammal Species of the World: A Taxonomic and Geographic Reference.* 2nd ed. Washington, D.C.: Smithsonian Institution. Excellent reference; now searchable on the World Wide Web at http://nmnhgoph.si.edu/gopher-menus/MammalSpeciesoftheWorld.html.

Sources of Information for Survey Techniques

GENERAL

Bookhout, T. A., ed. 1994. *Research and Management Techniques for Wildlife and Habitats.* Bethesda, Md.: The Wildlife Society.

Buckland, S. T., D. R. Anderson, K. P. Burnham, and J. L. Laake, eds. 1993. *Distance Sampling: Estimating Abundance of Biological Populations.* London: Chapman and Hall.

Davis, D. E., ed. 1982. *CRC Handbook of Census Methods for Terrestrial Vertebrates.* Boca Raton, Fla.: CRC Press.

Gilbertson, D., M. Kent, and F. Pyatt. 1985. *Practical Ecology for Geography and Biology, Survey, Mapping and Data Analysis.* London: Unwin Hyman.

Southwood, T. R. E. 1988. *Ecological Methods, with Particular Reference to the Study of Insect Populations.* 2nd ed. London: Chapman and Hall.

Yahner, R. H., G. L. Storm, G. S. Keller, W. Ronald, and J. Rohrbaugh, eds. 1994. *Inventorying and Monitoring Protocols of Vertebrates in National Park Areas of the Eastern United States: The Bibliographic Report.* Philadelphia, Pa.: National Park Service.

BIRDS

Greenlaw, J., and J. Swineboard. 1967. A method for constructing and erecting aerial-nets in a forest. *Bird-Banding* 38:114–119.

Hanowski, J., G. Niemi, and J. Blake. 1990. Statistical perspectives and experimental design when counting birds on line transects. *Condor* 92:326–335.

Heimerdinger, M., and R. Leberman. 1966. The comparative efficiency of 30 and 36mm mesh mist nets. *Bird-Banding* 37:280–285.

Karr, J. 1979. On the use of mist nets in the study of bird communities. *Inland Bird Banding* 51:1–10.

Ralph, C., and J. Scott, eds. 1981. *Estimating numbers of terrestrial birds.* Lawrence, Kans.: Allen Press.

Whitaker, A. 1972. An improved mist net rig for use in forests. *Bird-Banding* 43:108.

MAMMALS

Thomas, D. W., and S. D. West. 1989. *Sampling Methods for Bats.* Portland, Ore.: Pacific Northwest Research Station.

Tuttle, M. D. 1974. An improved trap for bats. *Journal of Mammalogy* 55(2):475–477.

Wilson, D. E., F. R. Cole, J. D. Nichols, R. Rudran, and M. S. Foster. 1996. *Measuring and Monitoring Biological Diversity: Standard Methods for Mammals.* Washington, D.C.: Smithsonian Institution Press.

HERPETOFAUNA

Campbell, H., and S. Christman. 1982. Field techniques for herpetofaunal community analysis. In *Herpetological Communities,* edited by J. Scott. Washington, D.C.: U.S. Fish and Wildlife Service.

Corn, P., and R. Bury. 1990. *Sampling Methods for Terrestrial Amphibians and Reptiles.* Washington, D.C.: U.S. Fish and Wildlife Service.

Heyer, W. R., M. A. Donnelly, R. W. McDiarmid, L-A. C. Hayek, and M. S. Foster, eds. 1994. *Measuring and Monitoring Biological Diversity: Standard Methods for Amphibians.* Washington, D.C.: Smithsonian Institution Press.

FISHES

Beamish, R. 1972. *Design of a Trapnet for Sampling Shallow Water Habitats.* Report no. 305. Ottawa, Canada: Fisheries Research Board of Canada.

Potts, G., and P. Reay. 1987. Fish. In *Biological Surveys of Estuaries and Coasts,* edited by J. Baker and W. Wolff. Cambridge, Mass.: Cambridge University Press.

Schreck C., and P. Moyle, eds. 1990. *Methods for Fish Biology.* Bethesda, Md.: American Fisheries Society.

INVERTEBRATES

Disney, R. 1986. Assessments using invertebrates: Posing the problem. In *Wildlife Conservation Evaluation,* edited by M. Usher. London: Chapman and Hall.

Southwood, T. R. E. 1988. *Ecological Methods, with Particular Reference to the Study of Insect Populations.* 2nd ed. London: Chapman and Hall.

References to Zoological Surveys

Erhardt, A., and J. Thomas. 1991. Lepidoptera as indicators of change in the semi-natural grasslands of lowland and upland Europe. In *The Conservation of Insects and Their Habitats,* edited by N. Collins and J. Thomas. London: Academic Press.

Murphy, D., and B. Wilcox. 1986. Butterfly diversity in natural habitat fragments: A test of the validity of vertebrate-based management. In *Wildlife 2000: Modeling Habitat Relationships of Terrestrial Vertebrates,* edited by J. Verner, M. Morrison, and C. Ralph. Madison: University of Wisconsin Press.

Zimmerman, B. 1991. *Distribution and Abundance of Frogs in a Central Amazonian Forest.* Tallahassee: Florida State University.

References to Lists of Globally Threatened and Endangered Species

BREEDING BIRD SURVEY

Bystrak, D. 1981. The North American Breeding Bird Survey. In *Estimating Numbers of Terrestrial Birds,* edited by C. J. Ralph and J. M. Scott. Studies in Avian Biology No. 6. Lawrence, Kans.: Cooper Ornithological Society.

Peterjohn, B. G. 1994. The North American Breeding Bird Survey. *Birding* 26:386–398.

Robbins, C. S., S. Droege, and J. R. Sauer. 1989. Monitoring bird populations with Breeding Bird Survey and atlas data. *Annales Zoologici Fennici* 26:297–304.

A very informative website that provides access to survey data and methodology: http://www.mbr.nbs.gov/bbs/bbs.html.

CITIES

Many countries have offices that maintain current lists. A downloadable and searchable list is available on the World Wide Web at http://www.ec.gc.ca/cws-scf/cites/intro_e.html.

IUCN

IUCN. 1996. IUCN Red List of threatened animals. World Conservation Union.

The IUCN list is searchable on the World Wide Web at http://www.wcmc.org.uk.

THE NATURE CONSERVANCY/NATURAL HERITAGE PROGRAM

Currently The Nature Conservancy's global rank information is not available in a published form. A web-searchable database of U.S. species is scheduled to go online (www.tnc.org). For information about Latin American and Caribbean species, contact the Chief Zoologist of the Latin America and Caribbean program at the Conservancy headquarters.

PARTNERS IN FLIGHT

Partners in Flight is a group of representatives from several governmental and nonprofit organizations. They are accessible through their website at http://www.pwrc.nbs.gov/pif/.

U.S. ENDANGERED SPECIES ACT

The species listed under the U.S. Endangered Species Act can be found at the U.S. Fish and Wildlife Service website at http://www.fws.gov. A database of species can be browsed or lists can be downloaded.

Equipment Suppliers

These suppliers are listed as a service to the readers of this manual. Listing does not constitute an endorsement on the part of the editors or The Nature Conservancy.

- *Amazon Books.* http://www.amazon.com. Sells a wide variety of books, covering twenty-four subject areas, only over the World Wide Web. The company's database can be browsed by author, title, subject or keyword.

- *Avinet, Inc.* Tel. 888-284-6387; international tel. 607-844-3277 and fax 607-8443915. http://www. avinet.com. Distributes field equipment, including mist nets, precision spring scales, banding tools, and leg bands. Permits may be required. International ordering available on the World Wide Web.

- *Ben Meadows Company.* P.O. Box 80549, Atlanta, GA 30366, USA. Tel. 800-241-6401; fax 800-628-2068. http://www.benmeadows.com. Offers a wide range of forestry equipment. Orders can be placed on the World Wide Web.

- *BioQuip Products.* 17803 LaSalle Avenue, Gardena, California 90248-3602, USA. Tel. 310-324-0620; Fax 310-324-7931. http://www.bioquip.com. Supplies entomological equipment.

- *Campmor.* tel. 888-226-7667; international tel. 201-825-8300 http://www.campmor.com. Distributes camping and hiking gear and other outdoors equipment. Provides international ordering services over the World Wide Web.

- *Forestry Suppliers, Inc.* Postal Address: P.O. Box 8397, Jackson, MS 39284-8397, USA. Tel. 800-647-5368; international tel. 601-354-3565. http://www.forestry-suppliers.com. Provides products for work in forestry, environmental science, life sciences, and surveying/engineering. Catalogs can be ordered on the World Wide Web.

- *Manomet Center for Conservation Sciences.* Tel. 508-224-6521. Supplies mist nets.

- *Patricia Ledlie Bookseller, Inc.* One Bean Rd., P.O. Box 90, Buckfield, ME 04220, USA. Tel./Fax 207-336-2778. http://www.ledlie.com. Distributes a wide variety of books, including field guides, checklists, and taxonomic standards.

- *REI.* Tel. 800-426-4840; international tel. 253-891-2500. http://www.rei.com. Distributes camping and hiking gear and other outdoors equipment. Provides international ordering services over the World Wide Web.

Chapter 7

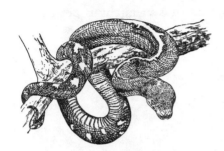

Assessing Threats

Ellen Roca

Most REAs include an assessment of existing and potential threats to the species and vegetation types in and adjacent to the study area. Threats assessments are based largely on observations made during the field surveys, and a threats assessment is usually conducted during or shortly after the fieldwork is completed. Understanding the threats that exist, which targets they impact, their intensity, and their distribution on the landscape will aid in the allocation of resources for conservation actions intended to abate threats. Information derived from a threats assessment can also be useful for developing conservation strategies, reserve boundaries, and management needs, and for assessing protection feasibility. Threats assessment is another essential part of a generalized site conservation planning approach (figure 5).

At site scales, threats are current or potential activities of a human or natural origin that interfere either with the maintenance of the ecological processes or species of an area or with the management and administration of the area (Machlis and Tichnell, 1985). A threats assessment is the identification, evaluation, and ranking of stresses and sources of stress to species, communities, or ecosystems at a conservation site (Fawver and Sutter, 1996). This assessment includes threats that alter processes (e.g., fire suppression, elimination of native herbivores, or alteration of hydrologic regimes) and affect species and communities either directly (e.g., hunting or cattle grazing) or indirectly (e.g., human population growth).

Methods for characterizing stress in environmental impact assessment (Westman, 1985), decision analysis (Maguire, 1986) and ecological risk assessment (EPA, 1992) are application specific and do not address the full range of anthropogenic and natural stresses that are necessary for conservation planning. In this chapter, we describe the threats assessment of an REA, which is modified and simplified from a robust threats assessment methodology used by The Nature Conservancy (Fawver and Sutter, 1996) and its network of global conservation partners. We draw from this work in presenting definitions, examples, and approaches to threats characterizations. We begin by characterizing stress and sources of stress. We then describe the threats assessment process for REAs and present a simple matrix for understanding threats at sites. We conclude by discussing threats abatement strategies.

Stresses and Sources of Stress

A stress is a process or event that has (or may potentially have) direct, deleterious ecological or physiological impacts on species, natural communities, or ecosystems. A source of stress is the action or entity from which a stress is derived (Mohan, 1994). Examples of stresses include habitat fragmentation, sedimentation, pollution, habitat loss, and reduced species populations. Sources of stress include agriculture, unrestricted cattle grazing, and road building. Differentiating the stress from the source is important because conservation action is directed at the source of stress. For example, in a protected area, habitat fragmentation may be a stress for a bird species at risk (conservation target species), while the source of that stress may be slash-and-burn agriculture by encroaching human communities. Conservation actions could therefore focus on enhancing protection through increased patrolling, fencing, environmental education in local communities, and seeking alternatives to slash-and-burn cultivation. An example of sources and stresses, and their interrelationships, is presented in figure 7-1. A source–stress hierarchy is presented in figure 7-2.

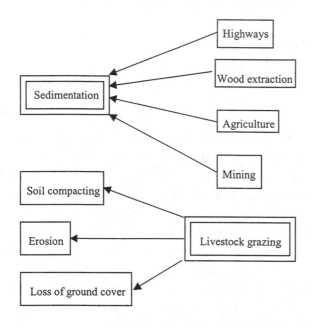

Figure 7-1. Sources and stresses and their relationships. A single stress can have multiple sources, and a single source can produce multiple stresses.

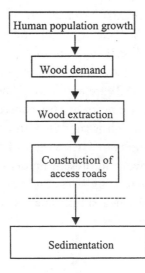

Figure 7-2. Source–stress hierarchies. A stress is produced from a proximate source but often is derived from a number of related sources, all organized hierarchically under an ultimate source.

Threats Assessment Approaches

There are a variety of different approaches to characterizing threats. The simplest and most common approach is a textual description of the threats that are known to occur in sites. While this method identifies threats, it generally does not adequately characterize them for conservation planning purposes. Matrix approaches are common and may be qualitative or semiquantitative. In a matrix approach, stresses are characterized either by source or by their impact on conservation targets or systems. Threats assessment may also involve visualization diagrams, ecological model development, or threats mapping. Some threats assessments incorporate stakeholder analyses and produce situation diagrams, which show the relationship between the human and ecological components of the site. Some of these latter approaches involve sophisticated sociological inquiry and are generally not part of the REA threats assessment.

The REA Threats Assessment

The REA threats assessment uses a simple, qualitative matrix to characterize stresses to vegetation types and target species. A template example of a typical threats assessment matrix is presented in table 7-1. Target species and vegetation types represent the columns of the matrix, and stresses are recorded in the rows. The cell values—to be determined by the individual or team doing the threats assessment—contain stress rankings, whose values are either very high (the stress is significantly impacting the target), high,

Stresses	Conservation Targets (Vegetation Types and Species)									
	Vegetation Type 1	Vegetation Type 2	Vegetation Type 3	Vegetation Type 4	Vegetation Type 5	Species 1	Species 2	Species 3	Species 4	Species 5
Stress 1										
Stress 2										
Stress 3										
Stress 4										
Stress 5										
Stress 6										
Stress 7										
Stress 8										
Stress 9										
Stress 10										

Stress Rankings	Stress-Ranking
Very High	Severity
High	Scope
Medium (or High Future Concern)	Reversibility
	Immediacy
Low	Likelihood

Table 7-1. The REA threats matrix approach. Individual stresses and their level of stress to vegetation types and species are recorded.

Stresses	Systems							
	Broad-leaved tall forest	Broad-leaved medium height forest	Broad-leaved inundated forest	Mixed mangrove forest	Coastal mangrove	Coastal dwarf shrubland	Marsh	Coral reefs/seagrass beds
Exotic Species	M	VH	L	L	L	VH	L	L
Illegal Hunting	M	H	M	M	H	M	M	-
Removal of Species for Sale or Consumption	L	L	VH	M	H	M	H	VH
Habitat Destruction	M	H	M	M	M	VH	M	VH
Accumulation of Solid Waste	L	M	L	H	VH	VH	M	-
Tourism	L	M	L	H	VH	L	L	VH
Contaminants	L	H	L	M	H	H	M	VH

Table 7-2. A threats matrix analysis from an REA in Parque Nacional del Este, Dominican Republic (modified from The Nature Conservancy, 1997). Levels of stress are low (L), medium (M), high (H), or very high (VH), and are determined by a consideration of the severity, scope, immediacy, and reversibility of the identified threats on the conservation targets (vegetation types). Results indicate that the coastal dwarf shrubland and coral reef/seagrass bed systems are highly impacted by multiple threats.

medium, or low (the stress is not significantly impacting the target). Criteria for ranking the stresses should include a consideration of the severity (potential impact), scope (geographic scale of impact across site), immediacy (current or potential), likelihood (probability of occurring), and reversibility (restoration potential) of the stress. Numerical values for the above rankings are sometimes assigned to allow for a semiquantitative assessment of the cumulative impacts of threats or the cumulative threat to a single vegetation type or species.

An example of a completed threats matrix for the Parque Nacional del Este REA in the Dominican Republic (The Nature Conservancy, 1997) is presented in table 7-2. This threats matrix was completed only for the vegetation types and does not include an assessment of threat for any species-level conservation targets. The threats assessment was conducted at a workshop held shortly after the completion of fieldwork, which was attended by all of the REA scientists, mappers, and managers.

Situation Mapping

In addition to characterizing stress with the matrix approach, a situation mapping diagram can be prepared for individual species or vegetation types. Situation mapping is a visual representation of the complex manner in which multiple stresses and their sources influence single elements of biodiversity. Cause-and-effect arrows are used to indicate linkages between sources and stresses. Situation mapping helps to convey the magnitude and complexity of threats abatement approaches, which may be necessary to reduce threats to conservation targets and their ecological contexts. Situation mapping is

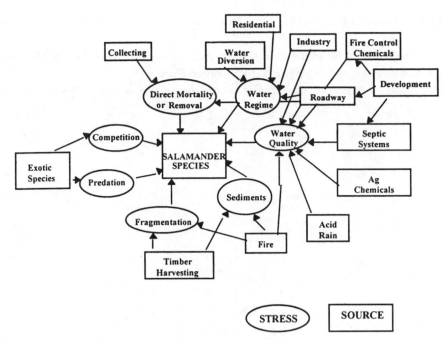

Figure 7-3. A threats situation mapping diagram depicting the stresses on a salamander and the sources of those stresses.

a visual modeling approach and can serve as a preliminary framework for the development of visual (nonquantitative) ecological models. A situation mapping diagram for a target salamander is presented in figure 7-3.

Threats Abatement Strategies

Major threats identified in the threats assessment should become the focus of threats abatement strategies, which should be proposed and detailed in the development of management recommendations. When the matrix is completed, summaries that describe the most effected conservation targets and the most severe stresses should be developed. Highly threatened species and communities identified from the threats assessment are logical candidates for increased protection. Widespread and damaging stresses should become the focus of threats abatement efforts. This will necessarily involve a subsequent determination of the important sources of those stresses because threats abatement activities must be directed at the source of the threats.

The threats assessment results are utilized in the Integration of Information step in the REA process, which is described in the following chapter. Threats assessment matrices should be included in the final REA report (see chapter 9).

Literature Cited

EPA (Environmental Protection Agency). 1992. *Framework for Ecological Risk Assessment.* EPA/630/R-92/001. Washington, D.C.: EPA.

Fawver, R., and R. Sutter. 1996. Threat assessment. Chapter 9 in *Site Conservation Planning Manual.* Unpublished technical document. Arlington, Va.: The Nature Conservancy.

Machlis, G. E., and D. L. Tichnell. 1985. *The State of the World's Parks: An International Assessment for Resource Management, Policy and Research.* Boulder, Colo.: Westview Press.

Maguire, L.A. 1986. Using decision analysis to manage endangered species populations. *Journal of Environmental Management* 22:345–360.

Mohan, J. 1994. *An Autecological Site Design Model for Nature Reserves.* Master's project, School of the Environment, Duke University.

Nature Conservancy, The. 1997. *Evaluación Ecológica Integral: Parque Nacional del Este, República Dominicana. Tomo 1: Recursos terrestres.* Arlington, Va.: The Nature Conservancy.

Westman, W. E. 1985. *Ecology, Impact Assessment, and Environmental Planning.* New York: John Wiley and Sons.

PART IV

INFORMATION MANAGEMENT, INTEGRATION, AND REPORTING

Chapter 8

Information Management and Integration

Ellen Roca

REAs generate substantial amounts of information in a variety of formats. This information needs to be managed, analyzed, and integrated for the presentation of results and the elaboration of conservation management recommendations. This chapter describes the information management tools and information integration approach central to an REA.

In this chapter, we begin by describing the multiscale dimension of REA data, and we continue with a discussion of database management systems (DBMSs) and database structures. We then describe the information integration dimension of REAs and consider approaches for combining and extracting relevant information for advancing conservation at the site.

Scale Considerations in Data Management

The coarse-filter/fine-filter REA approach generates different kinds of data at multiple scales, which need to be managed in an integrated fashion. REA data are usually organized by theme and scale, and much of this information is spatially hierarchical (e.g., point or plot data, organized by unique polygon types, and located in different sampling regions). When managing REA data, a general rule of thumb is to track information at the most spatially resolved and disaggregated level because, while it is always possible to aggregate information, it is rarely possible to disaggregate information into smaller units.

The complexity of data organization depends on the goal of the REA. For example, if the goal of the REA is only to map vegetation communities, then the data management approach will involve tracking polygons as the basic unit of analysis—a straightforward GIS data management application. If the goal of the REA also includes diversity estimates, the data management approach will include significant point/plot/transect data manipulations as well.

Field Data Forms

Well-designed, standardized data sheets for the collection of field data should always be used to maintain the consistency and quality of data gathered during field surveys. Examples of field forms are presented in appendix 2 and include data sheets for characterizing vegetation, flora, and fauna in sampling locations (points) and plots, and opportunistically. These example field forms are organized as follows:

Form 1: Sampling Region Description

Form 2: Sampling Location—Vegetation Structure and Dominance

Form 3: Sampling Location—Plant Survey

Form 4: Sampling Location—Animal Survey

Form 5: Plot Sampling

Form 6: Opportunistic Plant Observations

Form 7: Opportunistic Animal Observations

Form 8: Special Plant Elements

Form 9: Special Animal Elements

Transcribing Information from Field Forms

The transcription of information from field forms to a computer archive is necessary for data analysis. An appropriate data management strategy for the capture and manipulation of this information is essential and should involve a quality-control step. This quality-control function is usually provided by a second individual who spot-checks a subset of the entered records for accuracy, but the step can also be as rigorous as a complete independent review of all entered information or as sophisticated as double-entry techniques (discussed in chapter 6).

The organization and management of the hard-copy forms is as important as that of the computer files and records because these documents will always constitute the primary source of field-derived information. Referencing these forms requires that they be filed in a logical, organized manner that relates directly to the computerized database.

Database Management Systems

Management of REA data in a database management system (DBMS) facilitates data analysis, integration, and presentation. A database is an organized, orderly collection of information elements designed to serve a specific purpose. A DBMS is used to maintain and query data in a computer environment. The selection of a DBMS to use for an REA and planning the structure of that DBMS merit careful consideration by information managers. In general, the data management for most REAs is accomplished with the GIS because the GIS has a powerful DBMS "engine." The DBMS aspects of GIS were discussed in chapter 3. If it is determined that an additional non-GIS DBMS is necessary, it should have the following attributes:

- *Simplistic and logical formatting.* The data entry and field structure should facilitate the rapid and accurate entry of data.

- *Analytical capabilities.* Generally, the goal of REA is to provide coarse-level baseline data; therefore, complex statistical analysis will most likely not be required of the DBMS. However, conducting simple queries and calculations will be necessary.

- *Reporting.* Analysis and presentation of REA results may require the reporting of species organized by vegetation types and their conservation status, as well as by other species-specific characteristics. Therefore, flexible, user-friendly, customized reporting features are recommended.
- *Charting.* Depending upon the REA objectives, charting functionality may be necessary or desirable.
- *Relational capabilities.* Multithematic, multiscaled data may require relational table and key field linking capabilities.
- *Data types.* It will be necessary to manage and sort numbers, text, dates, percentages, and possibly other data types.

The first step in planning a database for the REA data is to determine what will be done with the data. What are the questions that need to be answered, and how will the data be manipulated and analyzed to arrive at those answers? The next step is to decide which data will be required and input into the database. The simplest approach is to make a list of the items that must be included and the types of data that will be incorporated.

REA data sets are complementary, and the integration of the different disciplinary datasets (e.g., vegetation, fauna, or socioeconomic) is necessary to interpret REA results and formulate management recommendations. Therefore, it is recommended that a single DBMS be used to maintain all datasets and that the datasets be interrelated. Integrating information about flora, birds, and mammals, for example, is difficult if that information is managed in three different DBMSs.

Database Structure

The type of information collected and the manner in which that information should be analyzed dictates REA database structure. The ultimate structure of the DBMS used—whether GIS or otherwise—will contain the following:

- *File.* A collection of information, such as a database file or a command file, stored as an identifiable unit.
- *Record.* An integral unit of data items. In some databases, a record is that information contained on a row in a rectangular table of rows and columns.
- *Field.* A field contains an item of information.
- *Value.* The actual data that is collected and stored for future analysis and retrieval.

Each entity for which information will be collected in an REA (e.g., individual plant or vegetation community) will have its own set of records. Because these entities occur at different spatial scales and representations (e.g., point, line, or polygon), a GIS is often the most comprehensive way to maintain REA information. This sophistication in feature representation, coupled with the intrinsic ability of a GIS to spatially integrate and visually represent REA information, makes a GIS an excellent candidate for the master DBMS function. In practice, the master DBMS for most REAs is almost always a GIS. Additional data management approaches (e.g., relational databases and spreadsheets) are considered if the master GIS database is unable to satisfy all information management objectives of an REA.

Integrating Information

One of the principal strengths of REA derives from the integration of different kinds and scales of information in order to generate final recommendations for conservation. In the integration step, all pertinent information and available data are gathered together, combined, and synthesized, often through the use of analytical tools, such as maps, tables, charts, and graphs. This synthesis permits a better understanding of the spatial relationships among the assessed elements of biodiversity and helps to identify conservation and management priorities. The results of each individual assessment (e.g., birds, vegetation, plants, mammals, and threats) are often effectively combined through the use of GIS to generate maps that characterize the distribution of vegetation units, conservation target species, areas of high biodiversity importance, and threats. This spatial integration capability is therefore an excellent tool for conservation planning. In addition to integrating the datasets, the single-discipline reports—with their individual threats analyses, conclusions, and recommendations—need to be integrated into one final, cohesive document. At one level, therefore, integrating information simply refers to the amassing, combining, and overlaying of all relevant REA information, which is often accomplished in a spatially explicit manner using a GIS.

Another approach to integrating REA information consists of asking questions relevant to conservation planning. The answers to these questions are then used to develop recommendations for management.

The Integration Workshop

The best forum for integrating the information from each of the disciplines, posing questions about management, and developing recommendations is a workshop attended by the chief scientists, managers, and protected area staff. Each disciplinary team should present their results to the group, and discussions should focus on conservation priorities and management requirements. The individual who is tasked with writing the final REA document often leads this workshop but not necessarily; strong facilitation skills are very important. The integration workshop is usually conducted shortly after the completion of fieldwork.

Assembling the Datasets

The integration step begins by assembling different REA-derived datasets and reports from the disciplinary teams (primary information sources), as well as from other secondary sources of information. Sources of secondary information may include regional and ecoregional maps (Dinerstein et al., 1995), thematic maps at national and site scales (Holdridge, 1967), topographic base maps, field guides, and existing lists of flora and fauna. Primary sources of information derived from the REA may include: the satellite images, the thematic maps of the site (including geology, elevation, roads, and rivers), disciplinary reports, vegetation maps, survey locations overlaid on vegetation, panoramic and detailed photographs from fieldwork and aerial reconnaissance, summary tables of classified vegetation, descriptions of vegetation, maps and matrices from the threats analysis, and resource-use data or other sociological survey information.

All of the spatial information should exist in the master GIS (chapter 4). It may be possible to have a real-time, interactive GIS capability that permits query and overlay analysis at the integration workshop; this capability is highly recommended. At a minimum, and whether or not interactive GIS is available, all hard-copy maps should be displayed in a sequentially useful manner. Prior to the workshop, the mapping team should prepare these maps by choosing a display scale that facilitates discussion and then printing out each of the maps at this same scale to allow easy spatial comparison by the integration group.

Analytical Approaches

Information can be integrated using a number of analytical approaches (e.g., spatial queries, tabular comparisons, and situation mapping), but the approach and desired outcome of these analyses should always be established by the objectives of the REA. Different data layers can be merged in the GIS so that they can be examined in one consistent spatial setting, providing an integrated perspective. Data of one type can be analyzed in the context of another type of data. For example, at-risk species can be mapped in combination with preferred hunting locations to identify locations that should be designated as off limits to hunting. The distribution of conservation target species can be mapped in the context of the vegetation units they occupy. Spatially integrating information about vegetation units, species, threats, roads and infrastructure, watersheds, and possibly other layers depending on the project produces useful perspectives. These results aid in developing zoning plans and prioritizing areas for conservation activities.

Another useful integration tool is tabular comparisons. Tables comparing vegetation types, area, taxonomic diversity estimates or number of species observed per major taxonomic group, and number of conservation targets from different sampling regions facilitate management planning. A similar table providing this same information but by sampling location provides even greater detail.

A Conservation Evaluation Framework

By posing a set of focused questions designed to extract information most relevant to conservation planning, conclusions can be made regarding the management requirements of the area. These conclusions lay the foundation for the formulation of recommendations. A set of example questions designed to frame the REA results in a management perspective follow:

1. *Which areas of the site are the most intact?* The first step in answering this question is to determine where the best representative examples of each type of vegetation are located and which areas of the site are least disturbed. Areas considered to be least disturbed may be those with few threats and whose fauna and flora species composition reflect a less-disturbed habitat. Sources of information to help answer this question include the fauna report, the vegetation characterizations and corresponding map, conservation target locations, threat locations, and resource-use areas.

2. *Are there areas with particularly high concentrations of conservation targets (species and vegetation types), and if so where are they located?* These areas may require strict protection. Conservation target maps, the fauna and flora reports, and tables of target species by observation point can help answer this question.

3. *Are there areas of particularly high species diversity?* Tables and maps (if available) of taxonomic diversity and/or diversity estimates by survey site and vegetation type address this question. Common areas resulting from questions 2 and 3 should be noted for their biodiversity importance.

4. *Are there any single occurrences of conservation target species or species with particularly restricted ranges?* The maps of target species locations or lists of target species per observation point provide this information. If an important conservation target species is believed to occur in a small range, this area may be a candidate for strict protection.

5. *Where are areas of high concentrations of threats, or where are the most heavily effected areas? Are these areas close to areas identified in questions 2, 3, and 4 above?* These may be candidate areas for threats abatement programs or restoration activities. These areas may also require future monitoring programs designed to measure the effectiveness of conservation programs and regeneration. Sources to consider when answering this question include the threats analysis matrices, characterizations of vegetation, and maps of threats, vegetation communities, and conservation target locations.

6. *What vegetation types, ecological processes (e.g., seasonal flooding and fire) or habitats are required by species targets to complete their life cycles? Are there any threats to these specific habitats or processes?* Because vegetation types or habitats are often used as basic planning units for most management decisions and practices, considering the range of environmental conditions needed by conservation targets is very important. Recommendations should promote protection strategies for conserving this environmental variation and for alleviating the impact of threats on these areas. Information sources for addressing this question include the conservation target maps, threats

map, and literature (REA results usually do not include habitat preference characterizations).

7. *What research is required in order to better understand and manage the conservation targets, ecology of the protected area, threats, and human communities?* REAs are most useful in characterizing the identification and locations of conservation targets, but they are more oriented to inventory than to research. Research to characterize the ecology of species and communities may be indicated.

8. *Are there problems with invasive exotics? What are their impacts on target vegetation and flora and fauna species? Are there management practices in place to eradicate these exotics?* Information sources for answering these questions include the floristic survey report, fauna report, and the literature regarding potential impacts of these exotics and management practices.

9. *What areas/habitats/vegetation types/natural communities are particularly fragile?* These are areas that may be easily degraded or difficult to restore and may therefore require strict protection. This information should be highlighted in the report on vegetation.

If the site being surveyed is a protected area, as is common, then the following additional questions should also be posed:

10. *Is there a need for buffer zones surrounding the protected area? If so, where should they be located and how far should they extend?* To answer this question, vegetation, threats, and human settlements surrounding the study area should be spatially analyzed. If encroachment is occurring, or if other human activities surrounding the site have a negative impact on the site, a buffer zone may be desirable.

11. *Have the boundaries of the protected area been legally declared? Are the boundaries clearly marked and identifiable by local people?* Legislation declaring the area protected should be examined for clearly described demarcation of boundaries. If boundaries exist that have not been legally declared, then such a recommendation may follow. In order to prevent encroachment and resource extraction, these boundaries should be clearly demarcated.

12. *Is the protection category of the protected area adequate for conservation of target communities and species?* The type and level of protection afforded to the protected area is important to consider because some sites may be designated as multiuse areas, extractive reserves, scientific reserves, or biological corridors. It is important to note how this will influence conservation targets and whether a different management or protection category is warranted.

13. *Do the current boundaries of the protected area adequately protect the habitats required by conservation targets for their persistence?* Secondary information regarding the habitat and range needs of conservation target species and ecological processes necessary for the persistence of those habitats is necessary to answer this question. A map of target vegetation types is also useful for determining whether the habitats extend beyond the boundaries of the protected area and whether the boundaries should be expanded to fully incorporate the habitats.

Asking and answering these questions will impart a conservation management emphasis to the integration process, and the questions should be discussed in the final REA document. As a result of this process, many management recommendations emerge as obvious, and the REA results are transformed from scientific survey information into motivation for conservation action.

Other Management Perspectives

Not all sites will be managed exclusively for conservation. Thus including information on nonconservation management dimensions in the integration process is also important. It is recognized that there may also be a host of other management dimensions at a site that will not be addressed in the analysis of the biological data. These dimensions include such management orientations as income generation from ecotourism, environmental education, border security, and protection of cultural and historical resources. These other approaches can be as important to the future use and planning of the area as management for conservation of biodiversity, and they should be considered during the integration workshop as well.

Site Prioritization

A specific goal of many REAs, especially those implemented at regional scales, is the prioritization of a subset of sites for conservation. Matrix approaches help to evaluate and compare sites based on a pre-established set of criteria. Prioritization matrices range from simple to complex. The most elementary matrices compare biological importance (defined by considerations of species diversity, endemism, ecosystem diversity, etc.) and conservation status (e.g., quantity and quality of remaining habitat, and actual and perceived threats, etc.) among sites. More complex matrix-based approaches rank sites according to predetermined criteria, such as the following:

- Presence of conservation target species and communities
- Ecological fragility
- Species diversity
- Centers of endemism/Endemic species
- Genetic diversity
- Condition of the habitat (in terms of disturbance)
- Connectivity between areas
- Landscape and ecosystem diversity
- Research value
- Economic value
- Viability
- Buffer potential
- Socioeconomic value
- Restoration potential
- Location in watershed
- Cultural value
- Aesthetic or landscape value

These criteria are then assessed for appropriate spatial planning units, such as watersheds, REA sampling regions, land cover classes, major habitat types, or sampling locations. A GIS greatly facilitates this type of prioritization analysis. The individual spatial planning units with the higher scores for these prioritization criteria are usually identified as priority conservation areas.

Developing Recommendations

One of the final stages of the REA includes the preparation of the conservation recommendations, which should inform decisions about allocating resources. Recommendations should be as specific as possible and should identify those parties responsible for carrying out the recommendations. They should be directed to the appropriate decision makers and should use appropriate language. While decisions to implement, or not implement, recommendations are usually beyond the control of the REA team, a broad dissemination of the results, coupled with effective communication with the stewardship-mandated entity for the area, will increase the likelihood that they are adopted.

Typical conservation recommendations are usually framed around the following:

- Development of park infrastructure necessary for the protection of biological resources
- Subjects for future investigation
- Species or vegetation that require management or monitoring programs
- Management practices for vegetation types (e.g., prescribed burning)
- Control of exotic species
- New protected area boundaries
- Creation of biological corridors
- Creation of buffer zones
- Zonation
- Environmental education
- Alternative practices regarding resource use (for local human communities)
- Practices to maintain watershed productivity
- Priority areas for conservation

For these recommendations to be most effective, they must be disseminated widely, preferably in a published format. The following chapter details the process for writing and publishing REA reports.

Literature Cited

Dinerstein, E., D. M. Olson, D. J. Graham, A. L. Webster, S. A. Primm, M. P. Bookbinder, and G. Ledec. 1995. *A Conservation Assessment of the Terrestrial Ecoregions of Latin America and the Caribbean.* Washington, D.C.: The World Bank.

Holdridge, L. R. 1967. *Life Zone Ecology.* San José, Costa Rica: Tropical Science Center.

Chapter 9

Writing and Publishing the REA Report

Gina Sedaghatkish

The field surveys and data analysis of an REA are an effective use of conservation funds if the findings and products are well presented and disseminated to appropriate audiences, especially those who can influence biodiversity conservation in the study area. The final REA document constitutes the ultimate representation of the REA and serves as the primary tool for highlighting recommendations. The document presents the major findings, conclusions, and recommendations for expedient delivery to managers and decision makers. REA reports can have powerful conservation impacts; thus they should be published with minimum delay so as not to lose the conservation momentum that most REAs catalyze. Although writing, publishing, and disseminating the document are the final steps in the process, preparation for these steps needs to begin in the planning stages.

We begin by considering the planning dimension of writing and publication, and we discuss the publication's target audience and the key components of the final REA document. We then consider the editorial review and publication development processes. We conclude with a description of the major issues to consider when publishing the report.

Planning for Writing

Determining authorship responsibilities early in the REA process is essential and improves efficiency at the time of writing. Each disciplinary team identifies a skilled writer to be responsible for the development and delivery of the team's respective disciplinary report. One or two individuals who are fully involved with the project and are good writers are identified for the writing, editing, and publishing of the integrated document. These individuals must offer the following:

135

- Strong writing and organizational skills, and fluency in the language in which the document will be written

- Dedication to the effort because writing and preparing the document for publication generally requires at least eight weeks of full-time work

- A complete understanding of REA methodology, the project's specific objectives, and the conservation information needs of the study area and the target audience

- Experience integrating data on plant and animal species with vegetation community and threats data, and an understanding of the principles of conservation biology

- Continuous involvement in the REA from the earliest conceptual and planning stages

- Experience preparing documents for publication, which may include desktop publishing skills

The table of contents for both disciplinary reports and the integrated document should be developed during the early planning for the REA as well. Developing a preliminary table of contents early on assists the teams in clarifying their focus, and the exercise tends to promote critical thought about the relationship between the project's objectives and field surveys. Chapters 5 and 6 discuss the types of data summaries and analyses that the disciplinary teams can produce to facilitate the writing of the integrated document. Box 9-1 presents a draft table of contents of a fauna report for an REA in Paraguay, in progress at the time of this writing. Box 9-2 presents a generic table of contents for a fully integrated document.

Example Table of Contents: Fauna Report

Four Sections:

    I. Executive Summary
    II. Ornithology
    III. Herpetology
    IV. Mastozoology

Each taxonomic section contains:

A. Names of the field data collectors
B. Summary
C. Background information
D. Methodology
E. Results
    1. Number of species per vegetation class
    2. Composition of species richness
    3. Special elements and their habitats
    4. Special elements per vegetation class
    5. List of threatened species according to the following:
        a. Threatened Fauna of Paraguay
        b. CDC
        c. IUCN
        d. CITES
    6. Density or abundance.
F. Map of the location of special elements
G. Discussion
    1. Identification of fragile areas
    2. Threats
    3. Comments on distribution
H. Recommendations
    1. Sites and species in need of monitoring (with map)
    2. Management programs
    3. Future research needs
I. Bibliography
J. Appendix
    1. Lists of all species observed per vegetation class

Box 9-1. Draft table of contents for the fauna report developed during the planning workshop of an REA in progress at the time of this writing in the Chaco region of Paraguay. The outline emphasizes data acquisition and analysis.

Generic Table of Contents for a Final REA Document

I. Executive Summary
II. Introduction
    A. Objectives
III. Study Area
IV. Methodology
    A. Remote sensing and mapping
    B. Vegetation analysis and floristic surveys
    C. Fauna surveys
        1. Mammals
        2. Birds
        3. Reptiles and amphibians
        4. Fish
    D. Human community assessment
    E. Threats analysis
V. Results and Discussion
    A. Vegetation types
        1. Background
        2. Results
        3. Description of the vegetation types
        4. Discussion
        5. Vegetation types of conservation concern
    B. Plants
        1. Background
        2. Results
        3. Discussion
        4 Species at risk
        5. Important habitats for plant species at risk
    C. Fauna (for each taxa)
        1. Background
        2. Results
        3. Discussion
        4. Species at risk
        5. Important habitats and vegetation types for fauna species at risk
    D. Human communities
        1. General context
        2. Historical background of patterns in land occupation
        3. Demography
        4. Characterization of the communities
            a. Brief history
            b. General statistics
            c. Domestic profile—structure and economics of the nuclear family
            d. Characterization of community organization—structure for decision making in the
                community (political, economic, and social institutions)
        5. Current natural resource use patterns
            a. General ecological context of the region
            b. Land use in the study area
            c. Typology of land and resource use
                –Agriculture   –Cattle
                –Forests   –Hunting and fishing
                –Agroforestry
        6. Community perceptions regarding the status of natural resources (changes over time)
        7. Participation in conservation, sustainable development, and management projects of protected areas
            a. Relations between the communities and the protected area
            b. Conservation and development initiatives in the communities (descriptions and analysis)
    E. Threats analysis
VI. Conclusions and recommendations
    A. Conclusions
    B. Recommendations

Box 9-2. Template outline for developing a table of contents for the REA document. Example sections are provided for vegetation, floristic, and fauna analyses; and for human community and threats assessments.

Target Audience

Prior to writing the final document, the ultimate target audience for the publication should be well defined. A pitfall for any publication is ambiguity about the intended target audience. For an REA, the audience can be extensive and diverse. Generally, the primary audience is the institution(s) charged with developing and administering conservation initiatives and resource management within the study area. Important secondary audiences need to be considered as well, including academic institutions interested in conservation-related research, funding institutions, and governmental and nongovernmental organizations that influence the allocation of resources and project implementation within and surrounding the study area. All REA document writers are challenged with determining the appropriate data presentation, language and style, and formatting and layout to meet the expectations of the target audience.

An REA of the Tempisque region of Costa Rica (Maldonado et al., 1995), exemplifies the diverse audience for which an REA document may need to be responsive. The 240,000-hectare region supports a mosaic of natural areas, agricultural lands, and transitional zones. A boom in agricultural production sharply increased the economic value of the region but also greatly reduced its natural forest and wetland coverage. The objectives of the REA were to document and display past and current land use patterns, land capacity, and species distributions. The REA products were needed to advance collaboration among stakeholders in conservation and resource management initiatives. The REA document needed to effectively present data to a large group of people diverse in their scientific literacy and interests: nongovernmental conservation, development, and agricultural organizations; landholders; and government agencies.

Key Components of the REA Document

The Executive Summary of the final document is very important because it is generally the section that is read the most, and it may in fact be the only section that is read by certain individuals who can exert influence on future outcomes at the site. An Executive Summary should not merely condense each chapter of the document but should provide the background for the project, state the objectives, and highlight the important findings for conservation and management. This section should emphasize the key recommendations made by the team. Including maps and tables of target species and vegetation types in the Executive Summary can focus attention on the REA results and the conservation value of the study area. Chapters 5, 6, and 8 detail the important data summaries and analyses that make up the major remaining content of the document.

The Executive Summary should not substitute for an Introduction chapter. The Introduction should state the objectives of the REA and provide pertinent background information on the study area, including settlement and natural history, location, geography, and climate. To save time in the REA writing process, much of the Introduction can be written before the fieldwork ends.

A chapter on Methodologies is another key component of the final document. The mapping and field teams will characterize their methods in their disciplinary reports. The mapping team should describe the sources of data for basemaps and imagery, scale and software used, ground-truthing procedures, and other details about mapping in the REA. A description of field methods must include the procedure for selecting sampling sites and the types of surveys conducted. Detailed sampling methodologies are necessary for the disciplinary reports, and syntheses of these methodologies should be developed for the final report.

A Results chapter should contain maps, tables, and textual descriptions of vegetation types and species. Detailed species lists are often best presented as appendices.

A Conclusions and Recommendations chapter concludes the main body of the report and presents the conclusions and recommendations derived during the Integration of Information step (chapter 8). This chapter embodies the purpose and future outcomes of the REA and should be very well crafted for maximum impact.

Maps are an essential element of the final report, and the vegetation, threats, species of concern, and proposed zoning maps should always be included. In fact, appropriate maps reduced in size to best fit with the document should appear throughout the document, illustrating survey results and integration concepts. Maps of sampling regions and sampling locations are essential and give the reader an immediate sense of the REA's level of survey effort.

Editorial Review

Because the ultimate purpose of the REA document is to present science-based information for more effective conservation and resource management, team members and certain stakeholders should review the document before publication. This editorial review enhances the value of the REA report as a conservation tool. Appropriate staff from the institution responsible for the application of REA recommendations should be invited to review the document. Their feedback can supply insights into additional or modified analyses that may be necessary. Science consultants contracted to advise field surveys have also proven to be valuable reviewers of REA documents.

Prior to sending the document to a printer, it should be copyedited. Copyediting is the detailed process of checking the document for spelling, grammatical, and consistency errors. Whether in-house or contracted, the copy editor must be fluent in the language of the report. The copy editor should probably not be directly involved in the elaboration of the REA document because a fresh perspective is helpful. Copyediting should not be initiated until the content and structure of the document is complete and all suggested changes from reviewers have been incorporated.

Publication

The REA document is usually more accessible and effective if it is published because publishing the report lends more credibility to the work and its authors. Budget, REA objectives, and target audience determine the type of publication necessary and the number of copies to be printed. These details tend to be project specific, but in general if the REA document will be used extensively in fundraising or advocacy for the creation of protected areas and other initiatives, a relatively significant investment in high-end graphics and stylized layout might be worthwhile. There may also be a need for a larger investment in publishing if the document has a leverage value beyond the site. For example, if the REA was conducted at a regional level or if it generated many lessons learned or new techniques, it may be wise to publish the report widely. The costs of the publication must be weighed against the perceived benefits because recovering these costs through the sale of an REA document is difficult.

In general, an REA document will not have sufficient sales potential to attract a publisher willing to fund the publication and manage the dissemination. As such, publication costs are usually borne by the institution funding the overall REA and need to be included in the overall REA budget. REA documents are rarely marketed for sale; rather, they are generally distributed without charge to interested parties. The tasks and costs of editing, designing, printing, and distributing the document are usually the responsibility of the implementing organization. Many cost-effective options for contracting the printing and binding are available, and some issues to consider in this regard are provided below. Many software packages are available for desktop publishing. An in-house individual with the skills, time, and enthusiasm for the job can be a valuable resource and should be engaged early in the REA process.

Key Publication Issues

A number of issues relating to contracts, copyright, and the costs of producing the final document merit careful consideration. Many references are available (in English) that provide guidance on style and publishing; some of these references are listed at the end of this chapter. We highlight some of the important document publication considerations below:

- *With whom is it necessary to establish contracts?* All parties involved in the publication who are receiving compensation should have detailed contracts regarding product content, deadlines, delivery of hard and electronic copies, and payment. Parties include writers, editors, publishers, printers, graphic designers, and translators.

- *What are the copyright issues with this particular REA document?* When using any photographs, artwork, or figures from other sources, copyright ownership must be researched and requested. Some sources might charge a fee for permission to reproduce the work. When working with a publishing company, avoid transferring copyright ownership; instead, grant a license to print and negotiate the details of the agreement.

- *How much money should be invested in the design and printing of the publication?* To determine the size of the investment, the distribution requirements and format for the document must be considered. The audience for the REA document defines the distribution needs. Printing too few copies is risky because the REA document is an important conservation tool that needs to be available to interested parties. The number of copies needed should be estimated, with an additional 10 percent for contingency. Regardless, a minimum of five hundred copies should be printed. Costs to produce reprints are greater than costs of making additional copies during first-run printing.

Format-related considerations include graphics, size, cover, and print technologies. High-end graphic design and color images and photos make for an attractive book, but they can be cost prohibitive. Maps generally need to be reproduced in color. A format size should be selected that is manageable and permits attractive, legible presentation of figures, maps, and tables. The cover should be durable. High-quality paper and lamination will add life to the document. Printing technologies change rapidly, and printing service costs fluctuate widely, so shopping around for an appropriate printing solution is a good idea.

- *Where will additional copies be stored, and who will distribute them?* Management of the distribution process is nontrivial. Requests for general information, copies of the document, contact information, and even solicitation for funding are common following the publication of the REA and require dedicated effort.

- *How will the digital information be archived and updated, and by whom?* The digital version of the REA document, and all supporting data and GIS files, should be archived in a secure location and maintained by the implementing agency. A long-term plan for storage and access of the data and report should be developed and implemented. Failure to maintain this digital archive can preclude future updating of the information. Wherever possible, REA data and reports should be available to the largest possible public and placed in the public domain by way of an Internet website.

Conclusion

Writing and publishing the final REA document brings closure to the REA process. At this point, the scientific assessment is complete, and the scientific information to support conservation-based management of the site is available. The stage is now set for subsequent policy and advocacy work to both highlight REA results and effect positive change for conservation at the site.

Literature Cited

Maldonado T., J. Bravo, G. Castro, Q. Jiménez, O. Saborio, and L. Paniagua. 1995. *Evaluación Ecológica Rápida del región del Tempisque, Guanacaste, Costa Rica*. San José, Costa Rica: Fundación Neotrópica.

Key Reference Books for Publishing

STYLE GUIDES

Chicago Manual of Style, The. 14th ed. 1993. Chicago: University of Chicago Press.

Lucy, B. *Handbook for Academic Authors.* 1990. Rev. ed. Cambridge: Cambridge University Press.

Strunk, W., Jr., and E. B. White. 1979. *The Elements of Style.* 3rd ed. New York: Macmillan.

PREPARATION AND PUBLICATION GUIDES

Chicago Guide to Preparing Electronic Manuscripts. 1987. Chicago: University of Chicago Press.

Dessauer, J. P. 1989. *Book Publishing: A Basic Introduction.* 3rd ed. New York: Continuum.

Lee, Marshall. 1979. *Bookmaking: The Illustrated Guide to Design, Production and Editing.* 2nd ed. New York: R. R. Bowker.

Skillin, Marjorie E., and Robert M. Gay. 1974. *Words into Type.* 3rd ed. Englewood Cliffs, NJ: Prentice-Hall.

Smith, D.C. 1989. *A Guide to Book Publishing.* Rev. ed. Seattle: University of Washington Press.

PART V

THE FUTURE OF REA

Chapter 10

The Future of REA

Roger Sayre

The REA methodology is expected to continue to evolve as the need for better biodiversity information at multiple scales increases and as technology improvements permit easier spatial information processing. In the future, we anticipate a greater number of ecoregional-scale REAs, which inform site prioritization initiatives and protected area network planning. REAs at site scales will be increasingly tied to management processes, and local communities will be more engaged in REA initiatives. REAs at either scale will be aided by higher-resolution imagery, and more powerful and easier-to-use spatial information technologies. In this chapter, we focus on scale changes, technology improvements, threats mapping, and community-based conservation initiatives as the most likely directions for future REA evolution.

Scale Dimensions

While the majority of REAs to date have focused on site-level assessment, it is anticipated that regional-scale REAs will be increasingly implemented. Biodiversity priority setting approaches at regional, continental, and global scales (Dinerstein et al.,1995; The Nature Conservancy, 1997; Olson and Dinerstein, 1998) are useful for making difficult resource allocation decisions. These approaches all require basic information about the distribution of biodiversity. REAs can provide this information, and it is likely that REA will be increasingly applied at ecoregional scales. In fact, the term REA could come to be associated with Rapid Ecoregional Assessments as well as with Rapid Ecological Assessments. While scale is a major challenge in most aspects of conservation, the scale-independent and scale-flexible nature of REA should secure its role in future regional and global conservation planning initiatives.

Technology Dimensions

Improvements in spatial information technologies will facilitate the acquisition, visualization, analysis, and presentation of information. As more and more satellites are launched, image data will become cheaper, and spectral and spatial resolution will increase. As image processing technologies evolve, the ability to utilize these improved data sources will become more commonplace. As geolocation and data recording technologies (e.g., GPS, laser rangefinders and profiling devices, and dataloggers) are improved, fieldwork will be facilitated. Real-time, in-the-field mapping capabilities are now available and will likely become important REA tools.

Threats Mapping

The ability to map the distribution of biodiversity is the essence of REA, and the approaches and available tools for this endeavor are advanced. The ability to characterize the spatial dimension of threats, however, is currently very limited. Threats mapping approaches are likely to evolve from simple, symbolic representation of threats on maps to spatially explicit characterizations of the geographic distribution of threats. Improved threats mapping will increase understanding of the spatial relationship between threats and conservation target health.

Community-Based Conservation

Future REAs will need to be more closely linked with community-based conservation initiatives. Surveying biodiversity is important, and knowledge of the conservation targets that occur in a site is a fundamental requirement for any conservation management focus. However, local people will always have a perception of and relationship with their natural environments, and these people need to be a strong (if not the strongest) part of any stewardship approach. There is little hope that biodiversity will persist otherwise.

Conclusion

REAs will continue to provide critical information for conservation action. We look forward to the continued evolution of the REA concept, and we believe that the information generated from future REAs will continue to be valuable. We understand that inventory is a relatively straightforward concept, whether rapid or not, and that the more challenging conservation tasks include building a community conservation vision, establishing a conservation management presence, maintaining a conservation focus, and securing long-term conservation financing. We call for more dedication in all of these fundamentally important conservation approaches.

We also call for an increased emphasis on informed ecological management. We advocate appropriate threats abatement approaches to protect conservation targets. We encourage research, when possible, to better characterize the relationships between the ecological processes occurring at sites and the distribution and condition of biodiversity. We encourage conservation planning and management approaches focused on maintaining and restoring the necessary conditions for the persistence of species and vegetation types.

While REA informs this active management approach, it does not drive it. That is the task of committed individuals and organizations. We wish these champions of biodiversity success in all such endeavors.

Literature Cited

Dinerstein, E., D. M. Olson, D. J. Graham, A. L. Webster, S. A. Primm, M. P. Bookbinder, and G. Ledec. 1995. *A Conservation Assessment of the Terrestrial Ecoregions of Latin America and the Caribbean.* Washington, D.C.: The World Bank.

Nature Conservancy, The. 1997. *Designing a Geography of Hope: Ecoregion-based Conservation in The Nature Conservancy.* Arlington, Va.: The Nature Conservancy.

Olson, D. M., and E. Dinerstein. 1998. The Global 200: A representation approach to conserving the earth's most biologically valuable ecoregions. *Conservation Biology* 12(3):502–515.

Appendix 1

An REA Case Study: Parque Nacional del Este (National Park of the East), Dominican Republic, 1994

In 1994, several nongovernmental and governmental institutions implemented the REA of Parque Nacional del Este. Encompassing the extreme southeastern region of the Dominican Republic, the park contains a unique assemblage of rare and endemic species within subtropical forests, mangroves, and fringing coral reefs. This protected area encompasses 77,000 hectares, including the island of Saona (map 9).

The implementing organizations determined that an REA was appropriate for the park because previous inventories had not produced a comprehensive vegetation map or identified conservation targets. In addition to the mapping of vegetation types and the surveying of plant and animal diversity, a speleology team surveyed the park's caves. This project included a socioeconomic analysis, ecotourism feasibility study, and threats assessment. Although the REA had a terrestrial and marine component, only the terrestrial component is presented here.

Implementing Institutions
- PRONATURA (a conservation nongovernmental organization)
- Secretary of Agriculture (government biologists and mappers)
- National Park Directorate (park service personnel)

- Espeleogrupo (speleological group)
- Acuario Nacional
- Fundación Mamma
- The Nature Conservancy

Objectives

The implementing institutions developed the following objectives for the REA:

- Characterize and map the vegetation types within the park.
- Survey the flora and fauna (birds, mammals, reptiles, amphibians, and fish) of each vegetation type and incorporate the data into conservation databases.
- Train Dominican personnel in the use of satellite imagery, aerial photography, mapping, and biological surveys.
- Identify and assess the threats (e.g., human encroachment and exotic species) to the park and design a program to monitor these threats.
- Assess the status and potential of ecotourism in the park from a local and national perspective.
- Conduct a socioeconomic assessment of the human communities within and around the park to better understand their use of natural resources. Also, identify the means necessary for obtaining community participation in the conservation of the park's natural resources.
- Survey caves (collect data on location, physical description, associated flora and fauna, and tourism activities within the caves) and make management recommendations.
- Identify mechanisms for coordinating the public and private organizations that are responsible for managing the park.

Methods

After delineating the unknown polygons from the satellite imagery (Landsat TM from 5/27/88 at the scale of 1:24,000) and aerial photography (scale: 1:24,000) (maps 1–6), the field teams divided the polygon map of the park into five sampling regions (map 8). The vegetation and mapping teams established sampling locations in at least one representative example of each distinct polygon type. The ability to access different polygons via trails was an important factor in determining the exact placement of sampling locations. This effort relied on the participation of park guards in pointing out the location of trails on the polygon map. The field teams spent one week within each sampling region. To characterize vegetation types, the ecologists collected data on vegetation structure and dominance, and on various environmental parameters, including slope, aspect, and topographic position. As part of the floristic survey, the botany team identified vascular plant species within sampling locations. The ornithologists set transects of 500 meters to 800 meters in length, in which they recorded birds seen and heard during 10-minute observations at each 100-meter interval. The mammalogist set mist nets at cave entrances and other locations to survey the bat fauna and made direct observations and recorded tracks and scats to survey nonvolant mammals. The reptile and amphibian team conducted general searches in strategic areas, such as under logs, or made observations of calling amphibians. Freshwater fish were surveyed in a few sites—such as pools of water within caves—using nets and minnow traps.

   In the REA, a species was identified as a target species for conservation if it was listed as threatened or endangered by the IUCN (International Union for the Conservation of Nature) Red Book or listed in appendix I or II of CITES (Convention on the International Trade of Endangered Species). For plants, target species were those considered rare in abundance.

Results

Map 9 displays the vegetation types and land use classes that resulted from the imagery interpretation and field surveys. The most extensive community was semihumid, broad-leaved, medium height forest (277.26 square kilometers). The following table lists the number of species observed for each taxa surveyed (a list of fauna species observed per vegetation community is located in chapter 6. The zoology disciplinary teams worked with the mapping team to develop a map of animal species at risk (map 10).

Species of Conservation Concern Encountered in Field Surveys

Taxa Surveyed	# of Species Observed	# of Endemics Observed	# of Target Species	# of Exotic Species
Plants	572	53*	12	35
Mammals	17	1	1	10
Birds	72	8	6	4
Reptiles	18	18	6	0
Amphibians	5	4	0	1
Fish	4	4	0	0

*Species endemic to Hispaniola.

Major findings that influenced the development of conservation and management recommendations include the following:

- Agricultural and pastural areas covered 18.09 square kilometers of the park. Much of the areas classified as agricultural were actually abandoned fields.

- Conducting bird surveys outside of the breeding and migrating times resulted in a low bird species count.

- With the exception of seven bird species, the ornithologists made observations of each bird species in both the tall and medium semihumid, broad-leaved, forest communities, indicating little habitat specificity at this scale.

- There were many first-time observations of species for the park: three plant families, twenty-eight plant genera, and forty-three plant species; four bird species; one fish species; and one reptile and one amphibian species for Saona Island.

- Exotic mammals appeared to be more prevalent than native mammals.

- One of the field teams opportunistically discovered a population of the endemic and rare solenodon (*Solenodon paradoxus*).

- The socioeconomic and threats analyses found that of the three human communities adjacent to the park, two are responsible for the majority of impacts. The impacts generated by each community differed in their type and intensity. For instance, some individuals from a nearby community collected animals for commercial sale and looted archeological sites. Much of the resource use from the community on Saona Island was at the subsistence level.

- The threats with the highest impacts on the park were exotic species, illegal hunting and collection, solid waste disposal, and habitat destruction. Map 11 displays the different locations in which these threats occur. This information allows park managers to focus threats abatement and sustainable resource use programs at the source of the threat, increasing their odds of successfully preserving the ecological integrity of this national park.

- To balance the priority goal of protecting the park's natural resources with human subsistence needs and tourism, the REA team proposed a zoning plan consisting of buffer, public use, and absolute protection zones (map 12).

Recommendations

The REA teams developed the following recommendations based on the integration of landscape and species data, and the results of the threats assessment and socioeconomic and ecotourism profiles:

Management/Natural Resource Use

- Eliminate or reduce populations of ten exotic mammals found within the park.
- Develop and implement a protection and management plan for native mammals.
- Reduce the accumulation of trash and abate damage to archeological sites and caves.
- Develop a management plan and determine the carrying capacity for ecotourism.
- Define which human activities will be allowed within the park and which will be regulated.
- Delineate and post the northern border of the park.
- Construct and staff park guard posts in the northern and central parts and on Saona Island.
- Increase the number of park guards and improve their working conditions.
- Coordinate with the Navy to protect the coastal zone and Saona Island.

Scientific Research

- Complete a botanical investigation in the park; include a survey of endemic species and the economic potential of different plant species.
- Establish permanent plots in each vegetation type.
- Carry out a census of birds and determine migration and breeding seasons.
- Locate the nesting areas of the White-crowned Pigeon *(Columba leucocephala)* and the Hispaniolan parrot *(Amazona ventralis)*.
- Assess the status of the exotic predator, the Pearly-eyed Thrasher *(Margarops fuscatus)* and establish a population control program.
- Determine whether marine turtles nest on the beaches of the park.
- Study the population and genetic affinities of the park's iguanas in the genus Cyclura.
- Study the fish and crustaceans occurring within subterranean freshwater.
- Study the population status of the endemic *Solenodon* and a rodent, *Plagiodontia aedium.*
- Study the distribution and life cycles of the different mosquito species to determine alternative mosquito control programs to alleviate the use of toxic pesticides.

Zoning/Reserve Design

- Consider adopting the zoning plan presented in the REA report, which divides the park into the following zones: buffer, public use, and absolute protection (map 12).

Ecological Monitoring

- Establish a monitoring program for *Solenodon paradoxus* and *Plagiodontia aedium.*
- Monitor the distribution of bat species in caves and other habitats.

- Continue to inventory and monitor the park's terrestrial invertebrates with emphasis on the *Lepidoptera* species, which are good indicators of vegetation type, and arachnids.

Human Community Support/Sustainable Development

- Consider the development of ecotourism in the towns of Adamanay or Mano Juan.
- Integrate microenterprises, such as ecotourism, into the economic activities of communities within and neighboring the park.
- Define areas on Saona Island where residents can sustainably use natural resources.

Restoration

- Reforest abandoned fields with native and endemic plants.

Post-REA Activities

Park managers and collaborating institutions are implementing several of the recommendations that resulted from the REA and socioeconomic study. The following projects and activities are under way.

Projects

- Evaluation of the abundance of economically important species, with the participation of local communities
- Development of programs for protecting target plant species
- Investigations of archeological sites and prehistoric settlements
- Development of an ecotourism management plan

Protection Activities

- Removal of some of the exotic animal species, such as cows, burros, horses, dogs, and goats
- Development of tourism regulations
- Construction of guard posts
- Increase in the number of park guards
- Delineation of the northern limits of the park

Research

- Located the nesting areas of the White-crowned Pigeon and the Hispaniolan Parrot.

Source

Nature Conservancy, The. 1997. *Evaluación Ecológica Integral: Parque Nacional del Este, República Dominicana. Tomo 1: Recursos terrestres.* Arlington, Va.: The Nature Conservancy.

Appendix 2

Field Forms

The field forms that follow have been included to enable REA practitioners to record field observations in a structured, comprehensive manner. These field forms have been revised and refined based on experiences from several REAs. These forms have been described in chapters 5, 6, and 8, and include the following.

- *Form 1:*   Sampling Region Description
- *Form 2:*   Sampling Location—Vegetation Community
- *Form 3:*   Sampling Location—List of Plant Species
- *Form 4:*   Sampling Location—Animal Sampling
- *Form 5:*   Plot Sampling
- *Form 6:*   Opportunistic Observations—List of Plant Species
- *Form 7:*   Opportunistic Animal Observations
- *Form 8:*   Special Plants Observed
- *Form 9:*   Special Animals Observed

Form 1: Sampling Region Description

REA Project Name _____ Field Team _____
(Circle the name of the person who records the data)

Sampling Region Name _____ Sampling Region No. _____ Date (d/m/yr.) _____
(Name established during the planning stage of the REA)

Name of the province, department or state where the sampling region is located _____

Is the sampling region located in a protected area? _____ If Yes, indicate the name _____

Sampling Region Centrum Coordinate: lat._____ long. _____

UTM: N _____ E _____ UTM Zone Number _____

GPS File Name _____

GPS Differential Correction: N _____ E _____

Directions to the Sampling Region _____

_____

Describe the dominant types of vegetation as well as general characteristics of the landscape _____

_____

Which vegetation types are shared with adjacent sampling regions? _____

Total Area (km²)_____ Map Name _____ Scale_____
(Note: 1km² = 100 ha) (National map series that includes the sampling region)

Property Owner: Name _____ Address _____

Occupation _____ Principal Contact Name (if not the owner) _____

Property Demarcation (check): _____ map _____ photograph _____ satellite image _____ other: _____

Additional Information about the Property _____

Land uses within the Sampling Region: (Check all that apply)

_____ Biodiversity Protection   _____ Agriculture

_____ Mining   _____ Livestock Production / Grazing

_____ Hunting   _____ Fishing

_____ Forestry   _____ Other (please indicate) _____

Land uses in areas adjacent to the sampling region _____

Principal threats within the sampling region: (Check all that apply)

_____ Slash and burn   _____ Changes in nearby land use

_____ Mining   _____ Looting of archeological sites

_____ Livestock Production / Grazing   _____ Colonization frontier

_____ Hunting   _____ Water pollution

_____ Fishing   _____ Drainage of wetlands

_____ Timber Extraction   _____ Dams

_____ Road construction   _____ Other (please indicate) _____

SKETCH OF SAMPLING REGION WITH SAMPLING LOCATIONS INDICATED
The space above may be used to sketch a map of the sampling region and sampling locations. Please note general information such as approximate distances between landmarks, the direction of nearby cities, and the names of settlements.

Form 2: Sampling Location – Vegetation Community

REA Project Name _____ Field Team _____
(Circle the name of the person who records the data)

Sampling Region Name _____ Sampling Location No.* _____ Date (d/m/yr.) _____

Directions to the Sampling Location _____

_____

Sampling Location Demarcation: _____ map _____ aerial photograph _____ satellite image _____ other: _____

GPS Coordinates: lat. _____ long. _____

UTM: N_____ E_____ UTM Zone No. _____

GPS File Name _____

GPS Differential Correction: N _____ E _____

Community Type (according to an accepted classification scheme) _____

Community Type (common name) _____

Indicate (check) whether the community is _____ Primary or _____ Secondary   Elevation (m) _____

Landform	Topographic Position	Slope	Aspect	Physiognomic Type *	Leaf phenology
Mountain (>300 m)		Flat - O°	Flat	Forest	Evergreen (<25% deciduous)
Hill (≤ 300 m)	Summit	Gentle - 0-5°	Variable	Woodland	
Plateau	High slope	Moderate- 6-14°	N 338 – 22°	Scrub thicket	Semi-evergreen (25-50% deciduous)
Plain	Midslope	Somewhat steep 15-26°	NE 23 – 67°	Dwarf scrub thicket	Semi-deciduous (25-50% evergreen)
Beach	Lowslope		E 68 – 112°	Shrubland	
Valley	Base	Steep - 27-45°	SE 113 – 157°	Dwarf shrubland	Deciduous (<25% evergreen)
Ravine		Very Steep - 45-69°	S 158 - 202°	Sparse woodland	
Other:		Vertical - 70-100°	SW 203 – 292°	Sparse shrubland	Annual (>50% annual)
			W 248 – 292°	Sparse dwarf shrubland	Perennial (>50% perennial)
			NW 293 – 337°	Herbaceous	
				Non-vascular	
				Sparsely vegetated	

Geology	Soil Type	Soil color	Soil Moisture	Non-vegetated surface	Depth of organic layer
Igneous: Volcanic	Clay	White	Extremely dry	_____% TOTAL	_____
Igneous: Plutonic	Silt	Gray	Very dry	_____% rocks	
Metamorphic	Sand	Brown	Dry	_____% bare soil	
Sedimentary	Sandy clay	Black	Somewhat moist	_____% litter, duff	Ecosystem
Unconsolidated	Silty clay	Ochre	Moist	_____% bedrock	Palustrine
Other:	Other:	Red	Somewhat wet	_____% deadwood	Terrestrial
		Other:	Wet	_____% water	
			Very wet		
			Periodically inundated		
			Permanently inundated		

Comments regarding soil, hydrological and environmental influences * _____

_____

* Please see instructions

Sampling Location – Vegetation Community Page 2

Sampling Region Name _____ Sampling Location No._____

Stratum Emergents; Canopy; Sub- canopy; Tall shrub (2-5m); Short shrub (<2m); Herbaceous; Non-vascular	Height (m)	Stratum Cover Class (% cover during growing season): 4=60-100%; 3=25-60%; 2=10-25%; 1=0-10%	List the dominant species and its cover class in each stratum (6=75-100%, 5=50-75%, 4=25-50%, 3=5-25%, 2=1-5%, 1=0-1%)	DBH (Largest individual of dominant tree species)	Epiphytic and non-vascular species associated with each stratum

Cite the general abundance of lianas, epiphytes and non-vascular plants at this sampling location where A=Abundant, C=Common, O=Occasional, and R=Rare

_____Lianas   _____Non-vascular plants   _____Epiphytes

CONSERVATION: Condition of the Sampling Location: _____ Excellent _____ Good _____ Fair _____ Poor

Level of Disturbance: _____ High _____ Moderate _____ Low _____ None

Principal threats within the sampling location: (Check all that apply)

_____ Slash and burn	_____ Looting of archeological sites	_____ Road Construction
_____ Livestock Production / Grazing	_____ Dams	_____ Colonization Frontier
_____ Timber Extraction	_____ Drainage of wetlands	_____ Mining
_____ Hunting	_____ Water Pollution	_____ Other: _____
_____ Changes in nearby land use	_____ Fishing	

Threats from adjacent communities _____

_____

Other comments (important species, ecological processes, aspects of the habitat, etc.) _____

_____

_____

Photographer _____ Roll No. _____ Frame No. _____

Instructions For Form 2: Sampling Location – Vegetation Community

<u>Sampling Location No.</u> Use a consecutive numbering scheme for sampling locations both within and between sampling regions. If the first sampling region contains sampling locations 1,2,3, then the second sampling region would start with sampling location 4.

<u>Physiognomic Type:</u>

Forest: Trees over 5 m tall with crowns overlapping (60-100% cover.) Shrubs, herbs and non-vascular plants may be present at any cover value.

Woodland: Trees over 5 m tall with crowns not usually touching (25-60% cover.) Shrubs, herbs and non-vascular plants may be present at any cover value.

Scrub thicket: Shrubs are 0.5 – 5.0 meters tall with crowns overlapping (60-100% cover.) Trees may be present but with 25% or less cover. Herbs and non-vascular plants may be present at any cover value.

Dwarf scrub thicket: Shrubs are generally less than 0.5 m tall (though known dwarf forms between 0.5 and 1 m can be included), and the majority of the shrub crowns are overlapping (60-100%). Trees may be present with 25% or less cover. Herbs and non-vascular plants may be present at any cover value.

Shrubland: Shrubs 0.5-5.0 m tall with 25-60% cover. Trees may be present with 25% or less cover. Herbs and non-vascular plants may be present at any cover value.

Dwarf shrubland: Shrubs are generally less than 0.5 m tall (though known dwarf forms between 0.5 and 1 m can be included), with 25-60% cover. Trees may be present with 25% or less cover. Herbs and non-vascular plants may be present at any cover value.

Sparse woodland: Primarily herbaceous vegetation (graminoid, forbs and ferns) with cover greater than 25%. Tree cover 10-25%. Shrubs and non-vascular plants may be present with 25% or less cover.

Sparse shrubland: Primarily herbaceous vegetation (graminoid, forbs and ferns) with cover greater than 25%. Shrub cover between 10-25%. Trees may be present with 10% or less cover. Non-vascular plants may be present with 25% or less cover.

Sparse dwarf shrubland: Primarily herbaceous vegetation (graminoids, forbs and ferns) with cover greater than 25%. Shrubs are generally less than 0.5 m tall (though known dwarf forms between 0.5 and 1 m can be included) with 10-25% cover. Trees may be present with 10% or less cover. Non-vascular plants may be present with 25% or less cover.

Herbaceous: Herbaceous vegetation (graminoids, forbs and ferns) with cover greater than 25%. Trees, shrubs, or non-vascular plants may be present with 25% or less cover.

Non-vascular: Non-vascular vegetation (bryophytes, lichens or other non-vascular plants) with cover greater than 25%. Trees, shrubs, and herbs may be present with 25% or less cover.

Sparsely vegetated: Substrate is predominantly not vegetated. Cover of trees, shrubs, herbs, and non-vascular vegetation combined is 25% or less.

<u>Comments regarding soil, hydrological and environmental influences:</u> Describe any other influences, which might affect the associated community. For example, soil pH, fluctuation in water level, seasonality, tides, climate, seasons, etc.

Form 3: Sampling Location – List of Plant Species

REA Project Name _____ Field Team _____
(Circle the name of the person who records the data)

Sampling Region Name _____ Date (d/m/yr) _____ Sampling Location No. _____

Record each species observed. Indicate the genus, family or common name when plants cannot be identified to species. Use one of the following categories to describe habit: tree (include estimated height in meters), shrub, herb, vine, liana or epiphyte. Estimate percent cover.

Scientific Name	Habit	Height (m)	Percent Cover	Collector Collection No.	Photographer Roll No. Frame No.

Form 4: Sampling Location – Animal Sampling

REA Project Name _____ Field Team _____

Sampling Region Name _____ Sampling Region No. _____

Date (d/m/yr.) _____ Sampling Location No. _____ Page _____ of _____ for this Sampling Location

Taxonomic Group(s) _____ Duration of Data Collection (hrs. or min.) _____

Methodology (check all that apply): _____ visual observations _____ nets _____ traps _____ leaf-litter plots ____other_____

Transect Description (if sampling occurred along a transect): Length of Transect (m) _____ Elevation (m) _____

Transect Coordinates: Start: Lat._____ Long. _____ Finish: Lat._____ Long. _____

Start: UTM: N _____ E _____ UTM Zone No. _____

    GPS File Name _____

    Differential Correction: N _____ E _____

Finish: UTM: N _____ E _____

    GPS File Name _____

    Differential Correction: N _____ E _____

Indicate how each species was detected (sighting, vocalization, pellets, excrement, tracks, nests)

Collection No. (if specimen collected)	Species	Evidence of Presence	Number Observed

Form 5: Plot Sampling

REA Project Name _____ Field Team _____

(Circle the name of the person who records the data)

Sampling Region Name _____ Date (d/m/yr.) _____ Sampling Location No. _____

Plot Number _____ Permanent plot: ___ yes ___ no   Sampling Plot Length (m)_____ Width (m)_____

Sampling Plot Radius (m) _____   Total Area of Sampling Plot (m^2) _____   Slope (in degrees)_____

Coordinates: lat. _____ long. _____ Elevation (m) _____

UTM: N _____ E _____ UTM Zone Number _____

GPS File Name _____

GPS Differential Correction: N _____ E _____

Directions to the Sampling Plot: (Include the number of meters the plot is located from a specific landmark)_____

_____

Record all the plant species encountered in the sampling plot. Measure the diameter at breast height (DBH) in centimeters for trees.

Scientific Name	Height (m)	DBH or Percent Cover	Comments (Morphological Characteristics)	Collection No.	Photographer Roll No. Frame No.

Form 5: Plot Sampling Page 2

Sampling Region _____ Sampling Location No. _____ Sampling Plot No. _____

Scientific Name	Height (m)	DBH or Percent Cover	Comments (Morphological Characteristics)	Collection No.	Photographer Roll No. Frame No.

Form 6: Opportunistic Observations – List of Plant Species

REA Project Name _____ Field Team _____
(Circle the name of the person who records the data)

Sampling Region Name _____ Date (d/m/yr) _____

Record each species observed. Indicate the genus, family or common name when plants cannot be identified to species. Use one of the following categories to describe habit: tree (include estimated height in meters), shrub, herb, vine, liana or epiphyte. Estimate percent cover.

Scientific Name	Habit	Height (m)	Percent Cover	GPS lat	GPS long	Collector Collection No.	Photographer Roll No. Frame No.

Form 7: Opportunistic Animal Observations

REA Project Name _____   Field Team _____
                                            (Circle the name of the person who records the data)

Sampling Region Name _____   Sampling Region No. _____

Provide the details for each observation on a separate line. Examples of evidence of presence include sightings, vocalizations, pellets, excrement, tracks, and nests.

Date (d/m/yr)	Observer	Closest Sampling Location	GPS lat/long	Species	Evidence of Presence	Number Observed

Form 8: Special Plants Observed

REA Project Name _____ Field Team _____
(Circle the name of the person who records the data)

Sampling Region Name _____ Sampling Location No. _____ Date (d/m/yr) _____

Scientific Name _____ Common name(s) _____

Habit: ____ Tree ____ Shrub ____ Vine ____ Liana ____ Herb ____Epiphyte

Light Intensity: ____ Open light ____ Filtered light ____Shaded

Photographs taken? ___ No ___ Yes Photographer_____ Roll No. _____ Frame No. ____

Coordinates: lat _____ long _____

UTM: N _____ E _____ UTM Zone No. _____

GPS File Name _____ GPS Differential Correction _____ Elevation _____

For collected specimens, indicate the collector, collection no. and herbarium where it is housed _____

_____

CHARACTERISTICS

Phenology	Approx. # of Individuals	Aprox. Population Area	Age structure	Vigor
___ In leaf	___ 1 - 10	___ 1m²	____% Seedlings	___ Very feeble
___ In bud	___ 11 - 50	___ 1 - 5m²	____% Juvenile	___ Feeble
___ In flower	___ 51 - 100	___ 5 - 10m²	____% Mature	___ Normal
___ In fruit	___ 101 - 1000	___ 10 - 100m²	____% Senescent	___ Vigorous
___ Dispersing seed	___ 1001 - 10,000	___ 100m² - Ha.		
___ Dormant	___ > 10,000	___ > 1 Ha.		

Briefly summarize size, condition, viability and other characteristics of the special plant population: _____

_____

_____

Describe the vegetation community in which the population occurs: _____

_____

_____

Observe and record approximately 5 of the dominant or codominant species of various strata and their percent cover:

_____

_____

Form 8: Special Plants Observed Page 2

Sampling Region Name _____   Sampling Location No. _____

List associated native species which are indicative of the habitat: _____

_____

_____

Exotic or weedy species: _____

_____

_____

List current and potential threats to local species viability: _____

_____

_____

Briefly describe current protection or management of the area in question: _____

_____

_____

Additional Comments: _____

_____

_____

<u>Summary of species occurrence</u>:

Quality: A-Excellent B-Good C-Marginal D-Poor   Comments:_____

_____

Condition: A-Excellent B-Good C-Marginal D-Poor   Comments:_____

_____

Viability: A-Excellent B-Good C-Marginal D-Poor   Comments:_____

_____

Defensibility: A-Excellent B-Good C-Marginal D-Poor   Comments:_____

_____

Rank :   A-Excellent B-Good C-Marginal D-Poor   Comments:_____

_____

Form 9: Special Animals Observed

REA Project Name _____ Field Team _____
(Circle the name of the person who records the data)

Sampling Region Name _____ Sampling Location No. _____ Date (d/m/yr) _____

Scientific Name _____ Time of Observation _____

GPS Coordinates _____

State/Province/Dept _____ General Weather Conditions _____

BIOLOGY

Observation Type: ____ Visual ____ Tracks ____Call ____ Excrement, Pellets ___ Other : _____
(check all that apply)

No. Observed _____ Estimated Number _____ Type of Estimation _____

Age and Gender of Individuals _____

Type of Occurrence: (Check all that apply)

_____Feeding Area   _____Colony

_____Territory   _____Den

_____Reproducing or Nesting Area   _____Wintering Area (for migratory birds)

_____Sleeping Area   _____ Permanent Resident

_____Corridor

Quality / Condition of Occurrence: (Select one)

_____Excellent   _____Marginal

_____Good   _____Poor

_____No Basis for Judgement

General notes on species behavior (indicate any activity: singing, feeding, territorial, reproduction, etc.) _____

_____

HABITAT

Record the immediate habitat where the observations are being made, e.g., tropical cloud forest, savanna, riparian forest. Note other pertinent information about the habitat (e.g., bromeliads and lianas abundant.) _____

_____

_____

Indicate the approximate extension of the habitat into the immediate vicinity (e.g., 2 caimans observed on a 50 m sandy bank of the Aponguao River 200 m upstream of waterfall) _____

_____

_____

Form 9: Special Animals Observed, Page 2

Characteristics of associated species which could affect the special animal (e.g., granivorous birds foraging between small shrubs in open areas may be displacing the special animal in pastures) _____

_____

CONSERVATION

Does the property owner know of the occurrence of this species? _____ Yes _____ No

Could this site sustain the species for several years? (Respond to this question in terms of the quality of the habitat in relation to the species survival and human or biological threats that are present)

_____ Yes _____ No   Explain:_____

_____

Describe evidence of population and/or habitat disturbance. Specify disturbance observed in the site and its effects on the population and habitat. (E.g., bird remains were found along with several gun shells) _____

_____

_____

Indicate direct and indirect threats to the population in the site _____

_____

How large an area is needed for a viable population at this site?
(Consider factors such as body size, diet and various habitat uses throughout the year) _____

Research Needs _____

_____

Should this site be monitored on a regular basis? _____ No _____ Yes (Indicate number of times/yr) _____

Comments _____

COLLECTION OF SPECIMENS

If the specimen is (was) collected, describe how:_____

_____

Where is it stored? _____

Collection No. _____ Source(s) used for ID:_____

Photographs taken:_____

_____

Conservation recommendations and additional information about the population _____

_____

_____

Appendix 3

Example Scope of Work for an REA

This document details the nature of work to be conducted in support of a Rapid Ecological Assessment (REA) of (study area) as well as the roles and responsibilities of the organizations participating in this activity. (Soliciting entity) has commissioned this biodiversity assessment from (primary contractor) in order to obtain information related to the biodiversity importance of the area. The REA is intended to produce baseline biodiversity information and a prioritization of areas of biodiversity importance.

Objectives of the REA

The REA has three primary objectives:

1. To characterize the vegetation types in the study area from imagery interpretation and to assess the biodiversity of these habitats by field study.
2. To assign biodiversity significance priorities to these habitat units for a more informed conservation management of the area.
3. To recommend candidate areas for the creation of permanent conservation areas within the study site.

Participating Organizations

The soliciting and funding agency for this REA is (soliciting entity). The organization charged with the management and overall responsibility of the REA is (contractor).

The (primary implementing agency, if different from contractor) will subcontract to (contractor) in the role of the primary implementing organization for the REA.

Study Area

The study area for the REA is (detailed description).

Scope of Work

The (contractor) agrees to conduct an REA for (soliciting entity) to characterize biodiversity in the study area. This REA will involve the following:

1. Interpretation of remotely sensed imagery for the determination and delineation of vegetation types within the study area. Imagery sources, in order of preference, are as follows:

   1:24,000 Color-infrared aerial photography (most current, best scale if not 1:24,000)

   1:24,000 Natural-color aerial photography (most current, best scale if not 1:24,000)

   1:24,000 Black-and-white aerial photography (most current, best scale if not 1:24,000)

   Landsat Thematic Mapper (TM) imagery

   Spot Multispectral imagery

   Spot Panchromatic imagery

   Radar imagery

   The most useful imagery source for the REA is a combination of color-infrared aerial photography and Landsat TM satellite imagery. This allows for aerial photo–interpreted vegetation polygons to be mapped onto a TM image base.

   (Soliciting entity) will also provide the aircraft (helicopter or fixed-wing) and pilot for two aerial recoinnascence missions (overflights) during which photographs and GPS positions will be obtained. A team of four to six scientists will participate in the overflight.

   (Soliciting entity) will furnish to (contractor or primary implementor) two (2) sets each of hard copy (as well as digital datasets where available) of the following:

   Imagery

   Topographic maps of the entire study area (all sheets) at (most appropriate scale)

   Other relevant and appropriately scaled thematic maps (geology, soils, precipitation isohyets, hydrographic resources and watersheds, vegetation, land use, etc.)

2. Planning and Training Workshops

   (Contractor or primary implementor) will organize and conduct on-site planning and training workshops for management and field personnel. These two workshops may be combined into a single workshop. These workshops will generate a sampling plan and chronology and will assign sampling tasks to responsible teams.

3. Fieldwork

   Vegetation types identified in the image interpretation phase will be field-verified by visits from teams of field biologists. All vegetation classes identified in the Initial Landscape Characterization phase will be characterized. Teams will visit predetermined sampling locations that represent an acceptable sample (to be determined in the planning workshop) of all identified vegetation class occurrences. At each sampling location or observation point, data will be collected on the following biological taxa: plants (primarily woody plants and trees), mammals, birds (migratory and resident), reptiles, and amphibians. Entemofauna and icthyofauna will not be characterized in this REA. Plants will be assessed by plot surveys; animals will be censused with standard observation and capture techniques; and birds will also be surveyed and captured through direct observation and mist-netting. Occurrence level information with geolocation will be emphasized. Abundance-level information will not be presented, but seasonality considerations will be addressed.

4. Synthesis of Information

   Information separated by discipline will be integrated into a single, cohesive analysis. Vegetation types will be characterized and mapped. Species-level biodiversity within these units will be characterized, with particular attention paid to the development of information about endemics and rare and endangered species and communities.

5. Assignment of Biodiversity Significances

   Individual polygon-level occurrences of vegetation types will be assigned biodiversity significance levels according to the following classes (these classes are preliminary and subject to modification):

   > Highest biodiversity significance
   > High biodiversity significance
   > Moderate biodiversity significance
   > Minor biodiversity significance

   Discrimination between these classes will be determined on the basis of biodiversity, condition of habitat, extent of habitat, threat, connectivity potential, contiguity with adjacent large blocks of landscape, and so forth. A precise description of these parameters and weighting levels will be produced during the planning workshop.

Products

The following products will be generated from this REA:

1. Draft final REA report.

2. Final REA report.

   The final REA report will contain textual descriptions of methodologies, results, analyses, and conclusions, along with supporting maps and graphics. It will also contain a description of the unique vegetation types and their spatial distributions, as well as a description of their biodiversity significance. While the report may contain a brief exposition of any obvious management recommendations generated from the results, the report will not contain comprehensive, explicit management recommendations. The report will present recommendations for candidate sites to be considered in planning for the establishment of permanent conservation areas.

3. 1:250,000-scale GIS-generated basemap showing roads and trails, villages, elevation, watercourses, and site boundaries.

4. 1:250,000-scale map showing vegetation types.

5. 1:100,000-scale maps showing vegetation types at a finer spatial resolution. These maps will also present occurrences of observed elements of special concern (species) when the display of this information does not risk the integrity of the element.

6. 1:250,000-scale map of biodiversity significance classes.

7. A series of 1:100,000-scale maps classifying all vegetation units into the biodiversity significance framework.

   For all map products, three copies will be delivered to (soliciting entity) in hard-copy format. Digital files of these maps, as PostScript or similar formats, will also be made. The digital GIS layers (data) will also be made available to (soliciting entity). These data layers will include the following:

   Basemap features (roads, rivers, villages, etc.)
   Sampling locations
   Vegetation types
   Biodiversity significances
   Candidate protected areas for permanent conservation

   All GIS data will be made available in ESRI/ArcInfo coverage export format (coveragename.E00 files for each data layer).

Data Sharing Agreement

Data generated from the REA will be archived at (all institutions). (Soliciting entity) retains the intellectual property rights to information generated in this study but will not unreasonably withhold the use of these data for publication or presentation purposes by (contractor or primary implementor), except in the case of locational information of a sensitive nature (e.g., locations of rare or endangered species or species of significant commercial or artesanal value). Permission to reproduce location-specific information to be released for public access must be obtained from (soliciting entity) prior to publication.

Additional Considerations

The Scope of Work is dependent upon the provision of imagery. The (soliciting entity) will also provide:

Access to all areas of the study site
A vehicle for the use of the field team for the duration of the field sampling effort
Two overflights of the study area
Accommodations and meals for field teams during the sampling season
An area for the processing of samples collected from the field as well as an energy source for light and to power equipment (laptops) and charge batteries
Permission, where consistent with legislation, for specimen acquisition, processing, registry, and storage
An overall point-of-contact person for site-related matters, who will respond to communications and requests for assistance

Reporting

(Contractor) will provide quarterly progress reports (Dates) as well as a draft Final Report (Date) and a Final Report (Date). (Contractor) will also submit a detailed Workplan and Sampling Strategy prior to commencement of fieldwork. Changes in this reporting schedule require prior authorization by (soliciting entity).

Disbursements

(Soliciting entity) agrees to pay (contractor) a total of (contract amount) for this work. This total will be disbursed according to the following schedule:

25 percent at signing by both parties of this Scope of Work

35 percent on delivery of the Workplan and Sampling Strategy

20 percent on delivery of draft Final Report

20 percent on delivery of Final Report

About the Authors

Shirley Keel earned her Ph.D. from City University of New York. She studied plant ecology at Emory University and plant taxonomy at the New York Botanical Garden. She has been an in-country technical advisor for the Conservation Data Centers in Peru and Paraguay and subsequently chief botanist of The Nature Conservancy's Latin America and Caribbean Region. Dr. Keel established the Conservancy's Latin American botanical database and helped develop the methodology for rapid ecological assessment. She has participated in more than a dozen REA projects since 1988, including a project under way in China. Her current interests are phytogeography of rare woody endemics, economic plants and their wild relatives in protected areas, and vegetation surveys that form part of The Nature Conservancy-sponsored rapid ecological assessments.

Thomas Lovejoy was the first person to use the term *biological diversity* in 1980 and has been credited as the originator for the concept of debt-for-nature swaps. Dr. Lovejoy is generally credited with having brought the tropical forest problem to the fore as a public issue and was founder of the public television series *Nature.* His Ph.D. thesis (1971) introduced the technique of banding to Brazil and identified patterns of community structure in the first major long-term study of birds in the Amazon. He has served in an executive capacity for World Wildlife Fund, Smithsonian Institution, and The World Bank and serves on numerous scientific and conservation boards and advisory groups.

Ellen Roca worked for The Nature Conservancy for six years, where she managed the rapid ecological assessment program for the Latin America and Caribbean Region. Ms. Roca participated in REAs in ten countries in Latin America, where she focused on project development, design, management, REA training, and technical support. She currently resides in Delaware working as a private consultant for rapid assessment projects.

Roberto L. Roca is the deputy director of the Wings of the Americas program of The Nature Conservancy. A native of Venezuela, he holds a Ph.D. in biology from State University of New York. Dr. Roca is a specialist in conservation biology and ornithology. Over the past four years he has focused his efforts on helping the Conservancy to develop conservation strategies and initiatives to protect birds at risk in the Americas. Previous to that he helped the Latin America and Caribbean Region of the Conservancy to refine the rapid ecological assessment methodologies and played a key role in the conservation of animal species in Latin America. His publications include papers as well as two books in the fields of avian ecology and conservation of protected areas.

Roger Sayre directs the Conservation Science Department of The Nature Conservancy's International Program, which includes programs in rapid ecological assessment, ecoregional and site-conservation planning, landscape ecology, zoology, botany, biodiversity information, community conservation, and conservation mapping. He has participated in almost two dozen REAs. He holds a Ph.D. in natural resources from Cornell University and is a specialist in conservation mapping technologies and approaches. Dr. Sayre also holds a M.Sc. in forest resources from Pennsylvania State University. He is currently developing approaches for mapping national portfolios of critical conservation areas. He has over fifteen years of experience in international conservation and sustainable development initiatives and has published several articles and book chapters on rapid ecological assessments, gap analyses, and biodiversity priority setting.

Tamara R. Sayre is a professional wildlife artist, graphic designer, and teacher. She lives with her husband, a research biologist, and two young sons in Fort Collins, Colorado.

Gina Sedaghatkish is the rapid ecological assessment specialist in the Conservation Science Department of the Latin America and Caribbean Region of the Conservancy. Ms. Sedaghatkish is the author of the Conservancy's Rapid Ecological Assessment Source Book and has coauthored several other conservation publications. She is a coeditor of *Cracidae: Their Biology and Conservation*. She holds a MSc in sustainable development and conservation biology from the University of Maryland at College Park.

Stuart Sheppard serves as the geographic information systems specialist in the Conservation Science Department of the International Program of The Nature Conservancy. As a member of the Spatial Information Program, Stuart has worked to build capacity in Latin America and Caribbean-based conservation organizations in the areas of spatial information, remote sensing, geographic information systems, and cartography applications for the REAs that were conducted in Belize, Brazil, Cuba, and the Dominican Republic.

Bruce Young is the chief zoologist of the Latin American and Caribbean Region of The Nature Conservancy. He specializes in faunal surveys and analysis and is currently researching the enigmatic declines of amphibians at a network of conservation areas throughout the region. Prior to working at the Conservancy, he was director of the La Selva Biological Station in Costa Rica. He has participated in the planning and implementation of several REAs and has participated in planning workshops for a rapid ecological assessment to take place in Río Plátano, Honduras. He holds a Ph.D. in zoology from the University of Michigan and is the author of over twenty scientific articles.

Index